From the Studio to the Streets:

Service-Learning in **Planning** and **Architecture**

Mary C. Hardin, Richard A. Eribes,
and Corky Poster, volume editors
William Zeisel, series editor

I

Acknowledgments

I thank Dana Buntrock, Lisa Findley, and Reed Kroloff for giving their broad and diverse perspectives to the task of reviewing chapter proposals. I also thank Tony Schuman for ceding the title of his introduction so that it could be used to entitle the volume. This entire project was a pleasure, made rich by interaction with old friends and new service-learning colleagues.
—Mary C. Hardin

AAHE is the former independent, membership-based, nonprofit organization dedicated to building human capital for higher education. Its publication program was acquired by Stylus in 2005.

Campus Compact

Campus Compact is a national coalition of more than 950 college and university presidents — representing some 5 million students — who are committed to fulfilling the civic purposes of higher education. As the only national higher education association dedicated solely to campus-based civic engagement, Campus Compact promotes public service that develops students' citizenship skills, helps campuses forge effective community partnerships, and provides resources and training for faculty seeking to integrate civic and community-based learning into the curriculum. Campus Compact comprises a national office based in Providence, RI, and 30 state offices in CA, CO, CT, FL, HI, IA, IL, IN, KS, LA, MA, ME, MI, MN, MO, MT, NC, NH, NY, OH, OK, OR, PA, RI, TX, UT, VT, WA, WI, and WV. For contact and other information, see www.compact.org.

Library of Congress Cataloging-in-Publication Data

From the studio to the streets : service-learning in planning and architecture /
Mary C. Hardin, editor.
p. cm.—(AAHE's series on service-learning in the disciplines)
ISBN 1-56377-100-4 (pbk. : alk. Paper)
    1. Architecture—Study and teaching (Higher)—United States—Social aspects.
    2. Community and college—United States.   3. Student service—United States.
    I. Hardin, Mary C.   II. Series

    NA2105.F76   2006
    720.71'173—dc22
        2006044317

From the Studio to the Streets: Service-Learning in Planning and Architecture (AAHE's Series on Service-Learning in the Disciplines)
Mary C. Hardin, Richard A. Eribes, and Corky Poster, *volume editors*
William Zeisel, *series editor*

    Stylus Publishing, LLC.
    22883 Quicksilver Drive
    Sterling, VA 20166-2102
    Tel: 1-800-232-0223 / Fax 703-661-1547
    www.Styluspub.com

ISBN: 1-56377-100-4
ISBN (set): 1-56377-005-9

Contents

About This Series
William Zeisel v

Introduction: The Pedagogy of Engagement
Anthony W. Schuman. 1

Part 1. Designing and Implementing Service-Learning in
Architecture and Planning Education

A Core Commitment to Service-Learning:
Bridging Planning Theory and Practice
Lorlene M. Hoyt 17

Institutional Support for Community-Based
Architecture and Planning Outreach Scholarship at Auburn University
Sharon Gaber and Daniel Bennett 33

Where Do We Go from Here? An Evaluative
Framework for Community-Based Design
Michael Rios 47

Part 2. Course Narratives

Research as Ethical Practice: When Academic Goals Align with
Community Needs
Mary C. Hardin 59

Achieving Large-Scale Community Development
Projects in a Teaching University
Hollie M. Lund and Gwen Urey 77

Sore Shoulders, Bruised Ethics:
The Unintended Lessons of Design-Build
Scott Wing. 91

Multiplying Knowledge:
Service-Learning x Activism = Community Scholars
Jacqueline Leavitt and Kara Heffernan 99

Beyond Boundaries, Weaving Connections:
Reflections on the American Indian Housing Initiative
David Riley, Michael Rios, Scott Wing, and Beth Workman 115

Shifting Ground: Design as Civic Action and
Community Building
Paula Horrigan 127

Service-Learning as a Holistic Inquiry and
Community Outreach Studios
Joongsub Kim and James Abernethy 139

Reflection and Reciprocity in Interdisciplinary
Design Service-Learning
Keith Diaz Moore and David Wang 155

Service-Learning in Texas Colonias
Anne Beamish 171

The Electric Greening of North Hollywood:
A Case Study in Environmental Design Education
Through Service-Learning
Julie A. Dercle 187

Funded Planning and Design Studios:
The Master of Infrastructure Planning Program at
NJIT's New Jersey School of Architecture
Darius Sollohub 203

Community Life and Places of Death
Umit Yilmaz and Daniel J. Nadenicek 219

Contributors 231

About This Series

By William Zeisel

This volume is the 21st in a series of monographs on service-learning in the academic disciplines published by the American Association for Higher Education in partnership with Campus Compact. The series was established as a venue for systematically exploring service-learning in a range of disciplines, through carefully designed essays providing background, salient issues, and important insights gained from experience by faculty and students. The editors of these volumes have been able to assemble cogent and persuasive essays that describe a wide array of approaches to service-learning in educational institutions and communities across the country. Truly, service-learning has become a part of the higher education landscape.

The concept of service learning emerged several decades ago as a potentially powerful instrument for both education and community development. Part of a larger constellation of terms including experiential learning and community-based education, it combines rigorous learning with meaningful service through courses in which faculty and students help community residents address problems or issues they regard as important. Service-learning fits easily into the pragmatic American tradition of education, as explicated by Dewey and others, yet it also rides comfortably with community-activist philosophies such as those of Paolo Freire and others.

Architecture would seem to be an ideal academic field for applying service-learning, since it requires mastery of theoretical concepts for direct application to human situations and needs. And in fact, as the essays in this volume show, the discipline of architecture has long included learning by doing in its mode of teaching. However, only in recent years have the field's hands-on aspects been subjected to a more systematic appraisal, with an eye to making them formal and even required parts of the educational process.

Not surprisingly, the proponents of service-learning, and their institutions, have often come face to face with significant problems and issues, both professional and ethical. This volume, assembled under the careful eye of Mary C. Hardin of the University of Arizona, identifies and addresses key issues of architecture service-learning, through the experience and reflection of educators who work both in the classroom and, often quite literally, in the field. It is a worthy companion of the first 20 volumes of this series, which appeared under the general editorship of Edward Zlotkowski. The new stewards of the series will strive to maintain the high standards that he set.

Introduction:
The Pedagogy of Engagement

By Anthony W. Schuman

A Dialectic

The concept of service-learning, as the essays collected in this volume demonstrate, embraces many impulses, depending on whether the emphasis is on the "service" or the "learning." Even when the two concepts are thus disaggregated there is still a variety of approaches reflecting different pedagogical and social goals. "Learning," for example, may refer to "field experience," the accumulation of practical training to supplement the intellectual foundations laid in the classroom. Co-op programs in schools of architecture or field placements in planning schools support this objective. Design-build programs in architecture schools provide intensive, hands-on construction experience, enabling students to understand what happens in the translation of a design from lines on paper to physical object. In either instance, when the beneficiary of the placement or the built facility is an underserved community or family, one may say that a service has been provided as well. For the learning to be truly service-based, however, implies a more formal connection between the pedagogy and the product, where the service component is also a learning experience and not simply a byproduct.

At the opposite end of the spectrum, advocates of "critical pedagogy" seek to have a more direct impact on contemporary social conditions. Drawing on work by critical theorists including Paolo Freire, Henry Giroux, and bell hooks, they ground their approach in the notion of a transformative process for students and community residents alike. Among educators using a critical pedagogy, in addition to those represented in this volume, one might cite Leslie Kanes Weisman for a consistent application of the principles, Thomas Dutton, whose theoretical investigations are informed by his work at the community design center he founded in Cincinnati's Over-the-Rhine neighborhood, and Kenneth Reardon, whose action research project in East St. Louis provided a model of interdisciplinary community engagement (Weisman 1999; Center for Community Engagement 2004; Dutton 1996; Reardon 1997; East St. Louis Action Research Project 2004).

Students are encouraged to challenge normative views of education in general, and technical knowledge in particular, in the context of a wider public debate about social equity, diversity, and the distribution of economic and political power in a democratic society. The neighborhood-based planning movement, for example, incorporates Freire's goal of empowering residents in poor communities through an emphasis on dialogue and reciprocity that values and acknowledges their own skills and knowledge base.

Two principles define the essence of service learning. The hallmark of pedagogy is *reflection*: What intellectual underpinnings inform the process and how is the field experience used to challenge and refine this thinking? The crux of engagement is reciprocity: What did the students learn and how did the community benefit; or, conversely, what did the community learn and how did the students benefit? Because many if not most service-based learning situations involve an unequal starting point in terms of technical expertise, access to information, and the ability to negotiate with public and private bureaucracies, there is an inherent risk of exploitation where the community setting is used as a laboratory to serve the university.

This essay focuses on two forms of service-learning: neighborhood-based planning and school-based community design centers. Both practices are rooted equally in the academy and in the professions, and the dialectic between the academy and the "outside world," between the studio and the street, gives these programs their immediacy and their dynamic tension. This dialectic also emphasizes the significance of the historical context in setting the tone and direction for service-learning, particularly in terms of response by the architecture and planning professions to broad social movements.

Advocacy and Activism

It is now 40 years since the launching of the first community design centers and the advocacy planning movement. In those heady days of social activism, when dramatic change seemed both desirable and possible, students and professionals alike were impelled by the moral and social imperatives of the Civil Rights movement. Communities marched under the banner "Power to the people" as they fought to stave off the ravages of urban renewal and to challenge the legacy of discrimination that had produced a society whose racial bifurcation was etched in its residential landscape. The turmoil in the streets was matched by intellectual ferment. In a span of five years, three seminal works challenged orthodox modernist thinking about planning, the environment, and architecture: Jane Jacobs' *Death and Life of Great American Cities* (1961), Rachel Carson's *Silent Spring* (1962), and Robert Venturi's *Complexity and Contradiction in Architecture* (1966). Socially committed professionals joined the fray. In 1963, architect C. Richard Hatch established the Architects' Renewal Committee in Harlem (ARCH), the nation's first community design center (CDC). The following year, at the annual meeting of the American Institute of Planners (forerunner of the American Planning Association), held in Newark, New Jersey, a group of planners including Walter Thabit, Paul Davidoff, David Stoloff, and Chester Hartman, and sociologist Frances Fox Piven founded Planners for Equal Opportunity (PEO) to legitimize social activism within the planning profession (Thabit 1999).

The early impulse toward activism in the planning and design professions was interdisciplinary as well. In Boston, planner Chester Hartman, urban anthropologist Lisa Peattie, architect Robert Goodman, and five others including two engineers, an attorney, a sociologist, and a psychologist established Urban Planning Aid (UPA), during the mid-1960s, to provide pro bono planning services to underserved neighborhoods (Hartman 2002a). UPA sought to help community groups fight urban renewal projects by crafting counter-plans through a participatory planning process. These organizations contained the roots of the advocacy planning movement that launched the neighborhood-based planning approach now incorporated into the municipal planning process in many cities. The significance of this movement was crystallized by Paul Davidoff in his seminal article, "Advocacy and Pluralism in Planning" (1965).

A New Pedagogy

During this period, planning departments were typically lodged in schools of architecture, and the early responses to the social challenges of the day involved students from both professions. My own first job, after receiving my architecture degree in 1970, was with the Community Planning Studio at Columbia University, directed by Robert Kolodny. Pratt Institute's Community Education Program, started by George Raymond in 1963 as an adult education program within the Department of City and Regional Planning, soon added an advocacy component when Ron Shiffman was brought in to work with a group of ministers from the Bedford-Stuyvesant community. A veteran of the Civil Rights movement through work with the New York chapter of the Congress of Racial Equality (CORE), Shiffman has described his approach as an urban application of the concept of "rural agents," part of the extension (outreach) service required of land-grant colleges under their federal charters. This collaboration bore fruit in 1966, when the Bedford-Stuyvesant Restoration Corp. was established as the nation's first community development corporation (introducing a second meaning of the acronym CDC). Architecture and planning students were initially involved in the Pratt Institute program as paid interns, gaining the right to work there for academic credit only after student protests in 1967 (Shiffman 2004).

At Harvard, Chester Hartman, then an assistant professor in the

Department of City and Regional Planning in the Graduate School of Design, established the Urban Field Service, in 1969, as a student version of Urban Planning Aid. Teams of Harvard and Massachusetts Institute of Technology (MIT) students from architecture, city planning, landscape architecture, and related disciplines, working under the supervision of faculty members or practicing professionals, offered free technical assistance to community groups in low-income areas.

In Pittsburgh, architect Troy West, then an assistant professor in the Department of Architecture at Carnegie-Mellon University, established Architecture 2001, in 1967, as a community studio at 2001 Central Avenue in the Hill District. He began the project in response to students' questions about why the architecture program was not engaged in the city around them. In partnership with psychologist Jay Greenfield and local artist Ed Ellis, West developed Architecture 2001 as an amalgam of architecture, planning, culture, and art. The principal project was renovation of a junk-strewn lot into a "Court of Ideas" with murals, performance space, and sitting areas. Other early school-based community assistance programs were Henry Sanoff's Community Development Group at North Carolina State University, started in 1966, and the Community-Based Projects Program created by Tony Costello at Ball State University, in 1969. Sanoff, notably, moved from Berkeley, where he was teaching, because the Agricultural Extension program at North Carolina State, a land-grant college, could provide the financial and logistical support for his community development projects (Sanoff 2004).

While these early forays into community activism varied considerably in their emphasis, ranging from political confrontation to artistic production, they shared a few salient characteristics. All espoused the philosophy of engaging students in the social issues of the day, and in supplementing classroom learning with direct neighborhood contact. Faculty and students proceeded from the belief that professionals had an obligation to make their expertise available to those lacking the economic or political influence to secure these services on their own, at a time when it was unusual for municipal planning agencies to seek input from neighborhood groups. And they believed that the planning and design professions could make a significant contribution toward improving living conditions in inner-city neighborhoods, a confidence in the social agency of design derived from the progressive social agenda of the Modern movement.

Taking the classroom into the community also meant grappling with the intrinsic problems, both within and outside the academy, of engaging the outside world. To begin with it is inherently difficult to synchronize the semester structure of most academic programs with the 12-month calendar of daily life. Second, academic institutions were often skeptical of these efforts, whose pedagogy was unorthodox and sometimes brought direct conflict with institutional goals, such as Urban Field Service's opposition to Harvard University's expansion plans. Both Hartman and West lost their academic positions as a result of their advocacy and, in Hartman's case, his open support of the 1969-1970 student strike at Harvard (Hartman 2002b; West 2004). West went on to a long career in architectural education at the New Jersey Institute of Technology, where he taught from 1972 to 2002. Hartman made his mark outside academe with various not-for-profit institutions including the National Housing Law Project, the Institute for Policy Studies, and the Poverty and Race Research Action Council, where he has been since 1990. Hartman was the founder and driving force behind the Planners Network, a national organization of some 700 progressive planners and related professionals and academics.

A New Planning Model

While it would be an exaggeration to suggest that in the late 1960s schools of architecture and planning enlisted wholesale in the cause of social activism, that is where we find the antecedents of the growing emphasis on service-learning in our professional schools. Since those common stirrings, however, schools of architecture and planning have followed quite different trajectories. Of the two, planning education followed the steadier course, mirroring a growing acceptance of neighborhood-based planning in the public sector (Chait 2002). Several factors helped account for this shift in orientation from centralized, technically driven "master planning" to a more inclusive, incremental approach. One was widespread public dissatisfaction with the quality of the urban environment produced by large-scale renewal projects. Another was the emergence of community development corporations as actors in reshaping their neighborhoods. The CDCs grew out of many sources including, notably, faith-based efforts like the New Community Corporation in Newark, New Jersey. More often, CDCs began as community organizing efforts formed in opposition to downtown plans for their neighborhoods.

These groups found that even when they were successful in fighting off highway projects and urban renewal demolitions, they were unable to implement their own counter-plans. A number of these organizations took matters into their own hands and moved into direct development activity as CDCs. Some fell by the wayside because they grew too fast or lacked the expertise to control the development process. Others encountered internal strife and, on occasion, corruption. But a hardy few survived to play an important role in determining the shape of their communities. The Cooper Square Committee on New York City's Lower East Side, for example, has waged a 40-year campaign to ensure that the Cooper Square Urban Renewal plan benefits the area's working-class residents in its implementation. Over that span, the committee has built 147 units of affordable housing, renovated 320 more, and created a mutual housing association with more than 400 units under its management. In fall 2003, construction plans were unveiled for a mixed-use, mixed-income development on the original urban renewal site, vacant since it was cleared for urban renewal in the early 1960s (Brozan 2004). In league with other tenant and community advocates, Cooper Square has succeeded in holding the line against the gentrification of the Lower East Side through several periods of superheated real estate markets.

The growth of neighborhood-based planning was helped by an evolution in public policy that favored local involvement. By the late 1960s, in response to local protests and citizen activism, "maximum feasible participation" became an important principle underlying the federal War on Poverty and specific programs such as Model Cities. Participatory planning was seen as a fundamental exercise in democracy. Still, it was not until the late 1980s that neighborhood-based planning began to gain acceptance as a legitimate practice and the concept of participation began to receive more than lip service. Gradually some cities began to institutionalize participation through mechanisms such as the establishment of local planning boards. Even in cases where these boards do not control final decisions about local development, as in the case of the "197-a" planning process mandated by New York City's Charter revisions of 1975 and 1989, the process gives communities leverage to negotiate eventual outcomes. Today, cities as diverse as Burlington, Vermont, Portland, Oregon, Rochester, New York, and Seattle, Washington, have adopted a neighborhood-based planning approach.

This shift reflects a growing recognition that neighborhood involvement produces better plans. It engenders local "ownership" of the plan that can foster long-term stewardship of public spaces. And it values local residents as assets for their skills and knowledge. As a practical matter, community endorsement means a smoother road to implementation. Communities alienated from the development process are more likely to throw up roadblocks, from demonstrations to lawsuits, that can produce costly delays.

The changing paradigm reflects tendencies from the earliest days of the planning profession as it emerged from a variety of sources: the urban design focus of the City Beautiful movement, the community organizing thrust of the social work and settlement house movements, the reform agenda of good government advocates, the sanitary concerns of public health organizations, and the technical orientation of civil engineering. A tension between physical planning and policy planning was evident from the first National Conference on City Planning, held in Washington, D.C., in 1909. One of the central debates at that meeting was whether the discipline of planning should focus on improving the physical appearance of a city or on improving the daily life of its inhabitants; in other words, whether the goal of planning was a more beautiful city or, in the words of English planner T.C. Horsfall, "a more beautiful life" (National Conference on City Planning 1909: 77).

These competing orientations continue to influence planning education. The debate over physical versus social planning explains both planning's attraction to architecture and its skepticism. The profession's roots in reform and engineering help clarify its faith both in technical expertise and in a government that is ready, willing, and able to address planning issues through a centralized authority, while its antecedents in the social work and settlement house movements emphasize planning at the neighborhood scale. This diverse background would explain both an initial resistance to bottom-up planning as well as an eventual embrace of the practice. In today's schools of planning, neighborhood-based planning is a significant presence, in some the dominant paradigm. This represents a substantial turnabout from the late 1960s, when the centralized master plan was still the most widely accepted model.

Accreditation procedures in planning education do not require a community-based studio or course, but they do mandate consideration of the role that values play in determining planning policy, including "issues of equity, social justice, economic welfare and efficiency in the use of resources," and "the role of government and citizen participation in a democratic society and the balancing of individual and collective rights and interests" (Planning Accreditation Board 2001: 22). The Association of Collegiate Schools of Planning (ACSP) offers two important awards that acknowledge and therefore encourage social engagement. The Paul Davidoff Award recognizes "an outstanding book publication promoting participatory democracy and positive social change, opposing poverty and racism as factors in society, and reducing disparities between rich and poor, white and black, men and women." The Marsha Ritzdorf Award recognizes "the best student work on diversity, social justice and the role of women in planning" (Association of Collegiate Schools of Planning 2003).

For a variety of complex reasons, analyzed in more depth elsewhere (Forsyth et al. 2000), service-learning has found a more congenial home in planning programs than in architecture departments. One factor is the tighter link between education and practice in the field of planning. While neighborhood-based work remains at the margins of architectural practice, it has entered the mainstream of contemporary planning practice. Key to this trend is a group of practitioner/educators who have moved back and forth between the two domains. Norman Krumholz, professor of urban planning at Cleveland State University, exemplifies this model. Krumholz served for 10 years under three mayors as director of the Cleveland City Planning Commission in addition to separate terms as president of the American Planning Association (APA) and the American Institute of Certified Planners (AICP). A growing body of literature, by Krumholz and others, chronicles the emergence of "equity planning" (Krumholz and Clavel 1994).

Service-Learning in Architecture

If planning has demonstrated a continuous evolution toward a socially engaged practice, architectural education has not. On the contrary, the social initiatives of the 1960s and 1970s were soon eclipsed. Robert Venturi's *Complexity and Contradiction in Architecture* opened the door to a rediscovery of figural design, and although Venturi and his partner Denise Scott Brown incorporated at least an ironic critique of the status quo in their work, this modicum of dissent was quickly lost in the historicist wave of postmodern architecture that ensued. With Philip Johnson's pedimented AT&T Headquarters in New York City (1984) as the iconic standard bearer, architecture began a retreat into its "autonomous discourse." The deconstructionist movement that followed claimed, in some quarters, to be based in a critique of bourgeois convention, but its trappings were more convincingly interpreted as a further retreat into a self-referential formal vocabulary. More recently, the ability to construct digitally produced forms that were heretofore unbuildable, as manifest in Frank Gehry's sculptural works, has strengthened this tendency to separate architecture from its social and historical context.

Against this trajectory it has been difficult for a socially based architecture to hold its own in the competitive world of the design studio. The successive design trends of the past 30 years, although enriching the design palette in formal terms, have reinforced a narrow spectrum of architecture practice focused on the elite designer and the signature building. Community design offers an alternative to the pervasive design studio exercise modeled on the "star architect" career model. It emphasizes neighborhood fabric over object-building, collaboration over competition, and process over product. It frees students to communicate their ideas in plain English, without the jargon that prevents lay audiences from entering the discussion. There is no "typical" community design project. Students can expect to develop a wide range of professional skills, including land use and building condition surveys, zoning analysis, demographic analysis, cost estimating, public presentation, site planning, urban design, participatory design process, public workshops and design charrettes, and measured drawings of existing buildings.

Community design programs have value far beyond the classroom

— for the individual, the school, the university, the community, and the profession. The service component that constitutes the core of the movement is increasingly recognized as part of the central mission of higher education, as the Carnegie Foundation report on architecture education and practice so firmly emphasized (Boyer and Mitgang 1996). Universities often have few initiatives that benefit local communities as directly as community design programs based in their schools of architecture. Community service is also central to professional work. The Internship Development Program operated by the National Council of Architectural Registration Boards (NCARB), a required part of the licensing process in most states, includes a community service component. Community service was a core theme at the American Institute of Architects (AIA) annual convention in 2000, linked directly the concept of leadership.

But community design programs are more than service activities. They are models of interdisciplinary teamwork, often engaging planners, urban designers, and landscape architects as well as scholars and professionals from related fields. They offer complex arenas for scholarship and research. Most importantly, they are proving grounds for creative work, where students and faculty must meet tight budgets and code constraints without compromising design intentions. Students are invariably enthusiastic about community work. As one of my own students exclaimed, "It's great to have real customers!"

Sustaining a school-based community design program over the long term requires a constant struggle with three economic exigencies. First, the programs and the communities they serve must secure funding for operational expenses and implementation of eventual proposals. Second, faculty salaries cover some basic costs, but operating a year-round program requires additional funding. Third, all community work is vulnerable to cutbacks in public programs that support neighborhood development. On top of this schools must arrange for insurance coverage on the construction site and ongoing liability coverage following occupancy.

Participating faculty must convince their schools that their work in community design is worthy of promotion and tenure. Community design work doesn't easily fit the standard academic evaluation categories of funded research or scholarly publication. While the work is intensely creative, the end product is rarely a substantial piece of new construction, the form of creative endeavor most likely to receive peer recognition through publication or prizes. In community design work, process is privileged over product, and benefit to the community over traditional esthetic preoccupations. Faculty must convince their colleagues that community design is an integral part of a professional curriculum. By situating practice closer to the routines of daily life than to the esthetic preoccupations of the discipline, community-based design also runs the risk of being marginalized, not only by architecture school administrators but by design faculty as well.

For community design to be more than simply a traditional design studio using a community client for site and program, there must be additional training in collaborative work methods, running public workshops, and identification of community needs and assets. Under the best of circumstances this would entail a constellation of courses to support the community design studio, and at the least it would require intensive seminars in conjunction with the studio.

To some extent, the difficulties in operating a university-based design program are shared by the independent community design centers. Both are vulnerable to shifting patterns of public policy and financial support; both were severely hurt by the withdrawal of funds during the Reagan years. But the university setting poses additional obstacles. How can "real life" problems be addressed during an academic schedule based on semesters? If projects result in actual construction, who stamps the drawings and assumes liability? Do students receive academic credit for service projects, and if so, what is the pedagogical focus of this work? Does the school-based work compete with local professional services? How are faculty compensated for the intensive time outside the studio?

In 1998, the Association of Collegiate Schools of Architecture (ACSA) surveyed member schools to establish an inventory of community design activity. Every school has an occasional design studio linked to local development issues, but ACSA wanted to know which had formal programs that permitted work to continue on a year-round basis, and to compile comparative data indicating how the programs were funded, staffed, and operated. The survey results were published in the *ACSA Sourcebook of Community Design Programs at Schools of Architecture in North America*, which includes entries on 46 school-based programs and profiles 24 independent centers affiliated with the Association for Community Design. The book also contains useful information on how community service is viewed by the five collateral organizations in the field of architecture, including related honors and awards programs. ACSA had two goals in publishing the book. The first was to help schools strengthen their programs by providing access to information and facilitating communication. The second was to support the visibility and credibility of community design practice at the schools. ACSA also offers annual Collaborative Practice Awards to honor the best practices in school-based community outreach programs. ACSA's acknowledgment of community-based practice constitutes peer recognition, an imprimatur that helps legitimize this work at schools and universities where community design is not properly understood or valued.

More than half the university-based programs responding to the

ACSA survey were started in the 1990s, a circumstance that may be read two ways. On the one hand, encouragingly, the founding of so many new programs gives clear evidence of an upsurge in interest by students and faculty alike. On the other hand, the data show how difficult it is to sustain a community design program. Only four programs can trace their origins back to the 1960s and an equal number to the 1970s. These surviving programs owe their longevity in large measure to the continuing involvement and commitment of their founding leaders.

To succeed in community-based design you have to do it every day. In November 2000, ACSA presented awards to the three oldest school-based programs — the Pratt Institute Center for Community and Environmental Development (1963), the Community Development Group at North Carolina State University (1967), and the Community-Based Projects Program at Ball State University (1969) — and the two oldest continuing independent CDCs: the Los Angeles Community Design Center (1968) and Baltimore's Neighborhood Design Center (1968). At the time, significantly, all three school-based programs were still run by their founders. In the words of Henry Sanoff, founder of the program at North Carolina State, "The key to survival for community-design programs is the faculty's life-long commitment to the principles of community service and to changing the way of how we practice architecture." Since that November evening in 2000, two of the three community-design veterans have stepped down from their positions. Ron Shiffman relinquished his post at Pratt Institute in 2003. Pratt is enjoying a smooth transition under a new director drawn from the community development movement. At North Carolina State, however, where the program was based entirely in the university and dependent on Henry Sanoff's leadership, the fate of the Community Development Group was uncertain when Sanoff stepped down in 2004.

As architecture programs moved away from social engagement, planning programs moved away from architecture, an estrangement manifest in the lack of joint activity between the two departments. At some schools the planning department moved its affiliation to other academic units: at the University of California at Los Angeles (UCLA), for example, the Department of Urban Planning moved from the School of Architecture to the School of Public Policy and Social Research; at Harvard the Planning Department switched over to the John F. Kennedy School of Government before reconciling with the Graduate School of Design. The current lack of cooperation between the two professional programs is of concern to both. In 2003, ACSA past-president Bradford Grant and ACSP president Wim Wiewel appointed a joint ACSA/ACSP Taskforce on Architecture and Planning and charged it to "survey graduate planning programs and architecture programs to identify the extent and nature of collaboration between these programs on courses and projects, and to use this as a basis for making suggestions to our member programs for such collaboration" (Wiewel 2003).

Seizing the Moment

Certainly the social vocation common to both professions offers an avenue for collaboration. Indeed, several schools already offer models of effective interdisciplinary teamwork: the East St. Louis Action Research Project at the University of Illinois at Urbana/Champaign involves faculty and students from architecture, urban planning, and landscape architecture; the City Design Center in Chicago is a multidisciplinary research, education, and service program in the College of Architecture and the Arts at the University of Illinois at Chicago, affiliated with UIC's College of Urban Planning and Public Affairs.

This is also a moment when socially engaged professionals have received the highest honors from the national organizations in architecture and planning. Planners Network (2004) received the 2004 National President's Award from the American Institute of Certified Planners (AICP) for promoting socially informed and community-based planning. Founded by Chester Hartman in 1975 as a newsletter to foster communication among progressive planners, academics, activists, and students, Planners Network evolved into a more formal organization that holds conferences, publishes the quarterly magazine *Progressive Planning*, and maintains a continuing dialogue about social issues in the planning and design professions. AICP President Daniel Lauber credits Planners Network with doing "more to advance the practice of sound, ethical, inclusionary, and discrimination-free planning than any other organization in America today" (Knack 2004: 27).

The AIA awarded its 2004 Gold Medal posthumously to Samuel Mockbee, founder of the Rural Studio at Auburn University, who died in 2001. Perhaps the best known design-build program in the nation, the Rural Studio earned Mockbee a MacArthur Fellow "genius" award in 2000 and has received notice in the mainstream press as well as professional journals. Mockbee required his students to live among the people in Alabama's rural Black Belt, where they constructed houses and community facilities ranging from a backstop at a sandlot baseball field to a Boys and Girls Club that brought not only a new building but a new institution into a small rural town.

There are other signs of revived interest in social engagement among architects:

• In 1999, Cameron Sinclair and Kate Stohr founded Architecture For Humanity (AFH) to promote architectural and design solutions to global, social, and humanitarian crises. AFH sponsors competitions, workshops, educational forums, and partnerships with other organizations to create opportunities for architects and designers from around the world to help communities in need. The project list includes transitional housing for displaced people in Kosovo and a mobile HIV/AIDS health clinic for sub-Saharan Africa.

• Also in 1999, the Enterprise Foundation, a national nonprofit housing and community development organization, established the Frederick P. Rose Architecture Fellowship to direct the "passion and skills" of new architects into service in low- and moderate-income communities. A three-year stipend links recent architecture graduates who share a belief in "the value of good design and the spirit of public service" with community development corporations or other community-based organizations. Their work is further supported through an intensive orientation program as well as the annual symposium and conference of the Enterprise Foundation Network (2003).

• San Francisco architect John Peterson founded Public Architecture as a nonprofit, public interest architectural firm in 2002. The project provides pro bono architectural services and has launched an ambitious "1% Solution" campaign to encourage private architectural firms to donate one percent of their billable working hours to pro bono activity (Public Architecture 2003). Bryan Bell, director of Design Corps, a nonprofit firm based in Raleigh, North Carolina, has edited *Good Deeds, Good Design: Community Service through Architecture* (Bell 2004), based on a series of conferences under the rubric "structures for inclusion." The essays describe school-based programs, mostly of the design-build variety, that promote community-based architecture. In that same volume, Robert Gutman argues forcefully that the concept of architecture as an autonomous discipline is an illusion, however useful it may have been for a period in the late 20th century in shaking the design professions from ingrained habits. He cautions about the difficulty in sustaining a high level of political activism, and points out that the impulse to use a specific built form to inculcate a desired set of social relations did not bear fruit. With these caveats, Gutman declares that architecture cannot ignore its social context and must respond to the political and social conditions that support its expression (Gutman 2004: 17).

• Architects/Designers/Planners for Social responsibility (ADPSR), founded in the early 1980s to protest the involvement of architects in building fallout shelters and to advocate for an end to nuclear armaments, has evolved to address other issues, from affordable housing and sustainable design to a current campaign to boycott prison design (ADPSR 2004).

The planning and design professions are enjoying an unprecedented level of public interest as a result of the extensive coverage of proposals for rebuilding the World Trade Center site. It is a rare moment, when both the underlying planning issues and the symbolic power of architectural expression are melded in a single cause — a propitious occasion for architecture to recover its political and social dimension and for planning to use a visioning process as a tool for engaging the public in a participatory process. Service learning, in its many guises, offers approaches through which architecture and planning can reestablish a symbiotic relationship with each other and contribute to the construction of a more beautiful city *and* a more beautiful life. The essays in this volume describe important work being done in our professional schools toward realizing this goal. They offer insights into both successful initiatives and roadblocks along the way. Most of all, they offer an exhilarating record of how service-learning contributes to a "more beautiful" education.

References

ADPSR. (2004). www.adpsr.org.

Association of Collegiate Schools of Planning. (2003). www.acsp.org.

Bell, B., ed. 2004. *Good Deeds, Good Design: Community Service through Architecture*. New York: Princeton Architectural Press.

Boyer, E.L., and L.D. Mitgang. (1996). *Building Community: A New Future for Architecture Education and Practice*. Princeton: The Carnegie Foundation for the Advancement of Teaching.

Brozan, N. (2004). "Rental Developer's Manhattan Debut: Lower East Side." *New York Times* January 4, Section 11: 1.

Center for Community Engagement. (2004). www.fna.muohio.edu/cce.

Chait, J. (2002). "Community-Based Planning: Building on Local Knowledge." *The Livable City*. New York: Municipal Art Society.

Davidoff, P. (1965). "Advocacy and Pluralism in Planning." *Journal of the American Institute of Planners* 31(5): 103-114.

Dutton, T. A. (1996). "Cultural Studies and Critical Pedagogy: Cultural Pedagogy and Architecture." In *Reconstructing Architecture: Critical Discourses and Social Practices*, edited by T. A. Dutton and L. Hurst Mann, pp. 158-201. Minneapolis: University of Minnesota Press.

East St. Louis Action Research Project. (2004). www.eslarp.uiuc.edu.

Enterprise Foundation Network. (2003). www.enterprisefoundation.org/RoseFellowship.

Forsyth, A., H. Lu, and P. McGirr. (2000). "Service Learning in an Urban Context: Implications for Planning and Design Education." *Journal of Architectural and Planning Research* 17 (3): 236-259.

Gutman, R. (2004). "Two Questions for Architecture." In *Good Deeds, Good Design: Community Service through Architecture*, edited by B. Bell, pp. 15-22. New York: Princeton Architectural Press.

Hartman, C. (2002a). "The Harvard Urban Field Service Program." *In Between Eminence and Notoriety: Four Decades of Radical Urban Planning*, pp. 367-374. New Brunswick, NJ: Center for Urban Policy Research.

_____. (2002b). "Uppity and Out: A Case Study in the Politics of Faculty Reappointment (and the Limitations of Grievance Procedures)." *In Between Eminence and Notoriety: Four Decades of Radical Urban Planning*, pp. 380-391. New Brunswick, NJ: Center for Urban Policy Research.

Knack, R. (2004). "AICP President's Award: Planners Network." *Planning* 70 (4): 27.

Krumholz, N., and P. Clavel. (1994). *Reinventing Cities: Equity Planners Tell Their Stories.* Philadelphia: Temple University Press.

National Conference on City Planning. (1909). *Proceedings of the First National Conference on City Planning.* Facsimile Edition. Chicago: American Society of Planning Officials.

Planners Network. (2004). www.plannersnetwork.org.

Planning Accreditation Board. (2001). *The Accreditation Document: Criteria and Procedures of the Planning Accreditation Program.*

Public Architecture. (2003). www.publicarchitecture.org.

Reardon, K. (1997). "Participatory Action Research and Real Community-Based Planning in East St. Louis Illinois." *In Building Community: Social Science in Action*, edited by P. Nyden et al., pp. 233-239. Thousand Oaks, CA: Pine Forge Press.

Sanoff, H. (March 26, 2004). Personal interview.

Shiffman, R. (March 28, 2004). Personal interview.

Thabit, W. (1999). "PEO: A History of Planners for Equal Opportunity." Unpublished manuscript.

Weisman, L. (1999). "Re-Designing Architectural Education: New Models for a New Century." *In Design and Feminism: Re-Visioning Spaces, Places, and Everyday Things*, edited by J. Rothschild, pp. 159-173. New Brunswick, NJ: Rutgers University Press.

West, T. (March 19, 2004). Personal interview.

Wiewel, W. (November 4, 2004). Email.

A Core Commitment to Service-Learning:
Bridging Planning Theory and Practice

By Lorlene M. Hoyt

Introduction

A longstanding and common criticism of planning education is the persistent gap between theoretical and practical modes of instruction (Perloff 1957; Rich et al. 1970; Schön 1970; de Neufville 1983; Sawicki 1988; Tyson and Low 1987; Garcia 1993; Friedmann and Kuester 1994; Baum 1997; Shepherd and Cosgriff 1998; Birch 2001). However, service-learning, especially when embedded in the core curriculum, offers a bridge for connecting theory-based instruction, where students study or conduct research on the planning process, and practice-based instruction, where they participate in the planning process.

This essay begins with an historical synopsis of the theory-practice divide in planning education and a detailed description of how and why the Massachusetts Institute of Technology (MIT) crafted a new service-learning model for the Master in City Planning (MCP) curriculum. Midway through, the focus shifts to a case study of one practicum to demonstrate how mutually advantageous university-community partnerships can occur and the benefits to be realized by community organizations and residents. The final part describes how MIT's service-learning model encourages students to integrate planning theory and practice, and considers the many challenges associated with institutionalizing service-learning.

The Theory-Practice Divide

Although MIT offered planning courses in the School of Architecture as early as 1921, it took more than 15 years for the nation's second independent MCP program to officially materialize (Garcia 1993). For the next three decades and in tandem with schools like Harvard University and the University of Pennsylvania, MIT's planning curriculum emphasized planning practice above theory, as evidenced by the volume of studio courses offered during this time. The 1960s proved to be both a promising and a turbulent time for planning schools (Ozawa and Seltzer 2000). First, planning education became more popular. For example, between 1960 and 1970, the number of planning programs increased by 50 percent (Birch 2001). Second, to further define the field and ensure that future professionals possessed the requisite skills, many schools adopted a core curriculum consisting of three parts:

basic knowledge, basic methods, and problem solving — a pedagogical paradigm that remains intact today. By contrast, this was also a time when schools of planning, including MIT's, experienced growing tensions between theory and practice.

The divide emerged as the value systems in universities shifted, and planning schools hired new faculty who were well-trained in the social sciences but had very little experience with planning practice (Sawicki 1988). Thus, a norm was established: planning professors were expected to conduct research and create planning theory, while planning professionals outside the walls of academia were responsible for its application. Throughout the 1970s and 1980s, the divide deepened, as the curriculum of most planning schools diverged from a focus on professional practice to a more theoretical orientation. For example, in 1967, MIT eliminated its core curriculum, which included a series of studios. A new set of core subjects, put in place by the mid-1980s, did not require studio courses (Rich 1970). The decision to exclude studios from the core accentuated the department's steady movement away from practice-based instruction. This trend continued in planning schools across the country, despite the cohort of educators who argued for the value of engaging students in professional settings to prepare them for the day-to-day reality of planning practice (Schön 1970; Schön et al. 1976; Tyson and Low 1987; Hemmens 1988).

For the past four decades, planning schools, like all academic professional schools, have faced the dilemma of teaching the art of practice within a system largely concerned with the advancement of theory. Nevertheless, many planning educators remain engaged in planning practice and committed to offering courses that expose students to professional planning practice. Some of these instructors provide opportunities for students to participate in service-learning, which is a type of practice that enables students to work with a client, confront place-based problems, and reflect on the consequences of their actions (Shepherd and Cosgriff 1998; Ozawa and Seltzer 1999; Frank 2002). Difficulties notwithstanding, the planning education literature shows that service-learning not only benefits students but also empowers community organizations and residents by building capacity and supplementing their efforts with additional resources such as information technologies (Grant and Manuel 1995; Dewar and Isaac 1998; LeGates and Robinson 1998; Rubin 1998; Baum 2000). Moreover, a movement to bridge the theory-practice divide via service-learning instruction is apparent in the contemporary literature on planning pedagogy (Grant and Manuel 1995; Dewar and Isaac 1998; Ozawa and Seltzer 1999; Baum 2000; Frank 2002).

This essay expands the burgeoning conversation by offering a more comprehensive approach, namely, the institutionalization of service-learning courses into the MCP core curriculum. What follows is one department's struggle to assemble a service-learning model that emphasizes the relationship between theory and practice and prepares students for the transition from the academy to the world of professional planning.

Crafting the Blueprints for a Bridge

In fall 2000, MIT's MCP Committee, led by Dennis Frenchman, a planning professor and practitioner with more than 25 years of experience, made a commitment to examining the core curriculum and revitalizing the MCP degree program. To confront the task of changing a curriculum that had been in place for nearly 20 years, the committee members designed a comprehensive and participatory planning process that included regular meetings with students, alumni, and instructors. After carefully reviewing their contributions and considering the requirements set forth by the Planning Accreditation Board (PAB), committee members decided to craft one educational experience for all incoming students and recommended that the new core curriculum focus on four basic competencies. It restructured the core so that each student would experience a common gateway course, take a course in an area of specialization, and acquire basic computing and quantitative skills. As the fourth competency, and for the first time in nearly 40 years, students would be required to advance their knowledge and skills by participating in a field-based practicum (Sanyal 2003). The committee quickly adopted "practicum" instead of "studio," because it is a term used by a wide range of professional programs to describe the experience of a professional-in-training and it accentuates the art of a profession, thus placing an emphasis on synthesis above analysis (Wetmore and Heumann 1988).

The notion of a required practicum surfaced (or resurfaced) for two reasons. First, urban design studios, which had been expanding from the early 1990s, began to attract students in other areas of planning — such as community development, environmental policy, or regional planning — who desired to gain real-world experience prior to professional practice. Second, some of the students had a different approach to planning that included an interest in working with community members, engaging in collective decision-making processes, and directly confronting issues of race, class, and gender (Kirschbaum 2003). Frenchman placed the idea of a required practicum experience on the core agenda, and argued that a professional planning education should require that students develop important leadership skills and learn how to synthesize innovative solutions to the complexities of real-world problems. In his mind, the practicum was the most appropriate way to meet these objectives (Frenchman 2003).

At the second MCP Committee meeting, Frenchman suggested that the department implement several practica, in a variety of national and international contexts. At this pivotal moment, Bishwapriya Sanyal, then department chair, deliberately guided the conversation toward a model of service-learning. For example, he pointed out that the faculty ought to strengthen relationships with institutions in nearby Boston. The practicum experience, he contended, would be more meaningful for students if the department pursued a model whereby university-community relationships were built on trust. A multi-year commitment, he added, would be the best way to foster such a relationship (Frenchman 2003).

Building the Bridge

In fall 2001, Frenchman launched and chaired the MCP Core Practicum Committee. Composed of faculty and student representatives, the group first focused on the development of course selection criteria and later managed the course selection and implementation processes. To ensure that the practica met essential pedagogical goals, the committee members identified and defined a distinctive set of requirements that each of the practica would be required to meet. Ultimately, they adopted six, which characterize the service-learning model adopted for MIT's MCP students.

The first criterion, "Involve Constituents and Issues at a Particular Place," draws attention to the intrinsic connection between service activity and learning. This requirement emphasizes the importance of establishing a long-term commitment with a client, such as a sponsoring agency, organization, or community group. In this framework, students build on the work done by their predecessors, achieving goals that have greater impact and more meaning to the community. Moreover, when students work within a community, the committee concluded, they need to balance the interests of a diverse set of stakeholders and confront issues related to diversity and planning. (Throughout this essay, the rubric "diversity and planning" includes confronting issues of race, ethnicity, gender, age, disability, and social exclusion.)

The second criterion, "Provide Opportunities for Reflection and Appraisal," encourages responsible civic participation by requiring students to examine their beliefs and assumptions and how past experiences affect their actions. The committee determined that each practicum course would require students to confront deep biases and assumptions about people and communities. Reflection takes place through class discussions, journaling, and self-learning assessments, thus creating a forum where faculty can guide students to become more conscientious citizens and planners.

The third criterion, "Include Opportunities to Put Theory into Practice," explicitly stresses the nexus between planning theory and practice. Student work that draws on experience with similar issues in other places, as well as the relevant literature, will facilitate the formulation of new theory. Moreover, faculty who are selected to participate must investigate linkages between the project and the development of theory, beyond the scope of the practicum, by supervising student involvement with community-based internships, research projects, and theses.

The fourth criterion, "Encourage Exploration and Innovation," is consistent with the spirit of MIT, an environment where students are encouraged to explore and take risks. Practica represent an opportunity to develop new tools and approaches for addressing problems. The expectation is that such an approach nurtures creativity and potentially introduces a wider array of solutions to the community.

The fifth criterion, "Address Cross-Cutting Issues and Involve Allied Disciplines," recognizes that planning practice involves interdisciplinary teamwork as well as the consideration of many perspectives and interrelated issues. Practica, therefore, must integrate different planning disciplines and involve faculty with divergent interests. In some instances, faculty invite outside specialists to offer expertise beyond what is available in the community or the university.

The final criterion, "Make and Test Proposals," reinforces the objective of giving students the experience and skills to develop proposals in the face of incomplete information and conflicting points of view. Such proposals become tools of decision making and consensus building as well as ways to engender constituent feedback for evolving plans and projects; they reinforce direct and meaningful client involvement. Finally, upon completion of each practicum, both the student and the client will have a tangible product that represents the culmination of their joint efforts.

After the adoption of the practicum criteria, the MCP Core Practicum Committee, now chaired by Karl Seidman, focused on course selection and implementation. To begin, Seidman conducted personal interviews with individual faculty members. The interview data enabled him to identify faculty members interested in developing a new service-learning practicum course. Simultaneously, committee members formed small working groups to tackle administrative concerns associated with computing, classroom space, funding, and matching students to classes, as well as pedagogical matters such as devising methods for incorporating reflection. To acquire additional feedback, the committee sponsored a student meeting and distributed a seven-page survey to faculty experienced in teaching studio courses.

In January 2003, the MCP Core Practicum Committee began a review of courses against the selection criteria. The committee prepared an instrument consisting of questions for each criterion that facilitated the review practicum proposals (Seidman 2002):

1. **Involve Constituents and Issues at a Particular Place**

Is there a long-term relationship with a specific client? Is there a process to engage students with constituents as part of formlating the plan?

2. **Provide Opportunities for Reflection and Appraisal**

How do students examine their assumptions and their engagement with the community? What approaches and tools for fostering this reflection are being used?

3. **Include Opportunities to Put Theory into Practice**

How does the course content relate to planning theory? In what ways does the course project allow students to apply these theories?

4. **Encourage Exploration and Innovation**

Does the course apply new tools to understanding problems and developing solutions? What new tools or approaches is it incorporating?

5. **Address Cross-Cutting Issues and Involve Allied Disciplines**

Do the course content and project address cross-cutting problems and issues? Does the course expose students to expertise from multiple disciplines?

6. **Make and Test Proposals**

Does the course project involve formulating specific plans and proposals? Is there a process to incorporate client feedback in the final plan?

Rather than require instructors to undergo an application process, the committee held a series of focused interviews to evaluate each proposal, and this instrument was helpful in structuring a two-way exchange of information with faculty, especially those who were less familiar with the selection criteria (Seidman 2003).

In March, committee members convened to choose a subset from the 11 courses presented. Beyond ensuring that the courses met the criteria, they attended to the emerging interest in diversity and planning articulated by both the faculty and the study body. Committee members established a complementary collection of three courses in diverse inner-city settings in Boston, Springfield, and Lawrence. (Practica courses in international as well as suburban contexts were recently introduced into the core curriculum.)

Destination: Lawrence, Massachusetts

The Lawrence practicum demonstrates one way that university-community partnerships materialize, and how service-learning not only prepares students for professional practice but also results in sophisticated and useful products for community organizations and residents.

Also, it sets the stage for describing how MIT's service-learning model supports a connection between theory and practice, and the difficulties with integrating service-learning into the core curriculum.

For nearly two decades, Lawrence has functioned as an urban laboratory for MIT planning faculty and their students. Faculty have taught planning studios with deliverables ranging from the development of commercial revitalization plans for the city's Office of Economic Development to a spatial analysis for Lawrence Community Works, Inc. (LCW). Moreover, at least 10 MCP students have written theses requiring intimate involvement with the city and its inhabitants, and countless others have participated in summer internships with nonprofit organizations and public-sector agencies throughout the city. A professional network has resulted from these ad hoc arrangements as evidenced by the number of MCP alumni who work and live in Lawrence. For example, several former MCP students work at LCW, while others hold key positions at the city's Planning Department, Groundwork Lawrence, and other local organizations.

Today, the Lawrence practicum, Information and Communication Technologies in Community Development, is the cornerstone of MIT's multi-year partnership with LCW, a community-development corporation dedicated to organizing, planning, and community building. This practicum presents a unique learning opportunity for students, residents, and instructors because it creates a single and continuous point of entry for MIT. Furthermore, through the alumni network, MIT forges a true partnership with the community, founded on trust and mutual respect (LeGates and Robinson 1998).

Lawrence is an ideal context for a service-learning-oriented planning practicum because it is a readily accessible, intensely diverse, and spirited community. Located approximately 25 miles north of Cambridge, Lawrence is easily accessed by bus, train, or automobile. Physical proximity permits students to attend community meetings and public hearings and work hand-in-hand with LCW staff and their constituents. This model of service-learning, although time-consuming, asks students to function as participants rather than consultants, so they can better understand the role of relationships in community building and neighborhood development. Furthermore, Lawrence, long known as the "Immigrant City," is a setting where issues of diversity and planning — a field explicitly supported by MIT's Planning Department — naturally converge.

Lawrence was established in 1847 as a highly planned industrial town and initially attracted immigrants from Canada, England, Germany, and Ireland. By the early 1900s, migrants from Italy, Lithuania, Poland, and Syria were living in Lawrence's company boarding houses and working in the textile mills along the Merrimack River. The next wave of newcomers, mostly from Puerto Rico and the Dominican Republic and some from Vietnam and Cambodia, arrived shortly after the United States changed its immigration laws in the 1960s. According to the 2000 Census, 60 percent of Lawrence's total population self-identifies as Latino, up from 3.5 percent in 1970. Like many older cities in the Northeast, Lawrence has experienced an exodus of manufacturing jobs. As a result, newcomers have fewer employment opportunities than did their predecessors. Anglo-Latino tensions, unemployment levels, and issues of bilingual education aside, the collective Lawrence spirit is hopeful. One explanation is the presence of the Reviviendo Gateway Initiative (RGI), one of the largest economic development projects in the Commonwealth. Reviviendo, "return to life," represents a long-term and resident-led strategy to redesign the entrance to the city from Interstate 495 and transform the surrounding neighborhoods.

Traversing the Divide

During the eight-month RGI strategic planning process, which included more than 350 residents, LCW identified the collection, analysis, and dissemination of information as an integral component of the project, yet lacked the means to implement the latest information and communication technologies. I was interested in exploring the role of information and communication technologies in community development, and recognized that there was a mutually beneficial way to solve the problem.

While LCW was eager to benefit from the technical support that MIT's faculty and students could deliver, they perceived the proposed practicum as more than a one-way flow of technical assistance. After some deliberation, MIT and LCW concluded that the practicum represented an opportunity to advance beyond an impromptu working relationship and embark on a focused, multi-year partnership. The practicum enabled students and faculty to become integral parts of the RGI vision by infusing the process with information and communication technologies. In broad terms, the partnership follows a participatory action-research model, whereby LCW members actively contribute to the design and implementation of a Web-based planning tool. In contrast to the conventional model of theory-based instruction and the most prevalent type of practice-based instruction, organizational members do not function as passive subjects, nor do the researchers act as experts whose principal responsibility is to deliver a specialized product (Whyte et al. 1989). In particular, LCW expressed an interest in working with youth to acquire data and develop a Web-based system, with mapping and other capabilities, that would enable the organization to share information, perform analyses, and foster greater community involvement in the RGI. This agenda, as depicted in Figure

1, constitutes the dominant framework for the partnership as well as the practicum. (Additional information about the MIT-LCW partnership is available at www.urbanrevitalization.net.)

Figure 1. MIT students and LCW working in Lawrence

Looking Back

In October 2003, the Lawrence City Council voted unanimously to pass the Reviviendo overlay district proposal, which went into effect immediately. The RGI's first initiative, the overlay district, represents an historic modification to the zoning code that streamlines the approval process for developers and property owners interested in building or expanding structures. This victory is meaningful to the MIT faculty and students who worked to promote the overlay district.

MCP students and LCW staff designed a Web-based neighborhood information system, or "sistema de informaci obre el vecindario," to publicize information pertaining to the RGI and the overlay district project. The site, which is fully accessible to the public and located at www.avencia.com/lcw/, consists of two parts. "Tell Me More about My Neighborhood" (Digame Más Sobre Mi Vecindario) allows users to explore neighborhoods with visual aids such as photographs, sketches, bar charts, and maps. For example, data from the U.S. Census Bureau enable LCW staff and residents to see how the population has changed over the past 30 years. Moreover, site visitors can view photographs of severely dilapidated as well as newly rehabilitated structures within the overlay district area, collected by youth who participate in LCW's Young Architects program. The other section of the site, "What Is Reviviendo?" (¿Qué es Reviviendo?), disseminates information about the working committees and tells residents how to get involved. It also offers access to the zoning overlay proposal and demonstrates how it will affect different groups, including homeowners, small businesses, mill owners, and artists.

Figure 2. RGI homepage

The most dynamic aspect of the site, the interactive address-mapping function, helps users understand the geographical scope and potential of the overlay district. For example, to determine if a property falls within the boundaries of the district, users simply enter a street address. As shown in Figure 3, the system responds by exhibiting a map along with the public information pertaining to the property, such as district status, size, deed date, deed book and page number, land value, building value, tax abatement, tax delinquency, and addresses of adjacent properties.

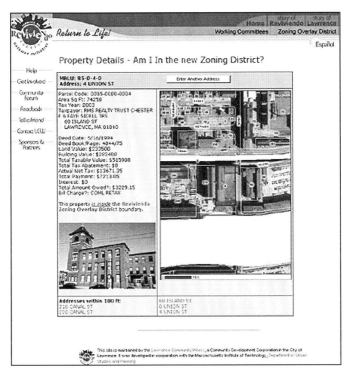

Figure 3. Interactive address mapping function

Maintaining the Connection

Although MIT has embraced service-learning, many challenges remain. Bringing the classroom into the community creates an occasion for faculty to explore the nexus between theory and practice. MIT's new service-learning model explicitly requires faculty to inform planning action with theory ("Include Opportunities to Put Theory into Practice"). In the Lawrence practicum, for example, students are expected to complete readings on the theoretical aspects of power relationships and the literature on collaborative planning; they are also expected to apply this knowledge as they work on the project in the field. Rather than passively accept how LCW staff and Lawrence residents interact, students rely on theories of planning to call into question the process by which stakeholders identify problems and build consensus; they test and expand planning theories. Furthermore, the second criterion, "Provide Opportunities for Reflection and Appraisal," encourages them to function as reflective practitioners, that is, practitioners who refine their practice by examining how their beliefs guide their decisions and actions (Schön 1983). This process often entails a synthesis of theory and practice. For example, each of the inner-city practica places a strong emphasis on working within diverse communities, which gives students an opportunity to compare a theoretical understanding of racial and ethnic discrimination with what they observe and experience on the site. It is important to note that while MIT planning instructors were eager to integrate methods of reflection into the practica, few possessed such skills, and most sought training through MIT's Center for Reflective Community Practice.

Despite MIT's recent success with introducing a service-learning model into the MCP core curriculum, there are several logistical and pedagogical challenges worthy of discussion. For example, continuity — maintaining relationships and momentum with community organizations within a discontinuous academic framework — is a formidable challenge. University-community partnerships are often difficult because meaningful relationships require students and faculty to spend a considerable amount of time at the site. Graduate students, with a two-year tenure that is interrupted with exams and long breaks, are often unable to engage fully with off-campus clients. However, service-learning that is part of the core curriculum and that obliges faculty to work with a community organization for several years ("Involve Constituents and Issues at a Particular Place") produces several opportunities. A multi-year schedule gives faculty ample time to acquire funding and conduct long-term research projects grounded in the community. Support from the department and assured external funding enable faculty to hire research assistants who work continuously with the community organization, including summers. In this way, the service-learning practicum is more than a teaching obligation for faculty; it is an important part of their long-term intellectual agenda. Moreover, students have a wider range of prospects for applying theory to practice within such a framework. For example, students may take the Lawrence practicum in their first year at MIT, work as research assistants during the second year, and construct master's theses that examine information technologies and community development in both practical and theoretical terms.

As mentioned earlier, the criterion "Address Cross-Cutting Issues and Involve Allied Disciplines" requires faculty with different interests to co-teach practicum courses. The intent is to engage students in interdisciplinary work; however, this is difficult because students possess divergent perspectives, abilities, and skills. However, this mandate also presents an opportunity to couple practice-oriented instructors with theory-oriented instructors and produce a classroom environment where students and instructors work together to bridge the seemingly dichotomous paradigms. Similarly, while MIT students have the ability to select a practicum that best matches their interests, the instructors review final enrollment to ensure that each course contains students with a wide range of expertise. This enables instructors to balance those students who prefer practice and those who subscribe to a more theoretical approach.

Other logistical hardships include the coordination of participant (faculty, student, and community member) schedules and agendas. For example, to produce meaningful products ("Make and Test Proposals"), participants must work to organize individual schedules both within and among practica offerings.

However, there are intellectual and economic benefits to coordinating multiple service-learning practica. For example, by deliberately focusing on a single substantive theme in the planning literature, participants can share their service-learning experiences. Although students are working on different projects, with different constituents, in different places, cross-cutting conversations can occur because a critical mass of MCP students and faculty coalesces around a common theme — namely, diversity and planning. Because the theme also reflects the department's broader agenda, other opportunities surface. For example, throughout fall 2003, the department sponsored weekly lunches with guest speakers who addressed questions like, "How Do Immigrants, Minorities and Excluded Groups Build Institutions, Power, and Networks?" Moreover, departments enjoy economies of scale when they synchronize service-learning initiatives. MIT's service-learning model urges faculty to "Encourage Exploration and Innovation." This may involve the use of technologies like the Web and GIS. Faculty members benefit from sharing both equipment, like laptop computers, network servers, and digital video cameras, and an administrative assistant. Instructors can direct their energies toward curriculum and research development (such as practice-theory connections) rather than becoming overburdened with administrative tasks.

The most formidable barrier to institutionalizing service-learning exists at the university level. Today, most universities reward planning faculty who participate in traditional research projects and publish work in refereed academic journals. The payoff for service-learning instruction has yet to materialize. Unlike schools of architecture or the fine arts, where practice-based teaching is essential to success, junior faculty in planning have yet to observe such activities as an effective strategy for advancing within the academy. However, the increasing demand for service-learning, and growing recognition of its benefits, may enable faculty to rally departmental support and challenge university-level policies, thus advancing the discipline. As Donald Schön and other renowned planning theorists have argued, city planning cannot advance solely on the basis of academic ruminations or analysis. Planning is a profession in action that must synthesize solutions, and therefore practice is the most legitimate route to planning theory.

References

Baum, H. S. (2000). "Fantasies and Realities in University-Community Partnerships." *Journal of Planning Education and Research* 20: 234-246.

_____. (1997). "Teaching Practice." *Journal of Planning Education and Research* 17: 21-29.

Birch, E. L. (2001). "Practitioners and the Art of Planning." *Journal of Planning Education and Research* 20: 407-422.

de Neufville, J.I. (1983). "Planning Theory and Practice: Bridging the Gap." *Journal of Planning Education and Research* 3 (1): 35-45.

Dewar, M.E., and C.B. Isaac. (1998). "Learning from Difference: The Potentially Transforming Experience of Community-University Collaboration." *Journal of Planning Education and Research* 17: 334-347.

Frank, N. (2002). "Rethinking Planning Theory for a Master's-Level Curriculum." *Journal of Planning Education and Research* 21: 320-330.

Frenchman, D. (September 30, 2003). Personal interview.

Friedmann, J., and C. Kuester. (1994). "Planning Education for the Late 20th Century: An Initial Inquiry." *Journal of Planning Education and Research* 14 (1): 55-64.

Garcia, R.B. (1993). *Changing Paradigms of Professional Practice, Education and Research in Academe: A History of Planning Education in the United States.* Ann Arbor, MI: UMI Dissertation Services.

Grant, J., and P. Manuel. (1995). "Using a Peer Resource Learning Model in Planning Education." *Journal of Planning Education and Research* 15: 51-57.

Hemmens, G. C. (1988). "Thirty Years of Planning Education." *Journal of Planning Education and Research* 7:85-92.

Kirschbaum, J. (September 29, 2003). Personal interview.

LeGates, R.T., and G. Robinson. (1998). "Institutionalizing University-Community Partnerships." *Journal of Planning Education and Research* 17: 312-322.

Ozawa, C.P., and E. Seltzer. (2000). "Our Bearings: Mapping a Relationship among Planning Practice, Theory, and Education." *Journal of Planning Education and Research* 18: 257-266.

Perloff, H.S. (1957). *Education for Planning: City, State, and Regional.* Baltimore: Johns Hopkins University Press.

Rich, W., K. Geiser, R. Goetze, and R. Hollister. (1970). "Holding It Together: Four Years of Evolution at MIT." *Journal of the American Institute of Planners* 36 (4): 242-253.

Rubin, V. (1998). "The Roles of Universities in Community-Building Initiatives." *Journal of Planning Education and Research* 17: 302-311.

Sanyal, B. (September 29, 2003). Personal interview.

Sawicki, D.S. (1988). "Planning Education and Practice: Can We Plan for the Next Decade?" *Journal of Planning Education and Research* 7 (2): 115-120.

Schön, D.A. (1983). *The Reflective Practitioner: How Professionals Think in Action*. New York: Basic Books.

_____. (1970). "Notes Toward a Planning Curriculum." *Journal of the American Institute of Planners* 36 (4): 220-221.

Schön, D.A. N.S. Cremer, P. Osterman, and C. Perry. (1976). "Planners in Transition: Report on a Survey of MIT's Department of Urban Studies, 1960-1971." *Journal of the American Institute of Planners* 42: 193-202.

Seidman, Karl. (October 1, 2003). Personal interview.

_____. (November 14, 2002). Memorandum. Department of Urban Studies and Planning, Massachusetts Institute of Technology.

Shepherd, A., and B. Cosgriff. (1998). "Problem-Based Learning: A Bridge between Planning Education and Planning Practice." *Journal of Planning Education and Research* 17: 348-357.

Tyson, T.B., and N.P. Low. (1987). "Experiential Learning in Planning Education." *Journal of Planning Education and Research* 7: 15-27.

Wetmore, L.B., and L.F. Heumann. (1988). "The Changing Role of the Workshop Course in Educating Planning Professionals." *Journal of Planning Education and Research* 7: 135-146.

Whyte, W., D. Greenwood, and P. Lazes. (1989). "Participatory Action Research." *American Behavioral Scientist* 32 (5): 513-551.

Institutional Support for Community-Based Architecture and Planning Outreach Scholarship at Auburn University

By Sharon Gaber and Daniel Bennett

Introduction

Strong research universities have historically undervalued the scholarship and benefits derived from community-based pedagogy in architecture and planning curricula, with faculty members cautioned not to pin tenure and promotion hopes to outreach activities. This perspective is changing.

It is not enough for a college to depend on the compassion of its faculty to engage in significant community-based outreach. Colleges and universities can sustain long-term partnerships with communities only by complementing their faculty's interests in outreach with institutionalized incentives, rewards, and financial support. Bringing outreach into the core values of scholarship makes community-based outreach part of the everyday business.

The College of Architecture, Design and Construction at Auburn University (which includes the Architecture and Community Planning programs) and Auburn University as a whole recognize the value of outreach and have developed policies for rewarding meritorious outreach scholarship. The university's new policy, built on Boyer's (1990) delineation of four types of scholarship, defines outreach as "applying academic expertise to the direct benefit of external audiences in support of university and unit missions" (Auburn University Vice President for Outreach 2002: 3). Outreach is defined to include extension work, distance education, service-learning, applied research, and technical education.

This essay explores service-learning and outreach scholarship, along with three types of concomitant institutional support, at Auburn University: (1) the integration of outreach scholarship into tenure and promotion guidelines and considerations at the university level; (2) the identification of outreach scholarship in college guidelines for tenure and promotion; and (3) the fiscal support for outreach offered by both the College of Architecture, Design and Construction and the university, as exemplified by support for the Center for the Study of Southern Rural Architecture (commonly referred to as the Rural Studio) in rural Hale County, Alabama, and the Center for Architecture and Urban Studies (the Urban Studio) in Birmingham, Alabama.

Figure 1. Urban Studio model, 2003

Background

Auburn University offered its first classes in architecture in 1907, and in community planning in 1978, but it was the development of the Urban Studio, in 1990, and the Rural Studio, in 1992, that marked the School of Architecture's leap into service-learning activities. The School of Architecture, consisting of the programs in Architecture, Community Planning, Interior Architecture, and Landscape Architecture, is situated within the College of Architecture, Design and Construction (CADC), one of 12 colleges at Auburn, the state's land-grant institution and largest university.

The Urban Studio was conceived of as a way for undergraduate architecture students to gain "an urban experience" while attending college in a small-town setting. The program enables fourth-year architecture students to do studio work in an urban setting, and to interact with many of the top design professionals in the state's largest city. Students typically spend one semester at the Urban Studio and receive 15 academic credits for their coursework-in-residence.

The Urban Studio began in 1990, with faculty member Frank Setzer named its first director in 1992. The interest by students in the opportunity to continue their education in Birmingham led to an expansion of the program, during the mid-1990s, to include fifth-year architecture students doing their thesis. The faculty worked closely with the main campus to follow the architecture curriculum model, but also included external constituencies in their studio work. The Birmingham-based faculty began affiliations with DesignAlabama and with the state's Small Town Initiative to perform urban design work for communities in the Birmingham metropolitan area that might not otherwise be able to contract with professional architects and planners. A studio class of 8 to 10 students would work with the faculty member in sponsoring a design charrette and developing a plan for the community. Students felt empowered by their close interaction with an appreciative client. Some of the students enjoyed their collaboration so much that they continued to a master's in community planning.

When Frank Setzer died in 2001, Cheryl Morgan became director of the Urban Studio and has continued the service-learning efforts to small towns in Alabama. In 2003, the Urban Studio moved to a new facility, in Birmingham's historic core, that it shares with the local planning commission, Region 20/20 (a visioning organization), and the Alabama chapter of the American Institute of Architects (AIA). These linkages allow students and faculty to become involved in metropolitan design and planning issues.

The Rural Studio originated in 1992, when Samuel "Sambo" Mockbee and D.K. Ruth, faculty members in the School of Architecture, did "a one year educational experiment" to investigate context-based learning and the notion of changing the curriculum from "'paper architecture' to the creation of real buildings; and to sowing 'a moral sense of service to the community'" (Dean and Hurley 2002: 1). It became clear, by 1993, that the Rural Studio provided two critical missing components in traditional architecture education — a client and social compassion. It was also evident that the Rural Studio should become a long-term part of the School of Architecture and the curriculum. The Rural Studio was organized to allow approximately 15 second-year and 10 fifth-year architecture students the opportunity to live, learn, and "give back" to Alabama's Black Belt, a swath across the lower third of the state named for its fertile soil. Unfortunately, it also houses the state's poorest residents and is one of the country's most impoverished regions.

The second-year students have typically worked on a group design-build residential project. Examples emerging from these efforts include the well-documented Bryant House (often referred to as the Hay Bale House), in 1994, and the Harris House (also known as the Butterfly House), in 1997 (Ho 2003: 93). Fifth-year thesis students, working in teams of four to five, usually take on larger community-based projects, such as a community center, a farmer's market, a religious facility, or park facilities.

The Rural Studio continues its success under new leadership. After Samuel Mockbee died in 2001, D.K. Ruth remained as director emeritus, but Bruce Lindsey, head of the Auburn University School of Architecture, and Andrew Freear now serve as co-directors.

Tenure and Promotion Guidelines as Institutional Support

As Kenny and Gallagher (2002: 20) have argued, and Auburn's urban and rural studios demonstrated, major developments in service-learning occurred during the early 1990s. But the questions remained: What is the role of service-learning on a university campus? How is it valued? (Kenny and Gallagher 2002: 23; Kezar and Rhoads 2001; Kenny et al. 2002).

Auburn University addressed these questions in 2002. The associate provost and vice president for outreach, David Wilson, and the assistant vice president for outreach, Robert Montjoy, in conjunction with the University Senate and the provost, agreed that they would more explicitly define how outreach scholarship is viewed and valued for tenure and promotion.

Figure 2. Rural Studio students working on Music Man house, 2003

The document and presentation developed to explain the role of outreach scholarship began with a definition of what Auburn University believes and values about outreach: "Outreach refers to the function of applying academic expertise to the direct benefit of external audiences in support of university and unit missions." Additionally, five general types of outreach were defined: extension, distance education, service-learning, applied research, and technical assistance (Auburn University Vice President for Outreach 2002: 3, 4). The presentations offered across campus frequently cited the Rural Studio as the prime example of service-learning outreach.

With the definition established, the document offered five key premises about outreach:

1. It is one of Auburn's three principal missions.
2. It is not required of all faculty.
3. It is more difficult to assess than research and teaching.
4. It is therefore typically undervalued in the reward system.
5. It is the subject of revisions to the faculty handbook aimed at improving documentation, assessment, and reward, as appropriate.

These points set the tone for the university's full commitment to the scholarship of outreach. The clear statement that outreach is "typically undervalued in the reward system" was met with resounding interest in changing the system. Also encouraging was the realization that faculty in the School of Architecture were engaged in outreach scholarship through the urban and rural studios and other service-learning projects (e.g., DesignHabitat and Alabama AIDS house).

Language from the new document was incorporated into the faculty handbook. Specifically, a faculty member's work can be regarded as outreach scholarship for purposes of tenure and promotion if it meets the following conditions (Auburn University 2002: 3.8.C):

• It has a substantive link with significant human needs and societal problems, issues, or concerns.

• It directly applies knowledge to significant human needs and societal problems, issues, or concerns.

• It uses the faculty member's academic and professional expertise.

• Its ultimate purpose is for the public or common good.

• It generates new knowledge for the discipline, audience, or clientele.

• It shows a clear link or relationship between the program or activities and an appropriate academic unit's mission.

Faculty members are now expected to document their outreach in a portfolio format consisting of supporting materials, allocation of time and effort dedicated to outreach, a self-reflective narrative, a description of the outreach scholarship, an analysis of how it meets university criteria, and an identification of activities and products (Auburn University Vice President for Outreach 2002). This seemingly prescribed and bureaucratic procedure was carefully developed to offer the same level of credibility for faculty who specialize in outreach as those who emphasize research. It also gives faculty clear benchmarks for measuring their progress toward tenure and promotion. The concept is that a faculty member undertaking outreach through service-learning is generating and disseminating new knowledge.

College of Architecture, Design and Construction Tenure and Promotion Guidelines as Institutional Support

Independently of the university's movement toward accepting outreach and service-learning in tenure and promotion (T&P) considerations, the CADC was seeking to define its own guidelines. Faculty in the School of Architecture (the programs in Architecture, Community Planning, Landscape Architecture, and Interior Architecture) had faced questions at the university-wide Tenure and Promotion Committee, which claimed not to understand the scholarship involved in a design-build project or an applied studio. The CADC School of Architecture and Department of Industrial design developed a T&P document, in 2002-2003, to demonstrate to the rest of the university what constitutes scholarship for faculty in these programs.

The CADC's School of Architecture and Department of Industrial Design, like peers at other institutions, strive for faculty excellence. Recognizing the need to identify guidelines and expectations for quality in education, scholarship, and outreach, the T&P document helps faculty, as well as stakeholders external to the college, in understanding the expectations and outputs of scholarship in the School of Architecture and the Department of Industrial Design. Faculty within the disciplines of architecture and industrial design, like those in the sciences and humanities, engage in scholarship and creative activity, but their scholarly outputs may take forms other than publication. For example, in architecture and industrial design, peer-reviewed design commissions are viewed as significant as, or more significant than, peer-reviewed journal articles. Faculty members may specialize in outreach scholarship that generates new knowledge (College of Architecture, Design and Construction 2003: 1).

The differences inherent in the disciplines in the School of Architecture led to establishing guidelines without overly prescribing or mandating types of research, creative activity, or outreach. Instead, the guidelines suggest that a strong body of good work is necessary for tenure and promotion. As Boyer (1990) noted, research and creative activity may include exploration and analysis of professional practice, original inquiry, outreach, and teaching, in addition to basic and applied research.

The School of Architecture's faculty first identified and prioritized three types of research and creative scholarship:

1. Highest Distinction Scholarship
- P.I. of external-to-university funded research grant or contract run through the university ($1,000,000 or more)
  - Publication of scholarly book
  - Major fellowship
  - Editor of scholarly book
  - National award (Guggenheim, Fulbright, MacArthur, etc.)
  - Major (national) architectural or design commission, with peer review accolades
  - External-to-university funded research grant or contract, run through the university ($500,000 to $999,999)
  - Refereed journal article (primary author or equal coauthor)

- "Best of Show" or finalist honors at national or international design competition
- External-to-university funded research grant or contract, run through the university ($100,000 to $499,999)
- Regional (multistate) award

2. Distinctive Scholarship
- P.I. of external-to-university funded research grant or contract run through the university ($20,000 to $99,999)
- Second author of refereed journal article
- Presentation of refereed or reviewed paper or project at international or national conference or meeting
- "Best of show" or finalist honors at regional (multistate) design competition
- Patent*
- Editor of major journal
- Paper in refereed conference proceedings
- P.I. of external-to-university funded research grant or contract run through the university (up to $19,999)
- State award
- Regional architectural or design commission, with peer-review accolades
- Expert witness testimony*
- Non-refereed journal article
- Publication of chapter in scholarly book
- P.I. of internal-to-university funded research grant or contract (greater than $50,000)

3. Adequate Scholarship
- P.I. of internal-to-university funded research grant or contract (up to $49,999)
- Recognition for professional practice or creative work (by professional associations, in journals, in newspapers)
- Local exhibitions, off campus (e.g., Auburn Museum of Art, Lee County Chamber of Commerce)
- Member of editorial board**
- Book review in international or national journal**
- Local exhibitions, on campus (e.g., a gallery)**
- Presentation related to professional practice or creative work**
- Reviewer for scholarly journal**

(* No more than two items in each of these categories may count toward promotion or tenure. ** No more than three items in each of these categories may count toward promotion or tenure.)

The faculty then addressed outreach. The faculty handbook indicates that outreach is not expected of all faculty, but it does point out that the College of Architecture, Design and Construction has a strong history of outreach: "The College of Architecture, Design and

Construction has provided a number of community outreach projects and services to the profession. Several architectural and community development master plans in the state and region have been supervised by faculty in the school" (Auburn University 2002: 6.3.B).

The School of Architecture's T&P guidelines (College of Architecture, Design and Construction 2003: 9) identify relevant examples of outreach activities:

- Community and regional-based class projects
- Summer industrial design workshop
- Supervision and/or participation in Rural Studio
- Supervision and/or participation in Urban Studio
- Participation on community advisory boards or groups
- Expert advice to a city, state, or nonprofit organization
- Supervision or participation in community projects or organizations (Cary Woods Playground, Habitat For Humanity House)
- Training of professionals in specialized skills or knowledge
- Provision of continuing education credit
- Organization of a state, regional, national, or international conference

The document (p. 10) advises faculty members to substantiate outreach activities in their dossiers, including:

- Description of the outreach activity
- Compatibility of the activity with the mission of the university, college, and department
- Faculty member's role in outreach scholarship activity
- Impact of the activity: evaluation and recognition
- Activities and products

The guidelines for the university and the college, although relatively new and not fully tested, provide the faculty in the School of Architecture with criteria for documenting their significant outreach work, assuring them that their work will "count." However, it is the financial commitment of an institution that allows the community outreach or service-learning activity to actually occur.

Fiscal Support by the College and the University

An institution must be willing to invest in an outreach activity in order to see it to fruition. Outreach or service-learning cannot be viewed as something extra or nonessential to the teaching mission of an institution. In Alabama, where the state government expects institutions of higher education to generate community and economic development, there is an understanding that the university must create opportunities for investment and reinvestment. The urban and rural studios are doing this and are therefore supported by the college and the university.

The Rural Studio has had tremendous success in developing funding, although initially it was a struggle. The college agreed to fund Mockbee and Ruth's salary for their studio, and the faculty agreed to solicit sponsors to pay for supplies. Both faculty members were very charismatic and had successful professional architectural careers. They were able to call corporations, companies, and vendors to request support. As Dean (2002: 4) reported, "the many benefactors ... supplied the studio with more than $2 million in grants and contributions between 1993 and 2000."

As the success and reputation of the Rural Studio grew, the cost associated with that growth also expanded. A full-time staff member was added in 2000 at Auburn to help with grant-writing efforts, solicitation, publicity, and on-campus coordination of students. (One recent grant, for approximately $20,000 from Major League Baseball's Baseball Tomorrow Program, enabled students at the Rural Studio to build a youth baseball facility.) Additionally, a full-time staff member was added to provide administrative support. The college still pays for all faculty from faculty lines, including one tenured member, co-director Andrew Freear, and two full-time visiting instructors and two part-time instructors.

The university has also demonstrated its financial commitment. For the first several years, the Rural Studio applied for, and received, one-time grants, usually from $50,000 to $75,000, from the Office of the Vice President for Outreach. The university saw tangible positive outcomes, such as buildings and improved living conditions, in Alabama's poorest counties. In 2001, the university memorialized Mockbee's death by earmarking $400,000 in permanent annual funding for the Rural Studio.

The college's financial support of the Urban Studio has been similar to its support of the Rural Studio, but this is not the case with the university's support. The college has covered the cost for two full-time tenured faculty members in Birmingham, with the faculty's contract or grant work paying for supplies, travel, and summer salaries. The death of Setzer left one faculty line open, which has remained unfilled after a failed faculty search. The salary line has been used to hire visiting lecturers and, in 2003, brought New York urban designer Michael Sorkin to Birmingham to teach. In addition to the salaries, the college has agreed to pay the rent and utilities of the Urban Studio, in its new co-located facilities, through at least 2005. It is hoped that the contract and grant work will become self-sustaining. (The Rural Studio does not pay rent because its quarters were donated or built by students as a part of their studio work.)

The university has provided minimal financial support to the Urban Studio. Several factors explain this but do not dilute the frustration felt by the faculty. The university administration understands and values a deployed, tangible product, but the Urban Studio offers designs, concepts, plans, and consultation — products that are usually "placed on a shelf." Second, the Urban Studio is in the backyard of the University of Alabama in Tuscaloosa, the state's other major research university, and must contend with strong competition for support. Third, the Urban Studio has not received as much publicity as the Rural Studio, because the latter's work and mission are unique. While the Rural Studio builds housing that is both sustainably constructed and architecturally significant, the Urban Studio offers a vision for the future and is similar to programs in architecture schools elsewhere across the country. Ironically, the Urban Studio's broad-based planning efforts actually touch more of the state's residents than the activities of the Rural Studio.

The Urban Studio's faculty have worked to garner financial support from the university, inviting vice presidents to Birmingham to view completed projects, but there is still no funding commitment. Likewise, while the city of Birmingham values and appreciates the studio's work, it has also failed to offer a major financial commitment. Nevertheless, the Urban Studio continues to receive grants and contracts from communities and planning organizations.

Lessons Learned

Auburn University's College of Architecture, Design and Construction and the School of Architecture are recognized leaders in community-based service-learning. They have succeeded after more than a decade of trial by fire that has taught them a few lessons.

First, service-learning or community-based outreach must be driven by dedicated, willing faculty eager to invest their students with an ethos of service and to work harder and put in more hours than in a traditional seminar or campus studio class. A college administration cannot require faculty to perform outreach; many faculty are not particularly interested in community-based work and would rather pursue more traditional forms of teaching and scholarly activity.

Second, we have always maintained that it is the role of the college and the university to provide financial support. We argue that this support is twofold: incentives and rewards, and programmatic funding.

Based upon Auburn's experience, it is difficult to encourage untenured or not fully promoted faculty to participate in outreach without written documentation that the college and university will value this work (specifically in T&P documents). Originally, all faculty participating in the Urban and Rural Studios were tenured full professors. Now,

Andrew Freear, the co-director of the Rural Studio, is a tenured associate professor. He will be able to count his outreach work at the Rural Studio toward his scholarship when he seeks promotion.

Additionally, in an age of "show me the money," it is clear that faculty and programs understand their perceived value by the dollars that are allocated to them from both colleges (local academic units) and the university. Community-based work requires significant financial investment and cannot succeed without permanent, allocated funding.

The final lesson is that institutional support for community-based architecture and planning is a value that a college or school has, or develops, and to which it remains true. Our learning in this area comes from the ongoing fiscal crisis of education in Alabama (and across the nation). The state and Auburn University have undertaken proration (budget reallocation) or budget cuts every year for the past five years. It would have been easy for the college to reduce its outreach efforts, but outreach is a core value to which the college and university remain committed. Accordingly, the college and school have worked harder to reallocate funds without damaging the investment in outreach learning or diluting the on-campus educational activities.

In the end, community outreach and service-learning entail a partnership and an institutional commitment among faculty, students, the college (or local academic unit), the university, and the community. All the participants may not be visible and active in the community, yet they are all integral to supporting the learning objectives and the community-based activity, and to effecting positive community outcomes.

Acknowledgments

We thank Cheryl Morgan of the Urban Studio, as well as Andrew Freear, Bruce Lindsey, D.K. Ruth, and the other faculty and staff of the Rural Studio, for their unfailing hard work in outreach and service-learning. We also thank John Gaber for his comments on this chapter.

References

Auburn University. (2002). *Faculty Handbook*. Auburn, AL: Auburn University.

Auburn University Vice President for Outreach. (2002). "Outreach Scholarship at Auburn University." Presentation.

Boyer, E. (1990). *Scholarship Reconsidered: Priorities of the Professoriate*. Princeton, NJ: Carnegie Foundation for the Advancement of Teaching.

College of Architecture, Design and Construction. (2003). *School of Architecture and Department of Industrial Design, College of Architecture, Design and Construction Guidelines for Annual Assessment and Promotion and Tenure*. Auburn University.

Dean, A.O., and T. Hursley. (2002). *Rural Studio: Samuel Mockbee and an Architecture of Decency*. Princeton, NJ: Princeton University Press.

Ho, C. (2003). "In the Stacks." *Architecture* 92 (2): 92-97.

Kenny, M., and L. Gallagher. (2002). "Service-Learning: A History of Systems." *In Learning to Serve: Promoting Civil Society through Service Learning*, edited by M. Kenny et al., pp. 15-29. Boston: Kluwer Academic Publishers.

Kenny, M., L. Simon, K. Kiley-Brabeck, and R. Lerner, eds. (2002). *Learning to Serve: Promoting Civil Society through Service-Learning*. Boston: Kluwer Academic Publishers.

Kezar, A., and R. Rhoads. (2001). "The Dynamic Tensions of Service-Learning in Higher Education." *Journal of Higher Education* 72: 148-171.

Where Do We Go from Here? An Evaluative Framework for Community-Based Design

By Michael Rios

Community design began in the late 1960s as an alternative to the traditional practice of architecture and planning. An interdisciplinary field, it can be defined by a commitment to building local capacity and providing technical assistance to low- and moderate-income communities through participatory means. This community-based approach to design is taught in many schools and practiced by numerous organizations and individuals in the public and private sectors alike. A 1997 survey conducted by the Association of Collegiate Schools of Architecture identified more than a hundred community design programs, centers, and nonprofit organizations in the United States and Canada (ACSA 2000). Of the 123 architecture schools that offer a professional degree in North America, over 30 percent run university-based community design and research centers. Technical assistance, community outreach, and advocacy characterize much community design work emanating from university campuses. While community design, built on a rich history of participatory practice, is growing within the academy, substantive dialogue and reflection about its contribution to community development are lacking. We urgently need to know about more promising practices and assessments of long-term impacts.

This essay examines the efforts of university-based programs within the field of community design and presents an evaluative framework for community-based projects as a starting point. My framework treats universities and communities as coequals and emphasizes criteria to measure the impacts of community-based projects for each. Measurements of organizational capacity building, policy generation and implementation, and the quality of service and input through community involvement are examples. My proposed framework suggests that methods such as participatory action research hold promise in meeting the goals of both communities and universities.

Introduction

Practitioners of community design identify and solve particular environmental problems that combine social, economic, or political aspects (Comerio 1984). It is a distinctive form of professional practice that links issues of social equity, the environment, and economic advancement. More than 80 community design and research centers are in operation nationwide, compared with a peak of 60 centers during the early 1970s (Pearson 2002; Curry 1998). A survey of university-based community design conducted in 2003 by Pennsylvania State University's Hamer Center for Community Design Assistance categorized more than 40 programs by service area, type of mission, projects and services, and funding support. Today's centers are more varied, on the whole, than the community design activity that grew out of the social activism of the 1960s or the economic pragmatism that followed.

One core value of community design is participatory decision-making, understood as a critical component in the implementation of local programs and achieving successful outcomes (Kretzman and McKnight 1993). Participatory decision making can include conducting community charrettes, using user-friendly models and technology such as GIS and Web-based delivery systems, inviting suggestions from the community throughout the design and development process, and offering technical assistance to residents.

Academics and practitioners offer several reasons for contemporary attention to community design, including changes in federal policy, economic restructuring, the emergence of sustainability as a design and planning paradigm, and a move toward integrating public service into design curricula. A review of recent surveys echoes these findings (Gabler 1999; ACSA 2000; Hamer Center 2003). Regardless of the underlying reasons for an increased focus on community design, the number of university-based programs suggests a desire and need for this type of activity. Evaluation of community-based design has been conducted in relationship to mainstream architectural practice, without consideration of its own body of work. Comerio published the first article (1984) that alluded to "defining success" in community design, but her central focus was to evaluate community design vis-à-vis traditional professional practice. Although community-based design has long been at the leading edge of integrating teaching with community outreach, it has contributed little to the growing literature on service-learning and public scholarship (but see Forsyth, Lu, and McGirr 2000).

If the community-based design movement is to grow, it will be critical for its proponents to share knowledge that can help guide design and planning education. The movement needs to disseminate knowledge and promising practices, publicize opportunities for education and training, assess long-term impacts, and create commonly accepted standards. The recent focus on university-based activity raises several questions related to the broader field:

• What goals do community-based projects serve for institutions of higher education?

- What contributions to community development are being made by university-based programs and initiatives?
- How is quality defined for community-based design education and practice in institutions of higher education?

In the following sections, I argue the need for evaluating community-based design. After giving a brief overview of approaches to assessment in community settings, I present a working framework for evaluation. I conclude with several challenges to university-based programs vis-à-vis communities and factors affecting the quality of evaluation.

Why Evaluate?

Evaluation is a key element of successful community development. It is used to measure neighborhood impacts and to assess the process of activities and the role of intermediaries and local stakeholders (Hyland 2000). Increasingly common is the use of indicators that measure the progress of project-defined goals linking benchmarks to desired outcomes (Kline 1995). Most indicator-driven projects use data and information readily accessible to the public, but they may also include volunteer programs to generate data and measure progress as a form of citizen science. Community indicator projects range in extent from metropolitan regions to cities and municipalities. Indicators that focus on community development are typically practice-based and include identifiable categories and themes such as housing, economic development, and community building (Development Leadership Network 2001).

Most efforts to assess and document design projects use the case-study method (Francis 1999). This is a descriptive approach to evaluation, initiated after project implementation, which concretizes generalizations and anecdotal information about projects and processes (Yin 1994). A staple of teaching in business and law schools, the case-study method can provide useful information to practitioners looking for precedents and can be a form of continuing education. Although it is beneficial in providing an in-depth analysis of a particular project, the case-study method does have some limitations. One is the difficulty of comparing across cases, especially when different types of information are being gathered. Evaluating projects comparatively is a critical first step before knowledge can be generated more systematically.

A promising alternative to the case-study method is participatory action research (PAR), which has emerged as an important approach to local participation in guiding and evaluating community projects. As an alternative to the scientific method of research, PAR is "a way of creating knowledge that involves learning from investigation and applying what is learned to collective problems through social action" (Park 1992: 30). Efforts in PAR have focused on community development, resource management, organizational decision-making, and community health, among other aspects (Reardon, Welsh, Kreiswirth, and Forester 1993; Chambers 1993; Whyte, Greenwood, and Lazes 1989; Wallerstein, Sanchez-Merki, and Dow 1997). Within schools of architecture, PAR offers the possibility of combining sound methods with the knowledge and scholarship of practice. As a teaching and community outreach approach, PAR also offers the potential to improve current models of service-learning that emphasize pre-professional assistance and pro bono services at the expense of research.

The results of community-based projects, if they are assessed using PAR, can also serve community groups as a tool to advocate for political resources (Nyden and Wiewel 1992). This is a vital area of assistance, given that community groups often turn to university-based design programs from a lack of capacity and resources. Many university-based centers get involved in projects at the initial, conceptual stage and help frame issues and problems, taking into account complex social, economic, and political considerations. Project designs, reports, maps, and other technical documents can serve a political purpose to highlight resource disparities, articulate environmental concerns such as the prevalence of toxic sites in low-income neighborhoods, or organize a community in support of neighborhood improvements such as public parks and recreational facilities (Hou and Rios 2003). PAR provides a means to measure results against initial goals and identify critical elements within a project to advance a community's agenda or desired outcome. In addition to measuring tangible benefits as a result of university involvement, a PAR approach can also "put less powerful groups at the center of the knowledge creation process (and) move people and their daily experiences of struggle and survival from the margins of epistemology to the center" (Hall 1992: 15-16). Shifting from "expert" to "local" knowledge opens up new sites of inquiry and discovery outside traditional academic settings, for both faculty and students. However, we can realize the collective benefits of work accrued by service-learning projects only if we share knowledge between schools *and* communities.

An important distinction between the case-study method and PAR is that the latter includes a theory- or goal-driven form of evaluation (Chen and Rossi 1992). While the method-driven evaluation of the case-study approach follows steps built according to predetermined criteria, theory-driven evaluation begins with a working hypothesis or goal established at a project's inception. It is important to note that the case-study method does not assume a given outcome or explicitly state an objective in evaluating the results of a project. For theory-driven evaluation such as PAR, hypotheses can be generated from abstract constructs, as well as hunches, to determine what is to be collected and what is to be measured to identify emergent patterns that match hypotheses. This approach permits tracking of the actual experience over time against the theory, and the testing of alternative hypotheses (Hebert 2001).

The decision to use theory-driven instead of method-driven evaluation in community design projects depends on the overall goal of evaluation — its purpose and audience and the potential benefits from the assessment. If, for example, we want to create a community facility on an abandoned, trash-strewn lot, we might hypothesize that our intervention will cause the surrounding physical environment to improve. We would develop a series of benchmarks to measure this hypothesis before and after completion of the project. One relevant benefit of this form of evaluation is that it provides a framework from which to plan a project from conception through implementation. Also, we could use evaluation as an argument for procuring resources from city agencies if crime rates dropped in the surrounding area, or as a strategy to attract private investment if a heightened sense of pride and ownership among local residents resulted in property improvements around the facility.

A Working Framework for Evaluation

The discussion thus far has focused on evaluation used outside the field of community-based design, and how the adoption of such methods could be beneficial to community-based design at universities. Given the emphasis on outreach by many university-based programs, one of the challenges will be the ability to integrate service learning activities into the language of research. A review of university-based programs conducted by the Hamer Center for Community Design at Penn State identified only 7 of 41 programs, or 17 percent, that evaluated projects (Hamer Center 2003). However, new paradigms in community-based research that emphasize mutual engagement and collaboration, such as PAR, suggest an unprecedented opportunity to do so without compromising the core values of community service and advocacy, while at the same time meeting pedagogical goals and curricular objectives.

The following table and section present a framework to evaluate the work of community-based design that proposes a twofold approach to assessment: (1) centrifugal knowledge, involving activities aimed toward the external goals of community groups and related community development intermediaries, and (2) centripetal knowledge, involving activities directed toward the internal goals particular to university-based community design programs. For each, questions

AN EPISTEMOLOGY OF COMMUNITY DESIGN	
CENTRIFUGAL KNOWLEDGE *Aimed toward the "external" goals of community groups and related community development intermediaries*	CENTRIPETAL KNOWLEDGE *Directed toward the "internal" goals particular to community design practitioners, educators, and students*
1) Technical Assistance Whose interests have been served and with what results?	1) Community Involvement To what degree did residents participate in a community design project, and what were the significant outcomes of their participation?
2) Capacity Building How do capacity-building efforts further the mission and goals of community groups and individuals?	2) Service-Learning How does service-learning in community-based design education benefit students as future practitioners?
3) Policy Support To what degree did a community-based project shape regulatory or policy change?	3) Promising Practices What are the standards used in community-based design projects and how do those standards compare with those established by the profession?

are posed as guides to evaluating community-based design projects and programs. This is not to suggest that the goals are mutually exclusive, but rather that they reinforce each other to meet the needs of both communities and universities.

Centrifugal Knowledge

Many community-based projects, rooted in the Civil Rights movement, have focused on the needs of low-income neighborhoods and disadvantaged populations. The emphasis of this work is largely to serve community organizations and likely users of designed environments. Projects range significantly — from design-build affordable housing to streetscape designs, and neighborhood plans to model code policy tools — and include both short- and long-term relationships with government agencies, nonprofit organizations, and community groups. Projects aim to support community goals and priorities and can be part of a triad focused on *technical assistance, capacity building*, and *policy support*. (This triad was developed by the Pratt Institute for Community and Environmental Development, one of the oldest community design centers in the country. See also Blake 2003.)

Technical assistance often takes the form of plans, drawings, studies, and reports that enable community groups to carry out their mission and objectives. Often, activities will be concentrated at the beginning stages to help gather information, frame issues, and provide documentation of the results. Technical assistance helps groups make key decisions and identify resources for implementation, and serves as a mechanism for developing consensus and support for a project. Thus, a key question is: Whose interests have been served and with what results?

Capacity-building activities conducted by faculty and students fulfill an important educational and advisory role in helping groups develop their own capabilities. Grant writing, development of budgets, zoning and data analyses, the use of technology, and meeting facilitation are some of the skills that can be shared with community groups. Several outcomes that measure capacity building include the strengthening of local institutions, increasing the ability of organizations and individuals to identify and secure resources for staffing or project implementation, gaining legal nonprofit status, or implementing a successful community-driven project or campaign. A challenge is to identify gaps and weaknesses in organizational capacity and use projects as vehicles to strengthen these areas. Thus, a key question is: How do capacity building efforts further the mission and goals of community groups?

Policy support through projects and studies carried out by service-learning activities often includes recommendations that lead to changes in policy and regulation. Policy support varies significantly and can also include recommendations for changes to city services, code enforcement, and other aspects of community regulation. A goal of policy support might be to educate community members, elected officials, and municipal staff about resource disparities, regulatory discrepancies, procedural problems, or other policy-related issues. Outcomes to evaluate the role of policy support in community design activities could include changes to policies, reallocation of municipal resources, or the creation of new tools that address regulatory barriers. Thus, a key question is: To what degree did a community-based project shape regulatory or policy change?

Centripetal Knowledge

In addition to advancing the goals of community groups, university-based projects and programs seek to improve the pedagogy and practice of design. Community engagement gives students feedback for making design choices that are responsive to the physical and social contexts of a given project. Community engagement also provides a space for experimentation leading to promising practices that emphasize mutual engagement between universities and communities. Additionally, service-learning done through mechanisms such as community design centers can advance research unachievable in professional and classroom settings. For example, the application of on-site building methods related to straw bale and rammed earth allow for problem-based learning while providing a vehicle for research in community settings. It is valuable to assess both what is being created and tested and the degree to which service-learning experiences enhance pedagogy, practice, and research. Assessing *community involvement* and *service-learning* and the identification of *promising practices* are considerations related to the internal goals of community design projects and programs.

Public involvement is an essential component of any community design process. Designers often solicit input, ideas, and criticism from neighborhood groups, municipal officials, and local residents in order to establish project goals and to guide the refinement of specific proposals. Faculty and students should assess their success in engaging communities in their work, since resident participation is crucial at various phases of the process and can contribute to success. One goal that bridges the external goals of community groups and of professional practice is community involvement. Outcomes in the assessment of participatory projects could include the level of public involvement, from project inception through implementation; increased levels of trust and volunteerism; skills development; or community awareness of a given issue. Thus, a key question is: To what degree did residents participate in a community design project, and what were the significant outcomes of their participation?

Service-learning has been identified as an important vehicle in creating a scholarship of engagement (Boyer and Mitgang 1996). The service-learning model of community-design education teaches professionals the civic relevance of design, facilitates interdisciplinary learning and collective problem solving, fosters professional ethics, and introduces diversity issues into practice. Service-learning is also important for research and outreach to communities that lack resources. Assessing university-based service-learning could include measures that benchmark civic and professional development, volunteerism, and social responsibility. Thus, a key question is: How does service-learning in community-based design education benefit students as future practitioners?

The quality of community-based design can be measured by the number of awards and commendations received, as well as by publications in peer-reviewed journals and external funding for community-based projects. However, the impact of community design can also be measured in terms of new methods and techniques that may be developed during design, and the quality of completed projects. Outcomes in the assessment of promising practices could include the adoption of new methods, the durability and usability of built works and community environments, or the long-term sustainability of proposed strategies. Thus, a key question is: What standards are used in community-based design projects and how do they compare with those established by the profession?

Conclusion

My purpose in proposing this framework is not to prescribe particular forms of measurement, but rather to define a starting point from which architecture schools, community-based programs, faculty, and students alike can begin to develop goals to assess the outcomes of projects and related activities in community settings. Nor does my proposed framework suggest an exhaustive list of criteria. To do so would not acknowledge the diversity within the field and the varying sizes and organizational capacities among curricular programs and university-based design centers. This evaluative framework should be viewed as an initial sketch, open to interpretation, critique, and further development. It is also an invitation to design faculty to be more reflective and critical of their work in communities and to contribute to the growing body of knowledge in community-based design.

While my suggestions may seem straightforward, they require addressing several challenges. Although community-based design projects are becoming more common in schools of architecture, they are undertaken for different reasons and reflect different interests and values among faculty. For some, they provide an enriching student learning experience; for others, they are either an outlet for alternative practice or a form of advocacy. Regardless of the motivation, service-learning presents challenges for faculty, students, and communities when it comes to time commitments and meeting expectations for the quality of work (Forsyth, Lu, and McGirr 2000). It is also important to note that although university-based programs and projects may appear in line with work conducted by nonprofit community-based organizations, the organizational goals and priorities of nonprofits are often different than the institutional goals of universities and colleges. Faculty should be cognizant of the limitations of institutions of higher education, especially when it comes to resource and liability issues, while community organizations should understand that the primary function of universities and colleges is education, not service delivery. Furthermore, universities risk creating dependency when they replace programs and support once provided by government.

Beyond these general observations, there are several specific challenges to academic programs conducting evaluation of community-based projects. Conflicting goals between researchers and practitioners, and methodological issues such as the objectivity of the evaluator when the same person is a participant, need to be considered, as do questions of context and scale. For example, how is the community defined and what is the scale for assessment (e.g., building, block, neighborhood)? Additionally, evaluation is often shaped by external factors, such as public agencies and foundations that fund community-based projects (Jenkins and Halcli 1999). How do these entities influence the goals of a project and the types of assessment to be conducted? Lastly, the issue of time is critical. The differences between "university time" and "community time" need to be accounted for in the planning and implementation of curriculum-based projects. Evaluating both effective process and project outcomes can ensure greater success in community-based design projects.

In sum, evaluation of community-based projects should not be entered into lightly and takes a considerable amount of individual faculty effort. However, the presence of programs at universities and colleges suggests that community-based design is here to stay. In order to deepen the knowledge within the field, community-based projects need to be viewed as an integral part of scholarship in teaching, research, and service. More reflective practice is needed in service-learning to illuminate the actions and activities of practitioners, both academic and professional. In the words of educator Donald Schön, we must "discover what [we] already understand and know how to do" (Schön 1991: 5). The changing landscape of our cities, towns, and neighborhoods provides an unprecedented opportunity for faculty and students to engage in issues of public significance through service-learning. Now is the time.

Acknowledgments

I would like to thank Ian Baptiste, who co-taught a 2003 graduate seminar with me in which the evaluative framework was developed; also Sam Dennis for his thoughtful comments on an earlier version of this essay, in particular for helping me to refine the framework.

References

ACSA Sourcebook of Community Design Programs. (2000). Washington, DC: ACSA Press.

Blake, S. (2003). "Community Design Centers: An Alternative Practice." In Time-Saver Standards for Urban Design, 4.11-1 - 4.11-8. New York: McGraw-Hill.

Boyer, E., and L. D. Mitgang. (1996). Building Community: A New Future for Architecture Education and Practice. Princeton, NJ: Carnegie Foundation for the Advancement of Teaching.

Chambers, R. (1993). "Participatory Rural Appraisal (PRA): Challenges, Potentials and Paradigms." World Development 22: 10.

Chen, H.-t., and P.H. Rossi. (1992). Using Theory to Improve Program and Policy Evaluations. New York: Greenwood Press.

Comerio, M. (1984). "Community Design: Idealism and Entrepreneurship." *The Journal of Architecture and Planning Research* 1: 227-243.

Curry, R. (1998). *History of the Association for Community Design*. New York: Pratt Institute Center for Community and Environmental Development.

Development Leadership Network. (2001). *Success Measures Project*. www.developmentleadership.net/smp/index.htm. Accessed June 11, 2001.

Gabler, M.L. (April 1999). "Survey of National Community Design Centers." University Park, PA: PSU School of Architecture and Landscape Architecture.

Forsyth, A., H. Lu, and P. McGirr. (2000). "Service Learning in an Urban Context: Implications for Planning and Design Education." *Journal of Architectural and Planning Research* 17(3): 236-259.

Francis, M. (September 1999). *A Case Study Method for Landscape Architecture*. Washington, DC: Landscape Architecture Foundation.

Hall, B. L. (1992). "From Margins to Center? The Development and Purpose of Participatory Research." *The American Sociologist* 23: 15-28.

Hamer Center for Community Design Assistance. (2003). "Survey of University-Based Community Design." University Park, PA: PSU School of Architecture and Landscape Architecture.

Hebert, S. (2001). "Structuring Case Studies and Other Forms of Self-Evaluation: Recommendations Regarding a Theory-Driven Approach." Presentation made on March 2, Pratt Institute Center for Community and Environmental Development, New York.

Hou, J., and M. Rios. (September 2003). "Community-Driven Place Making: The Social Practice of Participatory Design in the Making of Union Point Park." *Journal of Architectural Education* 57 (1): 19-27.

Hyland, S.E. (2000). "Issues in Evaluating Neighborhood Change: Economic and Community Building Indicators." *Cityscape: A Journal of Policy Development and Research* 5: 209-219.

Jenkins, J. C., and A. Halcli. (1999). "Grassrooting the System? The Development and Impact of Social Movement Philanthropy, 1953-1990." In *Philanthropic Foundations*, edited by E. Condliffe Lagemann, pp. 229-256. Bloomington and Indianapolis: Indiana University Press.

Kline, E. (1995). *Sustainable Community Indicators*. Medford, MA: Tufts University Press.

Kretzman, J.P., and J.L. McKnight. (1993). *Building Communities from the Inside Out: A Path toward Finding and Mobilizing a Community's Assets*. Evanston, IL: The Asset-Based Community Development Institute, Institute for Policy Research, Northwestern University.

Nyden, P., and W. Wiewel. (1992). "Collaborative Research: Harnessing the Tensions between Researcher and Practitioner." *The American Sociologist* 23 (4): 43-55.

Park, P. (1992). "The Discovery of Participatory Research as a New Scientific Paradigm: Personal and Intellectual Accounts." *The American Sociologist* 23 (4): 29-42.

Pearson, J. (2002). *University-Community Partnerships: Innovations in Practice*. Washington, DC: National Endowment for the Arts.

Reardon, K., J. Welsh, B. Kreiswirth, and J. Forester. (1993). "Participatory Action Research from the Inside: Community Development in East St. Louis." *The American Sociologist* 24(1): 69-106.

Schön, D. (1991). *The Reflective Turn: Case Studies in and on Educational Practice*. New York and London: Teachers College Press.

Wallerstein, N., V. Sanchez-Merki, and L. Dow. (1997). "Freirian Praxis in Health Education and Community Organizing." In *Community Organizing and Community Building for Health*, edited by M. Minkler, pp. 195-211. New Brunswick, NJ: Rutgers University Press.

Whyte, W.F., D.J. Greenwood, and P. Lazes. (1989). "Participatory Action Research: Through Practice to Science in Social Research." *American Behavioral Scientist* 32(5): 513-551.

Yin, R. (1994). *Case Study Research: Design and Methods*. Thousand Oaks, CA: Sage Publications.

Research as Ethical Practice:
When Academic Goals Align with Community Needs

By Mary C. Hardin

Architectural educators are challenged to find a relationship between the necessarily narrow and often arcane topics that are the focus of faculty research efforts and the more general format of problems they give to their design studios. To then reframe the research for exploration in the community proves especially difficult. This essay describes a fortuitous trio of collaborations at the University of Arizona that led from a research idea to full-scale improvisation in a design-build studio, and then to significant applications in impoverished Native American and Latino communities. Each of the projects involved different priorities for the researcher, the students, and the community being served. An examination of the projects from each of these priority systems allows the tracing of a research idea, from inception to current incarnation, and opens a discussion about the ethical questions that arise when many agendas are superimposed.

A holistic perspective reveals the research agenda as a thread connecting the projects, in ways that add value beyond their immediate contributions to the community or the students involved. Several years of residential design-build projects in low-income communities helped formulate the agenda, independent of any one project but linking all of them, focused on the evolution of low-cost methods of building with rammed earth. The agenda included determination of an affordable system of forming rammed earth, refinement of a reliable earth and cement mixture to meet performance-based building codes, and optimal use of rammed earth with respect to solar orientation. In short, the goal of the research was to discover a way of building inexpensively with a beautiful and environmentally correct material.

The service-learning projects themselves gave rise to the research goal, as I sought to use rammed earth for affordable buildings because of its good environmental attributes. The projects then provided vehicles for empirical investigations in a way that no university laboratory could have. The projects initiated and fueled the process, shaped the research, and were shaped by it. Tangential research topics spun off as necessary sidebars and then rejoined the primary investigation. Publications, conferences, and grant funding were all results of efforts to disseminate this research and, in turn, gave the academic payback needed to offset the enormous expenditure of time and energy.

Background

Rammed earth construction was once widely practiced by the indigenous peoples of the Sonoran Desert (Gregonis and Reinhard 1979). They achieved a load-bearing wall system by packing an earth and clay mixture between forms made of wood or cactus ribs. As with many populations dwelling in arid regions, the natives of Sonora built with earth because of its relative availability, ease of transport, and durability, as well as its potential for maintaining a comfortable interior environment. Rammed earth walls have almost no insulation value and function instead as thermal mass, which slows the transfer of heat from exterior to interior spaces during the day (and performs the opposite function at night). Heat transfers through a rammed earth wall at approximately one inch per hour. This means that as the sun's heat works its way through the 12-to-24-inch-thick walls, it does not reach the interior spaces before nightfall. The substantial drop in air temperature at night causes the walls to cool off again before sunrise, as heat radiates back into the desert sky. As a result, the indoor temperature fluctuates only 7 to 8 degrees F in 24 hours (Mazria 1979).

Rammed earth construction faded from use in the United States long ago and has only recently been revived as an alternative for custom homes. Since the mid-1990s, it has enjoyed a renaissance in the Southwest, especially in California and Arizona. Contemporary construction methods employ the stabilizing additive of Portland cement, pneumatic backfill tampers to compact the earth mix, and forms for cast-in-place concrete construction. Forms and labor are too expensive for most people, but rammed earth's good thermal and environmental attributes make it an alternative for reducing housing costs in the desert, if the construction methods can be made less expensive and the field practices more reliable.

The design-build faculty and staff of the University of Arizona School of Architecture were interested in learning the parameters, limits, and potentials of building with this construction method, which had very recently been adopted in the municipal building code. As is common with building codes, the text defines performance criteria but provides no recipes. Without a background body of knowledge or experienced local tradesmen with whom to apprentice, novices had no alternative but to experiment at full scale. Questions about soil composition, forming methods, strength, and plastic tolerance began to shape a research agenda. To blossom into an applied research project, however, the interest had to be cultivated through an opportunity to build.

The Research

Origin of the Research Idea – A Classroom off the Grid

The first project involving rammed earth construction was self-contained in terms of research — the professors and students learned about the material in order to construct the building. This initial collaboration developed in 1996, when the University of Arizona's Athletics and Recreation Department contacted the School of Architecture with a request for assistance with the design of a new classroom facility. One professor in the school, Richard Brittain, responded with an offer of a design-build project, and a partnership of two years' duration was formed. His fourth-year design studio took up the challenge to devise an environmentally conscious, low-cost classroom facility that could be built by novices. A second semester of design development and construction documents readied the project for ground breaking.

Figure 1. Conventional method of forming rammed earth walls using heavy, steel-reinforced forms.

Brittain and I, who would lead students through the construction of the rammed earth and insulated concrete block classroom, began to face the realities of functioning as building contractors with little budget for equipment and overhead. An obstacle looming very large in the path of the classroom facility — the need to do rammed earth work without the expensive commercial formwork used in contemporary projects — led to a research goal that would eventually affect the community beyond the campus itself.

Labor costs and formwork make rammed earth a high-cost choice for wall systems. Contractors form the entire building at once with many sets of steel-reinforced forms that are bolted together, and then tamp the earth and cement mixture intensively (Figure 1).

To reduce the cost, we found an alternative method of forming walls incrementally with formwork that could be managed by two or three people and then reused. We were willing to sacrifice the efficiency of the large-scale forming for a more labor-intensive system, if labor was plentiful and cheap. The problem of designing formwork for the classroom facility thus had implications for more significant research. It was, in fact, the same as the challenge of bringing rammed earth into the affordable housing arena.

Several rounds of formwork design and test walls prefaced construction on the classroom facility, focusing on the goals of mobility and reassembly. Examination of precedents from California, China, Morocco, and Australia (Easton 1996) led to the use of plywood walls, pipe clamps, and stiffening boards in a simple configuration. A few test runs with the revised formwork and some fine tuning of pipe spacing and placement allowed construction to begin (Figure 2).

**Figure 2. Incremental rammed earth forms assembled
using simple elements**

Developing a working method with the rammed earth forms and earth-mixing equipment involved a steep learning curve. The setting, squaring, plumbing, and clamping of forms was tedious until a logical sequence became obvious. The use of chamfer strips to create reveals between the rammed earth and concrete was time consuming and caused logistical problems. The need to mix earth by hand, in the absence of earth-moving equipment, slowed the tamping. While students working the tampers waited for delivery of earth by bucket brigade, they continued to tamp each layer beyond the compaction limits of the soil, which caused some wall sections to have a rough, muddy finish. As construction proceeded, however, the students developed a rhythm for the work, and synchronized the mixing of earth batches, the moving of scaffolding and forms, and the tamping (Figure 3). Eventually, they were able to understand the process and make suggestions for revised formwork, details, and earth-mixing techniques. The two-person system of incremental forming became a reliable system, for an investment of about $300 in plywood (Figure 4). As the students honed their expertise, they also identified the main challenges of working with rammed earth: *formwork design* and *reliable field practices* for mixing earth with cement and water.

Figure 3. Forms staggered to allow tamping at several locations simultaneously

Continuation of a Research Idea – Hughes Residence

Even as students shaped the classroom facility, Brittain and I realized the implications of the new forming system for the impoverished communities of the region. My next project involved designing and building a residence for Della Hughes and her four children on the Gila Indian Reservation. I wrote a grant proposal for an educational partnership between the School of Architecture and the Native American community, which was in dire need of additional housing. The Gila/

Pima community had rejected government-built housing that bore no affinity with their traditional building methods, and much had been abandoned or vandalized. Representatives of the tribal Housing Authority were seeking new ideas and attended student presentations of environmentally sensitive housing proposals; they had already requested assistance from the School of Architecture. The tribe was enthused about the notion of a partnership that would train members of the community to build rammed earth houses with inexpensive formwork and indigenous materials. When the W.K. Kellogg Foundation funded the proposal, a new collaboration was formed.

Figure 4. Rammed earth walls completed

Rammed earth had once been an important building technique of Native Americans in our region, along with wattle and daub (Easton and Nabakov 1989). Both were replaced in the last century by a composite wall system of wood and packed mud. Dwellings built with this composite system are called "sandwich" houses (Van Willigen 1970). Most of the reservation's residents live in sandwich houses or grew up in them. Tenants value the houses, despite the need to patch and replace the mud, because they keep a fairly stable interior temperature against the wide diurnal temperature swings of the desert. They also hold cultural value as a local tradition, and are built with found materials from the landscape (cactus ribs, plant stalks, earth) that remain part of the landscape when the houses deteriorate. Sandwich houses are still the most common dwelling type on the reservation, and new ones are constructed as a matter of preference and economy. The reliance on soil from the site and the uncomplicated construction techniques make rammed earth an easy fit in the arid regions of the Southwest.

My work with the next cohort of students on the design of the dwelling for the Hughes family raised new considerations. The soil mixture had to be changed to adjust for the site's very silty earth, and the family wanted to integrate other traditional materials, such as cactus ribs and arrowweed thatch, into the wall surfaces. Also, the formwork needed reconfiguration to reduce the number of breakdown and setup periods, which consumed more time and labor than the tamping. The 1999 design-build studio felt prepared to begin new construction only after a period of design and testing.

Figure 5. Second incarnation of forms: taller segments that stand alone.

The dwelling had a simple rectangular plan (similar to the typical sandwich house) on an eight-foot module, to correspond with the form's dimensions, and was adapted to the family's preferences for orientation, view, and outdoor living practices. I will not describe the process of defining the configuration, which was informed by discussions of space usage, indoor or outdoor plumbing, indoor or outdoor cooking, cooling and heating systems, the use of electricity, and the reuse of household water. Rather, I will concentrate on the considerations that directly affected the construction practices.

The experience of building the classroom facility led to changes in the forming system that included eliminating the use of plywood piers to support the forms (making them freestanding spared a great deal of plywood), doubling the height of the forms (cutting in half the number of breakdown and reassembly activities), and reducing the number of pipe clamps and stiffening boards (saving materials and handling time) (Figure 5). The revised formwork proved to be manageable by two people, although a third person was useful in tightening the clamps and checking for level and plumb.

Figure 6. "Flying formwork" for bond beam was difficult to support and level.

The walls of the Hughes residence were built in nine days with the participation of members of the Gila community construction crew. Tribe members formed and poured the footings for the rammed earth walls; four to six of the crew worked with the students each day and continued after the semester ended. During the first two days of wall building, the Gila crew mixed earth and cement and observed the forming process. By the third day they were engaged in the forming and eventually adapted it for special situations, such as the building inspector's request for a recess to contain the electrical panel box.

The last two days of wall building were done entirely by the Gila crew, as the design-build studio turned to the challenge of devising forms for the concrete bond beam that was required by the building code. Constructing a "flying" formwork on top of the wall proved difficult because of the uneven surface, and it was a challenge to find a method for leveling and securing the formwork for the concrete pour. Plywood strips were cut from wall formwork and clamped to the rammed earth walls with snap ties used in concrete construction. Two-by-four braces kept the forms a uniform distance from the wall footings, but the system was cumbersome and tedious to construct. Holes left in walls where pipe clamps had passed through turned out to be the most useful points for supporting the forms, a discovery that led to the refinement of the form design for the third iteration of building (Figure 6).

Refinement of the Research Agenda – The Felix Residence

My students and I designed and constructed a third rammed earth structure, this one a residence for Habitat For Humanity Tucson to house Maria Felix with her five children and their grandfather. The project involved a collaboration with Scott Merry, a University of Arizona professor of civil engineering, the local affiliate of Habitat For Humanity (HFHT). HFHT accepted the suggestion of an experimental rammed earth residence from its own Design and Technology Committee, which was advocating "green" building techniques. I was invited to address the committee about rammed earth and straw bale construction and had a direct influence on the final choices.

Figure 7. Bond-beam forms supported by pipe clamps put through wall at consistent height to ease the leveling process

In the pre-building phase, my students and I mixed small batches of rammed earth and broke test cylinders to ascertain compressive strength and other values necessary for obtaining a building permit. There is no formal body of knowledge about certain material properties of rammed earth mixtures, including stiffness and shrinkage potential. Deciding on the composition and compaction of a mixture is inexact, based on rules of thumb and experience. We needed more expertise about soils properties, and I sought the advice of Professor Merry. Together with a third cohort of design-build students and a research assistant in civil engineering, we devised a consistent earth and cement mix with constant water content and sufficient compaction. This involved creating tests and testing equipment in the university's soils lab to evaluate the relationship between the compacted dry density, water content, compaction energy, cement content, and compressive strength (Fritz 2001). This research led to the next goal: controlling the field practices to match the ideal practices established in the laboratory.

Construction of the residence allowed another round of form-work refinement. This time, extra pipe clamps were purposefully run through the top of each wall to establish holes all the way around the building, at the same level relative to the wall footings. Once the walls were completed, pipe clamps could be reinserted into the holes, as an armature for placing the bond beam formwork, which could rest on the pipe clamps and then be fitted with snap ties and carefully leveled. This eliminated the need for bracing below, and made the leveling a fine-tuning procedure rather than a struggle (Figure 7).

Even though this refinement proved clear and logical, another improvement became obvious. If a method of pouring an incremental bond beam could be developed, the need for separate "flying" forms for the bond beam would be wholly unnecessary. The required four-inch bond beam could be poured into the top of each eight-foot wall section while the rammed earth forms were still erect. Further research will investigate revisions to accommodate the passage of reinforcing steel bars through the end boards of the forms in order to make a continuous steel connection even with consecutive concrete pours (Figure 8).

Figure 8. Laboratory test illustrating one method of pouring concrete bond beam in top of rammed earth forms, holding concrete back to allow for a rebar splice

Dissemination of the Research

As we achieved the research goals of discovering and refining a method of building inexpensively with rammed earth, we began disseminating results of the service-learning projects in ways that brought academic recognition to the participants and led directly to additional resources and opportunities. We were able to give the three projects broad exposure by concentrating on the separate issues of technological innovation, pedagogical strategy, community outreach, design quality, and the history of local vernacular architecture.

The classroom building was honored in 2001 with a Sports Facility of the Year Award given by the National Intramural Recreational Sports Association. Technological and pedagogical aspects of its construction were the subjects of five peer-reviewed publications (three volumes of proceedings from conferences on technological innovations in architecture and two from conferences relating vernacular architecture to technological issues) as well as six scholarly presentations, from 2000 to 2003. The University of Arizona's College of Agriculture funded production of a video about the construction process and background information about rammed earth, for distribution throughout the state. Brittain and I received the Daryl Dobras Award for Excellence in the College of Architecture and Landscape Architecture, for our efforts in the service-learning project. The experience and success with this building were fundamental in winning two grants (a larger one from the W.K. Kellogg Foundation and a smaller one from the University of Arizona) for building the Hughes residence.

The results of further research on the Hughes house were included in four of the five publications mentioned above, as well as in a scholarly journal article, another peer-reviewed publication, two invited publications, and an additional scholarly presentation. The residence itself was selected in a peer-reviewed competition for inclusion in a national catalogue, *Design Matters: Best Practices in Affordable Housing*. In 2000, I won an honorable mention from the Design-Build Institute of America for "demonstrated leadership in the advancement of best design-build practices and of design-build as the project delivery method," and an Academy Teaching Award from the School of Architecture. The Hughes residence project was the cover story in an issue of *Outreach UA* magazine in 2000, generating citywide interest in the service-learning approach and opening doors for the collaboration between HFHT and the School of Architecture.

The Felix residence project's focus on the earth mixture opened the door for an interdisciplinary partnership with Merry. The questions about compressive strength, plasticity, and ideal water content piqued the interest of Wolfgang Fritz, a research assistant to Merry, who adopted the issues as the topics of his doctoral dissertation. His initial laboratory findings became the subject of a jointly authored paper (Fritz et al. 2001) presented at a national conference on thermal envelopes, and became the basis for two more collaborative papers (Hardin et al. 2003; Hardin and Comella 2004) published in the proceedings and chosen for presentations at international conferences on passive and low-energy architecture. The projects, when presented as a related trio, brought me the 2001 ACSA Collaborative Practice Award, a national honor for the best collaboration of professional practice, teaching, and community service.

I have presented this litany of publications, grants, and awards to show how a research agenda can come to fruition within service-learning projects. The research, running parallel to the service-learning projects, must have a coherent trajectory of its own. As research interests begin to define the nature of the service-learning projects and courses, they can suggest future projects while creating a basis of support for them. In this way, the service-learning projects can be made to do double duty for faculty, who are pressed for time to accomplish publications and other peer-reviewed activities aimed at promotion and tenure.

A faculty member's interest in conducting academic research as a part of service-learning courses should be balanced, of course, with the learning objectives of the students and the needs of the community. A review of the three rammed earth projects from these other two perspectives will highlight some of the student and community considerations.

The Student Perspective

For architecture students, a new type of learning takes place once the construction phase begins in any design-build project. Twenty-eight fourth-year and graduate students registered for the 1997 studio that constructed the classroom facility. Several teams formed to produce shop drawings for each wall and roof plane. Students organized and placed materials orders, met deliveries, and practiced skills such as welding, mixing mortar, and laying block. Carefully dimensioned sketches filled notebooks as students planned and prepared for each day's exertions. Tool belts lost their sheen, thumbs wore bandages, and vocabularies grew. Faculty and students from the Recreation Department joined in shoveling dirt and steering pneumatic tampers. The entire crew was energized by the participation of the clients. As the walls rose, the forming system was rethought, revised, and constantly improved until results became consistent.

Growing expertise with this system gave students more confidence in solving construction problems in the field. They tried innovative solutions, imagined how materials assemblies would come together, drew ideas in their sketchbooks, and relied on intuition about physical problems. The impact on their design thinking was immediate and tangible. For many of them, the palpable sense of material properties and the particularity of connections between materials were reflected in their final capstone and thesis projects the following year.

As with the previous studio project, the students who constructed the Hughes residence cemented abstract knowledge with an experience. Their study of materials and methods of construction, traditionally organized through a lecture format, expanded to include realizations and innovations that happen only in the field. Working alongside the Gila tribe members contributed to learning in unexpected ways. In spite of her obvious scarcity of means, Della Hughes invited the students and several tribe members to join her and her four children for lunch each day. While she made fry bread on a wood fire and cooked beans and meat for tacos, students talked with members of the Gila community about their jobs, pastimes, schooling, and career plans. The time and resources Della invested in her generous offerings made a strong impression on the group who gathered under her thatched ramada. The final course evaluations of several students reported an improved attitude about those on the receiving end of community service projects. The examination of beliefs about ethnic and socioeconomic differences and the confirmation of an ethic of community service may not appear on the course syllabus but are welcome learning objectives.

Ethical issues surfaced at the Gila reservation, in several ways. One related to deeply held views about appearance versus function. The Hughes family held a strong affection for their first home, now in bad repair, because it was built by a grandfather more than 70 years ago. They liked the look of the mud and saguaro rib walls and wanted their new home to have something of the same appearance. The challenge of incorporating saguaro ribs into the formwork and tamping system of rammed earth led students to experiment with strips of milled lumber and cactus ribs and different methods of embedding them into the earth or attaching them to the formwork. They finally achieved the desired result by laying the ribs against the formwork, one by one, as the tamping progressed, anchoring them into the rammed earth with three-inch drywall screws, and brushing them to subtract the covering surface once the forms were removed.

The experimentation created an opportunity to discuss professional ethics in the studio. Students resisted using materials in a way they considered gratuitous. Responding to solid modernist training, they saw the cactus ribs as ornamental, lacking in structural integrity, and insisted that the ribs be present only if they achieved a span, bore weight, or transferred loads. However, the saguaro ribs did none of these tasks. After several days in the company of tribe members, student opinions softened. The consensual decision was made to use the ribs, but to inset them 12 inches from the end of the form, which allowed the visual understanding that they served an ornamental rather than structural purpose. The students found an ethical compromise that enabled them to acknowledge a cherished doctrine (a construct of their own educational culture) while pleasing their clients.

As the educator, I too confronted an ethical issue: students had to drive 184 miles round trip to visit the site. The long travel time compromised other activities, and the learning sequence was interrupted by the periods between trips and delays in the delivery of materials and scheduling of tribal workers. While the project advanced my research agenda and the larger goal of achieving affordable housing with indigenous materials, some hardship fell upon the students. Furthermore, the terms of the grant provided funding for travel only for the rammed earth and concrete construction phase, leaving the Gila crew to finish construction. Students therefore did not witness the later stages of construction and completion of the residence. In this case, I faced the dilemma of balancing learning objectives with the logistics of the endeavor — and my decision was to favor the latter over the former.

For the duration of the Felix residence project, the proximity of the site to campus and the engagement of students in the entire spectrum of construction processes ensured a powerful learning experience. The final product was a well-crafted object of pride. Both students and faculty faced an ethical issue after the project ended, when an HFHT crew covered the natural earth walls with mint green paint. This was the result of a lapse in communication. I had not been consulted or notified of the intention of HFHT's Board of Directors president to paint the house to make it "blend in" with others in the neighborhood. The incident illustrates one of the difficulties in working with an institutional client. The institution has priorities that are defined by general policies and does not respond in an agile manner to the particular circumstances of an unusual individual project. In this instance, students saw the irreversible painting as a tragedy that defaced a year's labor to create a unique residence of all-natural materials with no painted, carpeted, or veneered surfaces. One act transformed the learning experience into a bitter perception of futility, potentially souring some of the students on community service work.

The Community Perspective

At the 1999 dedication ceremony for the rammed earth classroom facility, when Richard Ramirez, director of the Recreation Department, praised the final product as being "much, much more than the metal shed we would have settled for," it became clear that from the standpoint of the university the goals of the project had been met. A low-cost, functional building broke new ground in energy conservation and materials. Nevertheless, in retrospect it is clear that decisions made along the way had significant ethical dimensions.

When the students in the original design studio proposed constructing a building of rammed earth, they had no experience with the material or the construction methods. In design review sessions, they educated the clients about the thermal and aesthetic benefits of the material (thus steering the decision in this direction) but could not speak to the actual costs and technical requirements. Leaving these difficult issues to the professors and next cohort of students (the builders) is a behavior one would not encourage in professional practice. Most often this leads to inadequate technical solutions, poor design resolution in the hands of the builder, and associated cost overruns. However, Richard Brittain felt confident that novice builders could successfully address construction and cost issues after a period of research. The research did result in a commendable process and product, and the award-winning end seems to have justified the risky means.

In the case of the Hughes residence, community members sought out an earthen technology for home building and were willing research subjects. The many arguments for use of rammed earth on the Gila reservation underscore an ethical partnership between research and service. This instance, however, may be contrasted with the circumstances of the third project.

The recipients of the HFHT rammed earth residence, recent immigrants from Hermosillo, Mexico, liked the natural earth appearance and thermal resistance of their new home, which resembled the adobe construction they were familiar with. They did not choose to paint the interior rammed earth walls after the invasion of the HFHT exterior paint crew, and they felt the sturdy thick walls were superior to wood frame walls and would better resist fire and termites. But the larger community and HFHT's staff and volunteers were uncertain about the propriety of the earthen walls in the context of Styrofoam and stucco construction. The HFHT supervisor and others faced a steep learning curve, and construction demanded the use of rented equipment that added work for the staff. Finally, the rawness of the finished product puzzled those who were used to the mainstream housing market. In retrospect, we might ask if choosing a material so far out of the mainstream was the best solution for the challenges we faced in designing the residence.

There are several ethical concerns tied to service-learning here. Agreements between educators and community members should carefully describe the responsibilities and rights of both parties to communication and decision making. Educators should insist on an agreement that protects the work of the students from disrespect or degradation as far as is possible, and should shoulder the responsibility to educate the public about unusual aspects of the student work.

At the End of the Day

Research, teaching, and community outreach need not be considered as separate pursuits competing for the scarce resource of faculty time. By integrating service-learning into our studios, educators can model for their students the behavior of an ethical professional practitioner. By integrating teaching and service within a research agenda, the time and resources necessary for all can be spent to shape outcomes that are mutually beneficial to the professor, student, and community.

The three design-build studio projects reviewed here led me to these conclusions:

First, service-learning can be compatible with academic research; in fact, field experiences offer opportunities to ground research agendas in the exigencies of architectural practice and the most urgent issues of contemporary urban life. As an act of ethical professional practice, the refinement of an inexpensive way to use a valuable material in affordable housing is justified. Professional rammed earth contractors in the Phoenix and Tucson metro areas charge $26 per square foot of wall area for rammed earth construction. The development of an incremental form system reduced the cost, for the third project, to $3.17 per square foot of wall area. Factoring in the student labor at minimum wage, the total cost per square foot came to $8.77. The current cost of a wood-stud wall system (with R19 insulation, sheetrock interior, rigid insulation, and stucco exterior) is $7.42, and a concrete masonry unit wall system (with steel reinforcing, sheetrock interior, rigid insulation, and stucco exterior) prices at $11.17 (E-Crete 2001). This highlights the potential of rammed earth as a construction material for affordable housing, especially if the reduced long-term costs of utilities and maintenance are figured in. Viewed as the extension of a cultural tradition, this construction method merits further research and development. The research-driven development of building sound, low-cost housing brings the principles of the architectural profession into alignment with a pressing social issue.

Second, the tremendous time commitment for developing and teaching service-learning problems can be mitigated by strategic use of the circumstances for piggybacking grants, publications, awards, and other forms of peer recognition. Many educators testify to the necessity of spending much more preparation time on service-learning courses than on more traditional ones. The frequent community meetings, constant logistics planning, and individual student debriefings can claim much of the time usually devoted to research, writing, or service on school and university committees. Unless this extra time can yield academic results beyond the teaching objectives, tenure-track faculty may view service-learning projects as risky activity. But when mined for opportunities for peer recognition, service-learning projects can integrate the three prongs of academia (teaching, research, and service) in a way that describes a coherent and compelling case for tenure and promotion.

Third, a research agenda developed in conjunction with service-learning projects can be effectively combined with pedagogical and social agendas, although managing multiple agendas requires vigilance to avoid priority conflicts. All aspects of a service-learning project are important, but one of them will occasionally take precedence during some or all of the project's duration. The educator must review the project's priorities against the objectives for teaching, the research agenda, and the community needs, and adjust the goals and expectations of the involved parties to fairly balance the outcomes. A research agenda that ties a series of service-learning projects together into an overarching investigation or field of study ensures that the sum of the endeavors will be more significant than the list of discrete experiences.

References

E-Crete. (2001). "E-Crete Autoclaved Concrete Block." www.e-crete.com/build/build/buildingmain.html.

Easton, D. (1996). *The Rammed Earth House*. Vermont: Chelsea Green Publishing Company.

Easton, R., and P. Nabakov. (1989). *Native American Architecture*. Oxford: Oxford University Press.

Fritz, W., S. Merry, and M. Hardin. (October 2001). "Experimental Investigation of Optimum Compaction Parameters for Rammed Earth Construction." BETEC Symposium (The Building Environment and Thermal Envelope Council), Santa Fe, NM.

Gregonis, L.M., and K.J. Reinhard. (1979). *Hohokam Indians of the Tucson Basin*. Tucson: University of Arizona Press.

Hardin, M., and J. Comella. (2004). "The Avenue of Ideas: An Affordable, Sustainable Housing Project." PLEA conference, Passive and Low Energy Architecture, Eindhoven, Netherlands, September.

Hardin, M., S. Merry, and W. Fritz. (November 2003). "Towards an Affordable Rammed Earth Residence." PLEA conference, Passive and Low Energy Architecture, Santiago, Chile.

Mazria, E. (1979). *The Passive Solar Energy Book*. Emmaus, PA: Rodale Press.

Van Willigen, J. (1970). "Contemporary Pima House Construction Practices." *The Kiva: Journal of the Arizona Archaeological and Historical Society* 36 (1).

Achieving Large-Scale Community Development Projects in a Teaching University

By Hollie M. Lund and Gwen Urey

Students and faculty in the planning department at California State Polytechnic University, Pomona, have been involved in a multifaceted and highly political community development effort in the Angela Chanslor neighborhood, a predominantly immigrant community with high levels of crime and gang activity. Activism by the local councilwoman brought the area to the attention of the city of Pomona and of faculty at Cal Poly Pomona, a campus with a strong commitment to community service. In 2001, Cal Poly Pomona received a HUD Community Outreach Partnership Center (COPC) grant and formalized an emerging partnership with the city and the local school district. The planning department's contributions revolve primarily around service-learning courses and individual faculty efforts.

This essay describes how we integrated these activities throughout our planning curriculum, fostered connections with other design- and policy-oriented disciplines, and created possibilities for new benefits to accrue to our students and the community. Finally, we share our own learning process as we progressed through the partnership, including tips for carrying out service-learning activities and suggestions for dealing with the political nature of community partnerships. We hope that sharing our experiences will encourage others to engage in similar efforts and provide support for those embarking on such initiatives.

The "More Engaged" Campus

When universities shed their ivory tower image for that of an "engaged" campus, they shift paradigms in how they perceive themselves and are perceived by others. Recently, however, we have seen another important shift in university-community dynamics, from conducting work *on* or *for* communities to working *with* communities. This new relationship has been facilitated by increased funding for university-community partnerships. HUD's Community Outreach Partnership Center program and the W.K. Kellogg Foundation's University/Community Partnership grants program are among initiatives that have profoundly changed the nature of service-learning activities across campuses.

Early forms of service-learning typically involved instructors sending students into the community for volunteer work (often unconnected to the content of the course), or carrying out community-based projects following the consultant-client model (often without interaction with the affected community members). These were often one-time projects where students (and faculty) pulled up roots at the end of the course, leaving communities with a sense that they had just been used, rather than strengthened, by the university. In spite of good intentions, such approaches left the service activities open to criticism. The new generation of service-learning proponents emphasizes the creation of meaningful, lasting partnerships between universities and communities. Partnerships enable universities to (1) conduct large-scale, ongoing community development efforts while (2) providing communities with a sense of empowerment and with resources and enabling them to continue their community improvement efforts should the university end its involvement.

Schools of planning are at the forefront of this movement. The shift from working on or for communities to working with communities has paralleled a similar shift within the planning profession: at the same time that planning educators have been encouraging their students to work alongside community members and to be responsive to their concerns, planners have been increasing their efforts to engage communities in planning processes and to make more responsive decisions.

Planning's position at the forefront of the "more engaged" campus follows from its many years of association with community service. The involvement of planning students and educators in community service arose naturally from the field's interest in promoting social change; along with schools of social work, it originated during the social and environmental movements of the 1960s and 1970s. This history, plus the natural relationship between the profession and community service, has led to many valuable service-learning experiences that should be shared, both within and outside of the discipline. Urban and Regional Planning (URP) is among several departments at Cal Poly Pomona recognized for its long-term commitment to community service. Community-based projects have long been an explicit component of the planning curriculum. The department now serves as an example for other disciplines as Cal Poly Pomona and the California State University increase their efforts to promote service-learning. Even with a long history in community service, however, the departments finds service-learning to be an ongoing learning experience.

Service-Learning and the URP Curriculum

Taking on community engagement as a department, rather than as faculty members, facilitates individual engagement through the creation of informal support and the reduction of risk. A departmental commitment also enables faculty to develop longer-range views of the academic-community relationship. URP participated in an "Engaged Department Institute," sponsored jointly by Campus Compact and California State University in 2001. During that event, URP articulated two goals for community engagement: (1) to develop reflection and assessment mechanisms that support student learning and feed into scholarship and dissemination and (2) to develop strategies to select and manage community partner relationships. The latter goal recognizes that it is possible to map any given service-learning experience on two distinct continua. On the first, learning objectives lie at one end (with the curriculum driving community engagement) and a product desired by a community lies at the other (with community needs driving curricular decisions). Both ends of the continuum belong in a curriculum, but for educators the determining factor must be the course learning objectives. In highly structured classes, such as foundations in a core curriculum, learning objectives often need to be the driving force; in upper-division studios, where learning objectives are broader, a wider range of projects may be considered suitable.

In the context of the COPC-related work, community engagement in the introductory research-methods course is curriculum-driven: students must learn how to create empirical knowledge about places. To meet this objective, students have learned about designing and implementing exploratory and descriptive research designs by investigating aspects of the target COPC community. In 2000, the product of the students' research was used to prepare the successful COPC grant application (thus providing a concrete community benefit). It was also used to guide future service-learning classes at the other end of the spectrum: one piece of knowledge gained was that safety and fear of crime are primary community concerns. Responding to this need (for a safer community), students in an upper-division studio worked with community members to develop proposals to the city for programmatic and design interventions to enhance the neighborhood's ability to prevent crime. The project organizers were careful to meet the course learning objectives but guided the effort primarily by responding to community need.

The second continuum is defined at one end by a broad educational agenda of fostering good citizenship and at the other end by the discipline-specific knowledge, skills, and values to be taught in an urban planning course. The "good citizenship" end of this continuum drives much of the interest in service-learning outside of design- and social-science-based curricula. California State University's system-wide service-learning program distinguishes between community service programs, which promote the creation of opportunities for student-initiated service without connecting them to a curriculum, and academic service-learning programs, which promote faculty adoption of the service-learning teaching method. Within our disciplines, however, it is more appropriate to think about degrees to which community-engaged learning activities relate to discipline- and course-specific learning objectives, including the explicit value of good citizenship.

The Engaged Department Institute helped us to place more deliberately each community engagement project along the two continua, and to articulate our new thoughts regarding community engagement more fully into documents that shape our future, both as an organization (the strategic plan) and as a collection of individual faculty (the review for tenure and promotion document). The Pomona COPC provided a timely opportunity to use our new tools to help revitalize a distressed community in our own backyard.

"Angela Chanslor" and the COPC Grant

Through the COPC proposal, Cal Poly Pomona created partnerships with the city of Pomona and the Pomona Unified School District. Each partner contributed various combinations of resources and staff: URP's primary contributions were faculty release time and student involvement through service-learning, in the "Community Planning and Capacity Building for Neighborhood Revitalization and Crime Prevention" focus area.

Figure 1. Barricaded alley (to minimize "escape routes" during police chases) and gang territory markings in Angela Chanslor neighborhood, 2002

**Figure 2. Boarded-up homes and graffiti tagging
in Angela Chanslor neighborhood, 2002**

Angela Chanslor is an immigrant neighborhood in south Pomona that experienced severe social and economic decline during the 1990s. As the table shows, incomes and education levels declined while households became linguistically isolated and increasingly crowded. Criminal activity also rose, culminating in a rash of gang-related homicides that brought the neighborhood to the attention of the city in 2000. The physical conditions (shown in Figures 1 and 2) help complete the picture of this distressed neighborhood.

	Block group		City of Pomona	Los Angeles County
	1990	2000	2000	2000
Share of population that is:				
Foreign-born (%)	41	46	37	36
Linguistically isolated (%)	22	35	17	16
Share of households that have:				
6 or more people (%)	28	38	20	10
Share of adults (25 years & older) with:				
Less than 9th grade education (%)	26	37	26	16
Bachelor's degree or higher (%)	6	2	13	25
Median household income:				
In current $	$34,609	$32,200	$40,021	$42,189
In 1999 $	$46,500	$32,200		

Source: U.S. Census 1990, 2000

**Demographic characteristics of Angela Chanslor's Census
Geographic Areas, 1990-2000**

Articulating Activities across the URP Curriculum

The COPC program provided a unique opportunity to define a long-term, comprehensive approach to the problems of the neighborhood. URP thus made a conscious decision to fully integrate COPC service-learning activities into its undergraduate curriculum.

As part of URP's accredited professional-oriented planning program, undergraduate students begin building practical, theoretical, and ethical foundations for "working in the real world" right from the start. During their first two years in the program, students participate in service-learning through small projects, many of which have been connected in recent years to the Pomona COPC. Gradually, their involvement in real communities increases, culminating during their senior year in a variety of studio-based service-learning opportunities, many of which recently have focused on the COPC project. This process is diagrammed in Figure 3.

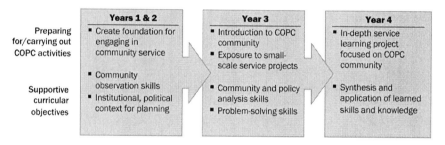

Figure 3. Students' progression through the service-learning components of the URP curriculum

Years 1 and 2: Creating a Foundation. Students begin to form a foundation for the practice of planning, on which they will build as they begin their community service work. Among the first skills that students learn are how to observe communities from various perspectives and how to present this information to different audiences. They also begin to understand institutional and political frameworks for planning: where planners fit in the larger picture and the various roles they play. Although students have limited interaction with community members, through, for example, meeting with city planners, speaking informally with homeowners, and making presentations to the city planners, they learn the value of talking to residents in order to understand a community and the importance of balancing city-wide goals with neighborhood needs and concerns. They also begin to overcome their natural apprehensions as they leave the security and protection of the classroom.

Year 3: Introduction to COPC. Students continue to build a theoretical and practical foundation for future community work, and (in recent years) are introduced to the target COPC neighborhood (Angela Chanslor). Learning objectives shift from *observing* communities to *analyzing* and *understanding* them through policy analysis, quantitative and qualitative research, and other problem-solving skills. Students are also exposed to professional ethics and the legal framework for planning.

Year 4: In-Depth COPC Studio. A capstone studio requires students to apply all they have learned to an in-depth, two-quarter community-service project. During the first year of the Pomona COPC, URP dedicated one of these studios to work in the COPC community. Students developed and carried out two community workshops about how to enhance safety and livability within the neighborhood (see Figure 4) and made recommendations to the city of Pomona based on what they heard from the community members. They also made recommendations for follow-up projects to future URP classes. (Many of these ideas were pursued in an elective studio the following summer.)

This was our first intense interaction with Angela Chanslor residents and our first opportunity to begin establishing trust within the community. It was critical that our students be prepared and able to "connect" with the residents while also acting responsibly and professionally. The students succeeded. More than 20 adult residents attended each of the two workshops, engaging in open discussions about their neighborhood. Local youth, at least 10 per workshop, were engaged in separate activities and provided their own unique perspective on the community.

The success of these and other workshops must be placed in the context of the URP curriculum as a whole. Without the three years of preparation leading up to the capstone studio, this project would have been much more difficult, because it is impossible to fully prepare the students for conducting responsible, effective, and meaningful work in the community in the short time frame of 10-week academic quarters.

Electives. COPC-based service-learning activities have also been incorporated into a number of department electives. In an elective course during the summer following the community workshops, planning students elaborated ideas put forth by residents during workshops: an open space and youth activity plan, a streetscape plan, and a strategy for mitigating the displacement of residents. Students also organized and facilitated a neighborhood improvement day that included a clean-up component and a mural painting by children (Figure 5). In a subsequent upper-division interdisciplinary studio, students from planning, landscape architecture, and architecture worked with the Pomona Police and Angela Chanslor adults and youth on crime-prevention approaches that combined design solutions and community empowerment strategies. The COPC partnership has opened the door to interdisciplinary opportunities that are important to the success of any large community development and were explicit components of the Pomona COPC.

Connecting to other Courses and Disciplines

The comprehensive nature of COPC has provided opportunities to connect across disciplines and to involve additional faculty. In the first year of the grant, the university's president provided funding for a mini-grant program to encourage faculty participation in service-learning projects that would benefit Angela Chanslor. Among other projects, students created graphic materials designed to enhance the cultural identity of the project, using community members as "cultural informants" and design judges; regenerative studies students hosted sustainability workshops for sixth graders; and environmental design students produced a video documentary about life in Angela Chanslor.

Observed Benefits

An intensive approach to service-learning — particularly in the context of a single large community project such as COPC — has many potential advantages, as witnessed within the Pomona COPC:

Student Benefits. By taking a curricular approach to this service-learning endeavor, we have observed that our students are

• constantly experiencing and examining how they can synthesize theories and skills learned throughout the program and apply them to a real-world problem (thus enhancing their educational experience);

• adequately prepared for the intensive (and very sensitive) COPC-related projects;

• gaining the experience (and patience) for working on long-term efforts;

• able to see their contributions develop and become visible in the community as they progress through the program (thus contributing to their sense of empowerment);

• more actively involved in and enthusiastic about the course as a whole; and

• producing higher quality work (as a result of seeing the community's interest in their work and realizing how much they truly have to offer).

We also witnessed an increased effort and commitment to the project by previously marginal students, particularly those with first-hand experience of similar neighborhoods. They seemed to suddenly realize the value of their insight and expertise. A final advantage of the curricular approach is the reduction of risk when individual events fail to unfold as anticipated. Students aware of the big picture can more easily remain engaged in learning even when political and other changes disrupt an activity.

Figure 4. URP student Jorge Perez sharing residents' input at community outreach workshop for Angela Chanslor neighborhood

Community Benefits. The most visible community benefits thus far have been in capacity building and empowerment. Given the original lack of trust expressed toward "outsiders," the simple fact that residents attend our community workshops and project presentations and participate in student-organized events has been extremely encouraging. Aside from supporting our efforts and demonstrating an interest in collaborating, they have had the opportunity to work together and begin building capacity among themselves.

For further evidence, however, we must look beyond the activities of URP. Early during the COPC grant, a group of women from Angela Chanslor participated in a series of leadership trainings organized by a faculty member from the Department of Political Science. This leadership group has since helped to organize events and activities within the neighborhood and has been instrumental in encouraging participation by other residents. The most profound display of their new sense of confidence came in recent efforts to reinstate the community coordinator, whose abrupt termination was the fallout of a political shift during the COPC's first year. While the COPC representatives from the city and school district did not view this grassroots effort favorably, those of us working in the neighborhood saw it as very encouraging.

Faculty and University Benefits. The university and its faculty have benefited, most notably through increased cross-disciplinary interactions and collaborations that probably would not otherwise have occurred. The COPC prompted our college to offer its first upper-division design studio in years, involving interdisciplinary collaboration at both the student and instructor levels. Across the campus, the COPC has fostered communication among participating faculty and has provided a common forum for discussing service-learning in general. Finally, the COPC has helped participating faculty to develop ties to practitioners and other community partners that may serve as resources in the future. This is important not only for achieving our long-term goals in Angela Chanslor, which will require sustained partnerships beyond the three years of the grant, but also for facilitating additional service-learning activities outside of the COPC.

Lessons Learned

As the COPC project enters its final stages, we can see where we excelled, where we missed opportunities, and where we simply wish we had approached things differently. The following five lessons are the most critical to the overall success of the project. They are also the challenges most likely to be faced by other institutions seeking long-term community partnerships.

Lesson 1: Begin a Dialogue with the Target Community. We learned not to underestimate the power of talking with and listening to community residents. Dialogue helps generate support for activities and deepens our understanding of the community beyond what could be achieved from second-hand information and perceptions. For instance, students learned from the early community safety workshops that crime was just one of the community's primary concerns. The students also gained insight into the sources of crime and residents' ideas about strategies for combating it.

By engaging residents in a conversation rather than a more formal "presentation," students helped the neighborhood articulate what really concerned them, such as landlord-tenant relations, lack of trust in the police, and lack of opportunities for their children. The results of the workshops were used to make future COPC activities responsive to the concerns of residents. Subsequent service-learning activities in both URP and the Political Science Department have addressed the various concerns through the organization of tenant-landlord meetings, projects with the Pomona police, and creation of a "public space and youth activities" plan for the neighborhood.

Dialogue has enabled our students to challenge common misperceptions about the neighborhood, such as the incorrect assumption that Angela Chanslor is an entirely transient community — a misconception that prevented the city from understanding the true nature of the community's problems. Students from URP and other disciplines were able to show that the neighborhood had long-term residents, including some who had lived there for more than 20 years. These residents have become leaders in the community and represent a tremendous resource for our community development efforts.

Figure 5. Children from Angela Chanslor neighborhood painting mural on alley wall during URP-organized Neighborhood Improvement Day

Lesson 2: Create and Maintain Trust within the Target Community. We are not the first to emphasize the importance of creating trust with members of the target community. The fragility of this trust, however, and the profound impact that a loss of trust can have on a project became an all-too-real learning experience for us. We want to strongly emphasize it here. The following elements are critical in engaging with a community that distrusts outsiders:

• **Important community connections**. While developing the COPC proposal, Cal Poly Pomona created a relationship of trust with the local councilwoman, who is highly respected within the community. Without her support, it would likely have been very difficult to establish any relationship with the community.

• **Dedicated faculty**. Faculty commitment is obviously important for pushing through obstacles and sustaining efforts over time; it is also something that can be sensed by community members. If they sense a lack of dedication, they may be apprehensive about your involvement and the efforts of your students and less likely to make significant contributions.

• **Effective community coordinator**. A project coordinator with a strong presence in the neighborhood proved critical to our establishing trust. The coordinator facilitated making links between each of the partners involved and the community. Readily accessible to residents at her workspace in a school district facility, with the right personality for engendering trust, and articulate and bilingual, she helped us to overcome a primary barrier, language, while also becoming a trusted and appreciated voice for residents.

• **Ongoing commitment**. This aspect is best described with an example. In 2003, the community coordinator position described above was reorganized so that it lost almost all its community coordinating responsibilities, and the current community coordinator was replaced — much to the dissatisfaction of the local residents, who felt that they had lost their main source of trust and support. They responded by essentially boycotting activities associated with the project. At the urging of the just-released community coordinator, the residents slowly returned to the COPC activities, but the trust had already been damaged. Our future efforts may be fruitless unless we can regain their trust.

Lesson 3: Partner with Organizations That Value the Meaning of Partnership. Our most frustrating challenge has been working with partners who prefer to do things the way that they have been doing them for years. As a university participant whose contributions come in the form of knowledge and recommendations (as opposed to direct service activities), our efforts can have no long-term impact without implementation. Even the capacity building gained by involving community members will be lost if they see no return on their efforts. Unfortunately, our partner with the power of implementation, the city, has done very little. Much of this relates to a difference in approaches to community development — the university's community-based approach and the city's top-down approach, each of which is deeply rooted and not easily broken down. We hoped that the city's willingness to enter a partnership signified that they were open to a more community-based approach in Angela Chanslor, as this was a clear component of the COPC.

Unless partners recognize each other's strengths and trust and value their contributions, the pieces of the puzzle are unlikely to come together, and the potential benefits of community development will fail to become a reality.

Lesson 4: Be Clear (and Realistic) in Setting Goals. We now realize that the responsibilities of each partner in achieving the goals of the grant should have been spelled out more precisely. We also should have responded more strategically to the political change that occurred in year one, such as with a revision to those responsibilities and goals. Ultimately, partners will share responsibility for a program's outcomes, while each partner will also pursue independently its own project-related agendas. It is important to articulate a set of goals explicitly related to the partnership itself, as well as laying out more explicitly how accountability for outcomes would be shared.

It is also important to consider the timing of project goals. Partners are likely to meet disappointment if they expect dramatic results too soon. And if they pass these expectations to community members, they may lose their trust early. Establishing trust, the first task in a community partnership, takes time, especially in a community where trust has not been fostered or has even been destroyed. Both faculty and the off-campus partners may need a third party other than a grant writer to facilitate the negotiation of goals and objectives.

Lesson 5: Keep Spirits High. We have emphasized the need for setting realistic goals and not expecting to see dramatic changes immediately; we must also emphasize the need for visible signs of progress. Continued involvement by students, faculty, and the target community, while critical to the success of any long-term service-learning project, can be lost all too easily if any of these groups feel that their efforts are fruitless. Achieving small successes can thus do wonders for maintaining enthusiasm. Successes could be a neighborhood clean-up day or other community event, or making small-scale physical improvements such as new mailboxes or landscaping. Be careful, however, not to overuse the same small success; activities such as neighborhood clean-ups, unless combined with other new successes, lose their excitement over time and may leave participants feeling that little or no progress is being made.

Another factor is the potential for burnout among faculty members and students. It can arise from continually dealing with the same community and issues, quarter after quarter, and having to cope with the demanding nature of the essential communication and coordination. Remedies include having a variety of faculty involved, rotating responsibilities, and providing students with a range of community experiences. Exposing students to different communities and service activities is also important for their planning education as a whole. A planning curriculum that gives students all of their practice-oriented experiences from a single community may leave them ill-prepared for work in other settings.

Recommendations from a Teaching University

Departments in teaching-oriented universities can succeed in large community-development projects. In spite of our setbacks, we have seen tremendous benefit to our students, on a variety of levels, as well as a visible increase in the capacity and empowerment of the target community. It is too soon to know the long-term effects, or how our efforts will be perceived in the near future (as the political environment continues to shift), but it is clear that we have established a strong base.

Such an endeavor can succeed, however, only if the core faculty support it and if it is regarded as central to the department's way of operating. In addition, since most of the activities (especially in a teaching-oriented university) will rely on service-learning, the faculty must agree that service-learning is an appropriate and broad interest in the pedagogies of community engagement. Faculty members need to value discussions about how and where specific levels of service-learning fit into the curriculum. Department support is also critical for managing the workload both of engaging in instruction, which is particularly heavy for faculty in a teaching university, and of nurturing relationships with community partners. Balancing these workloads can become burdensome unless faculty members share responsibility for maintaining the relationships and agree that they have value. These contributions need to be seen as important by the rest of the faculty and must also be explicitly acknowledged in faculty evaluation criteria, especially for untenured faculty.

Finally, student learning must remain foremost. An opportunity to follow a real-life project through its many stages, and to be involved in many, if not all, those stages, simply cannot be simulated through projects or achieved in one-time-community service projects. Students get to know the community and its residents, become invested in the outcomes of their projects, and gain a sense of empowerment as they see how their knowledge and skills can contribute to real community improvement. Even the setbacks and disappointments provide learning experiences that may not be gained elsewhere: a properly handled "bad" service-learning experience can be a great lesson for students. Of course, if the students can help to transform the community for the better along the way, the reward is clearly that much greater.

Sore Shoulders, Bruised Ethics:
The Unintended Lessons of Design-Build

By Scott Wing

Design-build projects in architectural education, proponents argue, aid the professional development of students by teaching them technical skills complementing those gained through standard classroom study. Opponents of design-build complain that the act of construction limits design complexity, requires great expenditures in time and money, and presents risks not worth the rewards. Construction knowledge, they say, is better left to technology courses and professional internship. However, these debates about merit or inadequacy obscure one of the central values of design-build projects for teaching construction skills and processes: when situated in conditions of social consequence, they provide an educational platform on which to present architecture as a complex structure of ethical positions and actions. As students confront material consequences and cope with physical exhaustion, struggle to reconcile the divergent missions of clients and classmates, and ponder limits of time and money, they experience the act of construction as a process of forging personal definitions of "doing the right thing." Rather than a professor "teaching" a predetermined code of conduct, ethical conduct emerges from the students' confrontation with difficult choices.

Experiences in a series of service-learning design-build projects at the University of Arkansas, including the careful dissection of an early 20th-century house, the erection of a 140-foot pedestrian bridge, and the making of a prototype Habitat For Humanity (HFH) house, suggest that design-build projects can extend their value beyond technical issues. In these projects, led by Eva Kultermann and me, students had to weigh concerns for personal risk, public safety, and legal liability against the responsible reusing of resources, improving the quality of the physical and social environment, and honing design skills through the act of making.

In the course House Dissection: A Crash Course in Building Pathology, the difficult ethical questions centered on the choice between demolition and resuscitation, as a class of first-year students delaminated a 1908 wood-frame house over a three-week period (Figure 1). Emphasizing safety, we preached careful demolition while the students received tetanus shots.

Figure 1. Students dissecting a house to reveal its inner structure

The house had been condemned by the municipality and was heading for a bulldozer-to-landfill death. We realized that our participation in the demolition made us accessories to the crime, but judged that the educational value of the project, our focus on construction-waste recycling and material reuse, and the public awareness we could amplify through print and television justified our involvement.

Students stripped the frame bare, revealing a glorious white oak frame. We recorded the house's successive additions, deduced the technical weaknesses leading to its decline, and rummaged through the remains above and below ground. We catalogued nails and boards, pipes and plaster, and everything in between. The components of the house were then reconstituted and displayed in 30 gleaming galvanized steel trashcans for a gallery exhibition. Still, in the end, four 30-yard dumpsters went to the landfill. We did escape without injury and with wood and stone for future projects.

Ethical considerations expanded from student safety to public safety in the building of a pedestrian suspension bridge in the town of Chester, Arkansas, population 90 (Figure 2). Our objective was to design and build a bridge connecting the town to a public park on the site of three previous bridges washed out by storms over the past one hundred years. Fortunately, we were again working with first-year students who didn't know it was impossible to design and build a bridge of this size in less than four weeks. In the absence of zoning or building codes in this small town, we faced an ethical issue: while code-free rural building sites often enable design-build projects to progress quickly, without official review, life safety issues are the sole responsibility of students and faculty.

**Figure 2. Pouring of concrete abutment for
a pedestrian bridge in Chester, Arkansas**

Students researched and designed individually and then in groups, before choosing one scheme — a suspension bridge — to build during the remaining two and a half weeks. While we oversaw the geotechnical and structural issues, students cut wood planks (from the frame of the demolished house), assembled cables and hardware fittings, built formwork, and poured concrete. Relative to the norms of professional practice, the speed of our efforts might seem irresponsible, yet I have typically found sufficient value in taking these risks. In turn, the students, given the seriousness of their work, have shown greater maturity in their personal conduct and performance.

Unfortunately, we failed to complete the second anchorage and never gained the satisfaction of walking the bridge. (The bridge was later completed to an altered plan as a river overlook.) While we addressed the probability of not completing our work with the town's representatives at the outset, the students were disappointed. Nonetheless, the people of Chester were deeply grateful and the students experienced one of the great gifts of design-build public service work: the feeling of genuine appreciation from the people they were assisting.

Our design and construction of the House of Modest Means, an HFH house, for the Brown family, clarified the ethical questions prompted by construction. Aside from issues of student and public safety and legal liability, we debated the following questions:

• When is it ethical to reject a client's directive?

• To what degree should the mission of architectural education conform to the mission of a nonprofit building partner?

• What obligations do we have to future inhabitants for adaptation and change?

• What obligations do we have, beyond the site, to the neighborhood and region?

• What are our obligations to address long-term costs in durability, energy efficiency, and resource use?

Students were asked to design a 1,200-square-foot, wheelchair-accessible, four-bedroom house on a south-facing slope, 75 by 150 feet, with a $50,000 construction budget. Complicating matters, the slope varied between 5 and 15 percent, with a stormwater drainage swale carved through the middle of the site. Students developed individual designs during the fall semester and later in teams, as proposals were refined. The executive director of the HFH chapter in Fayetteville, in consultation with the Browns, made the final choice of design. Construction extended through the spring semester and the Brown family took possession in May 2000.

Figure 3. The House of Modest Means, east entry elevation

We identified the issue of long-term costs, not just first costs, as our ethical imperative for affordable housing design. To that end, we sought to diminish life-cycle costs through use of durable building materials and energy-efficient building components and systems. Durability began with the foundation: two-foot-diameter concrete piers, 10 feet on center, drilled to resistance and interlocked by a reinforced grade beam. Unstable weathered shale on the hillside had undermined recent HFH houses (as well as much more expensive ones);

therefore our ethical position began with a foundation that would last no matter what the cost. Unfortunately, at $10,000, the cost was 20 percent of our total budget.

The south-facing slope allowed us to easily control solar exposure with overhangs while maximizing daylight (Figure 3). The hillside provided natural ventilation through daily microclimate breezes, while a vertical air stack in the house with rooftop mechanical fan supplemented air movement in the summer. Wood-frame construction was upgraded, from HFH standards, to two-by-six walls with energy-conserving detailing and cellulose insulation throughout. We rigorously sealed the building to prevent air infiltration; a blower door test for tightness showed the house was within the top 1 percent in the state. The efficiency of the shell allowed us to downsize the mechanical system. Local materials, including stone gathered from the site during construction, formed site walls, drainage beds, and walkways. Fortunately, responsible design methods and materials often coincide with having no money for any other option.

Many of the ethical dilemmas we faced resulted, in part, from two communication lapses. First, our design documents were not thorough and left many design details unresolved. This was largely intentional, as we encouraged individual student design initiatives to "fill in the blanks" in the process of building. Unfortunately, HFH discouraged changes during construction. While a few important changes and refinements were made, the semester-long period for construction restricted our ability to fully consider and present alternatives to the Brown family. We all would have learned more by slowing down, working more deliberately, and debating the merits of varied design approaches, but our ethical decision to ensure the completion of the house drove a construction schedule that conflicted with the ethical imperative to teach.

The second communication lapse existed between the Brown family and us. Despite our close contact and friendship with the Browns, HFH made all design decisions, usually without homeowner involvement. Understandably, HFH wished to maintain control of their primary mission: providing basic, uniform, affordable shelter to worthy families. We came to understand that our studio's educational mission ran tangentially to HFH's charge. In our view, HFH's search for equity resulted in designs, divorced from the particularities of people and place, that were inexpensive and easy to build but not to maintain. Our mission sought to make distinct and intelligible the specificity of family organization, and align it to site, region, and cultural heritage (Figure 4). Additionally, in our role as builders, we had the means to control and implement design in direct response to opportunity and budget constraints. Here, the ethical debate centered on equality versus quality.

Figure 4. The House of Modest Means. Brown family children enjoying the shade of the south-facing porch

The gap between HFH's mission and ours fueled a continuous debate and critique of our role as architects. We were often reminded of the danger of custom design if other HFH families perceived inequities ("design creep," it was termed). Students were asked to take responsibility for their work as it affected the wider community, and to understand HFH's challenges in negotiating neighborhood opposition to affordable housing. We, in turn, asked HFH to consider adjusting their standards for particular site, region, and family circumstances, to attain a qualitatively better living environment built for longevity and change.

As we struggled to respect HFH's mission and our own, fundamental differences emerged that created a stream of difficult choices. For instance, we battled HFH's standard "maintenance-free" vinyl siding, on the grounds it was not adaptable to the homeowner's changing tastes in color. Habitat agreed only reluctantly to the use of painted cement-board siding, finally recognizing that Mr. Brown's occupation as a house painter made for a unique case.

Some of our ethical dilemmas were of our own making. Tight budget constraints frequently pushed us to debate the merits of designing for safety versus durability. For example, in one 15-minute span, we decided not to use safety glass in the dormer window, reallocating the $300 for a waterproof roof underlay. We traded a potential safety gain for long-term durability. These daily judgments affecting public welfare and pleasure were, for me, a joy as an educator and an all-too-rare alignment of practice and education.

Disagreements with HFH centered around matters considered trivial in most student design projects: a window in a bathroom, a shade of blue paint, transom windows for natural ventilation, an alternative kitchen cabinet layout modestly increasing storage space, a glass panel in the front porch door, and so on. I found these mundane details of design, rarely discussed in conventional student project critiques, to be the core of our work. As students made impassioned pleas for the smallest of design issues, we realized the power of design-build to provide an educational platform for the ethical practice of architecture.

On occasion we refused to change our work. After receiving approvals early for paint colors, we declined the directive to repaint our two-tone color scheme when HFH notified us that they only allowed one-color houses. More commonly, we attempted to convince them of the wisdom of a design change by building it and showing it to the director. This approach was rarely successful. In one instance, students proposed a change in a second-floor bedroom space that would increase usable area by removing a wall to the storage room, improve light and room proportions, and avoid a building code violation. HFH refused the alteration, correctly pointing out the new design exceeded their 1,200-square-foot space limit. We rebuilt the wall as directed. The decision was devastating to students who were convinced of the wisdom and "rightness" of their position.

For many, the project was successful. It met the budget, while creating a building that is significantly more substantial than in typical HFH projects. It is more energy efficient and has wonderful light. The students loved making it, and the Browns love living there. But for me, the project failed in its central mission. As architects, we failed to convince an important provider of affordable housing of the benefits of better design. Despite the enthusiasm the project received, it was understood as an anomaly, built under special circumstances and not to be repeated. In short, our labor was respected, but not our work. Although Habitat has continued building houses in the neighborhood, they bear no witness to our efforts.

University of Arkansas students, under the direction of Eva Kultermann and Greg Herman, completed a second house in spring 2001, with a similar budget and less technically challenging site, although this time not through HFH. A local bank financed the house, which was not sold until after all work was completed. In this case, the students' frustration during construction was a result of the distant involvement of the bank's representatives and uncertainty about who would buy the final product. Like most architects doing affordable housing, the students had to design for hypothetical clients and could not make a personalized design. While detachment eliminated conflict, the absence of client provocation did not force the students to fully shape their beliefs in order to respond directly through design. In hindsight, our conflicts and failures with HFH had a productive end: they provided a circumscribed space challenging the students to explore and construct definitions of ethical conduct. This is an appropriate activity for future architects and a worthy goal of a university education.

Multiplying Knowledge:
Service-Learning x Activism = Community Scholars

By Jacqueline Leavitt and Kara Heffernan

Introduction

This essay describes the development and accomplishments of the University of California at Los Angeles (UCLA) Community Scholars Program (CSP) as one prototype of service-learning. Service-learning is defined and practiced in many ways: reciprocity, method, citizenship, and activities organized to meet actual community needs are a few defining keywords and phrases (Communications for a Sustainable Future 2000). Another dimension of service-learning links it to traditions of applied research. We begin with an overview of the CSP and the several themes informing it, discuss the steps involved in founding and sustaining the program, and conclude with lessons learned.

Program Overview

The CSP is the first program of its kind in the University of California system.[1] It turns resources outward by engaging Los Angeles labor and community activists, the Scholars, in collaborative projects with graduate students. Launched in 1991, the program is housed in the Department of Urban Planning and co-sponsored by the Center for Labor Research and Education. On June 27, 1991, applications from activists in the region were solicited. By the start of the 1992-93 school year, a pilot program was launched with a small grant from the Rockefeller Foundation. One hundred and twenty scholars have participated so far, in numbers varying from 8 to 17 per year, and the class of 2003 was the largest ever.[2] Approximately 12 students a year take more than one class in the two-quarter sequence, and altogether more than 300 students have enrolled in at least one class in the sequence. Scholars must take the entire sequence to fulfill the requirements of the program, and students can fulfill graduate requirements if they take both classes.[3]

Program Philosophy

A distinguishing mark of the CSP is that research informs action; the action can take place during or after the more formal "learning" takes place. This enables learning to be reconceptualized as action research and applied practice. The nature of the research is based on utility to activists and meets university standards of research. Gilda Haas, the first director of the program, explained: "Someone coming from outside to do research has the advantage of objectivity, but the disadvantage of ignorance... We look to those experiencing the problems as the touchstone for the values underlying our research" (National Committee for Responsive Philanthropy 1998). Learning is nonstop, dynamic, and fluid, changing in response to the context, and the context changes as the research is applied.

The program can be described as horizontal or peer learning (Freire 1973), which blurs the boundary lines between student and teacher. Teaching and learning occur between and among students, Scholars, and faculty, and often continue after the program ends. The program strives to create a bridge between participants, regardless of educational level, and to open the university's doors to communities that might otherwise be denied access to its resources. Scholars share their experiences in ways that are accessible to those outside the experience, and in turn gain a reflective space in which to exchange views and reflect on social-justice issues. To paraphrase one Scholar, "The Scholars program allowed me to expand and learn about the experiences, views and struggles of other people, which are very similar to the cause of the Central American and Latino communities" (Perez 2000).

Through the program, students deepen their understanding of policy problems and put a human face on statistics and analyses. They get practical experience in the nature of coalition-building, and engage with activists from different fields who have a multiplicity of views and experiences, all in pursuit of a common goal. Students are generally following their interests, both in collaborating with activists and in working on projects that can have real utility to the larger community, as opposed to writing reports that may just sit in faculty offices.

The program has five objectives: (1) advancing activist networking by erasing boundaries separating unions, community organizations, and community and economic development corporations; (2) breaking down the academy's insularity by helping it connect to the world beyond the ivory tower; (3) turning resources outward through an applied research project that encourages students to collaborate with Scholars and, by extension, with the sponsoring organizations; (4) exposing students to labor research and broadening the content of more traditional classes in community development and community-based planning; and (5) laying a foundation for future partnerships.

The program is structured around production of a final product, whether reports, maps, posters, timelines, or brochures. Products intentionally target a broad nonacademic audience, and many have been widely used by community and labor groups; they often have value beyond any one Scholar's organization, and have even led to the development of new institutions, housed in the community. The first project, "Accidental Tourism," set a precedent for this. It critiqued the city of Los Angeles's tourism promotion strategy and proposed alternatives that would bring economic benefits to working-class communities and communities of color. The report supported the work of the Tourism Industry Development Council (TIDC), which evolved into the Los Angeles Alliance for a New Economy (LAANE). In turn, LAANE spearheaded passage of the city's living-wage ordinance. The products of CSP projects also have resonance in training. For example, in 2003, the Liberty Hill Foundation used "Connecting LA's Community Organizations & Labor: Towards a Social & Economic Justice Landscape" in its training of leaders and organizers. Products have very practical applications but still meet, and often exceed, academic standards; the report "Care in Organizing: Building Coalitions in Los Angeles, Lessons from the Homecare Workers Campaign" won local and state planning awards for excellence.

Program Threads

The CSP draws on numerous traditions within not only urban planning and architecture but broader social movements including civil rights and labor. The most influential traditions include popular education, labor and neighborhood colleges, and institutes that focus on leadership and organizing. Table 1 provides an overview of the many different influences; their boundaries are fluid and each has competing strains within itself. A short discussion of these traditions begins with those that have the closest relationship to architecture and planning, then moves to colleges and institutes, and concludes with popular education.

Tradition	Emphasis
Community-based university studios	Education-based, frequently joint architecture and urban planning; clients typically cannot pay for assistance; making issues more visible.
Advocacy planning	Active responses and projects to urban renewal and redevelopment projects.
Community design centers	Architectural and financing projects; clients range from community groups to local government; includes fee-for-service and pro bono.
Labor colleges	Labor-based and worker rights.
Neighborhood colleges	Community issues and residents' experiences become subjects of classes.
Freedom/citizenship schools	Cultural rights; preserving language and traditions; citizenship rights.
Organizing institutes	Techniques/methods; leadership building; capacity building for organizations.
Popular education training	Experience-based; critical thinking; use of theater; English as a second language.

Table 1. Traditions Influencing the Community Scholars Program

Community-Based University Studios

Reflective thinking about community can be partially simulated, even if students' experiences are dissimilar from the groups with whom they work. Several UCLA joint architecture-urban planning studios that worked with two L.A. public housing developments (Nickerson Gardens, 1990 and 1991, and Pico Aliso, 1992-1993) were developed as a way for students to understand the lives of public housing residents. Even though none of the students had grown up in public housing and some had never set foot in a development, the class provided a structured way for them to meet with residents on a regular basis. The groundwork for the studios involved the professor being introduced to leaders and slowly gaining their trust. Classes frequently met at the development, often in homes, where residents controlled the space. Students had a chance to listen to the residents' opinions and ideas. One studio addressed the fact that 1,100 households of a development lacked onsite common laundry facilities (UCLA Joint Planning Studio 1990). With architect Judith Scheine as co-instructor, planning students researched tenants' laundry expenses and identified other needs, such as lack of meeting space, and this information enabled architectural students to define the needs, such as the number of washers and dryers and the specifications for meeting spaces. For the final assignment, architecture students presented models of laundry buildings and meeting rooms to a jury of residents.

Other studios may follow the example of Anthony Ward when he was on the architecture faculty at the University of Auckland, New

Zealand. Ward pioneered a studio informally known as the Maori studio. Otherwise underrepresented Maori students were a majority in the class and were encouraged to draw on their culture in developing design alternatives on a range of projects (Ward 1991).

Advocacy Planning

The social and physical turbulence of the 1960s and early 1970s, including the Civil Rights movement and the large-scale urban renewal projects that were wiping out entire communities, spawned advocacy planning, an activist orientation grounded in social and economic justice and an explicit focus on improving the lives of low-income communities and communities of color. Early advocacy planning was pioneered by Walter Thabit, who worked in Cooper Square, New York, where an organized community warded off a Robert Moses highway plan that would have displaced thousands of households. While advocacy planning addressed the voicelessness of residents living in threatened communities, it generally stopped short of giving them a major voice in directing the planning and making them true collaborators.

Community Design Centers

The community design movement can be traced to a 1968 speech in which Whitney Young chastised the members of the American Institute of Architects (AIA) for their inaction in the Civil Rights movement (Association for Community Design 2003). As with advocacy planning, the community design movement arose in response to urban renewal and the climate of change caused by the Civil Rights and antiwar movements. Groups like The Architects Resistance (TAR) in New York City protested the segregated bathrooms that Skidmore Owens and Merrill were including in plans for a South African project. Other architects formed design centers to work directly with residents; storefront architecture offices were set up and local youth were encouraged to learn architectural skills. One of the best and oldest design centers is the Pratt Institute Center for Community and Environmental Development (PICCED), which today works with residents on architecture and planning projects to address gentrification and industrial retention, and offers a wide range of leadership and community organizational courses.

Labor Colleges

The three most notable labor colleges, founded in the 1920s to advance the labor movement, were the Work People's College in Duluth, Minnesota, Brookwood Labor College in Katonah, New York, and Commonwealth College near Mena, Arkansas. Labor colleges eschewed the traditional hierarchical educational system in favor of "democratic settings [that] encouraged a co-operative feeling which transferred to the development of fraternal attitudes among workers who belonged to a common union and to a radically new social arrangement" (Altenbaugh and Paulston 1978: 251). Rutgers University, the University of California, and others offered extension courses under the rubric of workers' education (McElroy n.d.). Union education departments and universities offer worker education in many countries today.

Neighborhood College
The National Congress of Neighborhood Women (NCNW), with offices now in Appalachia, was founded in Williamsburg, Brooklyn, during the 1970s. Fueled by the women's movement, and in pursuit of strengthening grassroots voices in domestic affairs, the congress organized a neighborhood-based college for local women. Participants wanted more education to preserve their communities from the closing of services and displacement. Classes were designed to build local leadership by training "students" in the skills needed to speak knowledgeably at public meetings and in content built on neighborhood issues that students brought into the classroom. Class times were arranged to recognize that family responsibilities had to be managed along with school (Leavitt and Saegert 1990). The NCNW later turned to international networking as a member of the Huairou Commission. One part of the network has been Grassroots Women's International Academies, in which women are teachers and students (Leavitt and Yoder 2003).

Freedom Schools/Citizenship Schools
During the Civil Rights movement, schools born of Freedom Summer in Mississippi educated black students in basic subjects and black history. Septima Clark, fired from her job as a public school teacher of 40 years because she was a member of the National Association for the Advancement of Colored People (NAACP), became director of education at the Highlander Center. With Highlander and the Southern Christian Leadership Conference (SCLC), Clark organized schools to train leaders to pass the reading and writing tests required for voting. Throughout the Deep South, schools trained thousands of people, changed the face of local government, and led to the first federal Head Start program.

Organizing Institutes
Institutes, found in both the labor and community organizing traditions, have functioned as a method for training new activists and advancing the skills of existing ones. In pursuit of building power for social change, institutes equip individuals with techniques for organizing membership organizations and building coalitions. One of the best known is the Midwest Academy in Chicago, Illinois (Bobo et al.

2001). Some organizing institutes are offshoots of university programs, such as UCLA's Center for Labor Research and Education, which recently introduced an all-Spanish organizing workshop to its ongoing research activities on labor and community issues.

Popular Education Training

The popular education tradition is best exemplified by the work of Myles Horton at the Highlander Center in Tennessee and Paolo Freire in Brazil. Freire used literacy education to politicize community members to become more active citizens. He sought to help participants "read the world and be able to connect the world with the word" (Freire and Macedo 1998: 9). Highlander, similarly, was founded as an educational facility to educate workers and "common people," and later civil rights activists. Its work was rooted in a fundamental respect for "the intelligence of the students and their capacity to help you teach them" (Kohl 2002: 7).

The Scholars Come to UCLA

A convergence of interests within the Department of Urban Planning, in 1990, led faculty who worked in the community and community planning to discuss a new role for the university. For 20 years they had been working with poor and underrepresented communities around planning problems. While the federal "war on poverty" had made marginal gains, people of color, poor and working-class people, women, and other marginalized groups were still feeling the brunt of discrimination and of the increasing gap between the haves and have-nots. Los Angeles was becoming a place of multiculturalism and home to Third World conditions. The involved faculty discussed new ways to engage with nonstudents in these communities.

Gilda Haas, an adjunct lecturer who would head the Scholars Program, subsequently convened a series of meetings with community-based groups to identify research topics that could be useful to their work. The overwhelming agreement was to focus on economic development. At the time (and even today), Los Angeles lacked a Department of Economic Development per se, and community economic development was of great interest to groups. Over a series of meetings, the concept of a Community Scholars program emerged, and the first class was admitted for the 1990-1991 school year.

The program has been offered every year since then, except for 1997-1998. The most significant partner has been the UCLA Center for Labor Research and Education, whose director, Kent Wong, helps formulate each year's program and recruits Scholars, especially from the labor community.[4] Two directors have run the program; despite this change in leadership, the program has remained true to its original principles, striving to include equality in the classroom, minimal hierarchy, accountability to Scholars in the form of products that are useful to their organizations, commitment to building long-term relationships with Scholars, and valuing all forms of knowledge, especially those gained through direct organizing and service by Scholars.

Who Are the Scholars?

Scholars have hailed from 77 organizations, which work on a range of issues across the L.A. region, including immigrant rights and services, economic development, community development, social services, the arts, environmental justice, labor, and education. Most come from nonprofit community-based organizations or labor unions, but others come from the public sector and faith-based organizations. At first, Scholars tended to be drawn more from community-based organizations, while in the last few years union representation has been heavier. The racial and ethnic breakdown of Scholars is estimated (since the program keeps no formal data on race or ethnicity of participants) as 48 percent Latino, 23 percent white, 15 percent African American, and 14 percent Asian. These figures are generally representative of the region's population, with whites slightly underrepresented and Asians and African Americans slightly overrepresented.

Scholar Projects

The annual planning for the program involves establishing a loose framework to give structure, while at the same time allowing enough flexibility for the class to pursue its research interests. When the program began, Scholars largely shaped the topics, but later it became the norm to identify topics prior to recruitment, though there is still leeway for change. In one recent class, for example, where the plan had been to examine relationships between worker centers and unions, the Scholars wanted instead to respond to breaking events about the California budget crisis by developing a poster as a popular education tool for organizers. (Worker centers are community-based organizations, largely immigrant-oriented, addressing worker rights, housing, and related needs.) Table 2 documents topics since the program's inception.

While projects may be shaped by current events, as just noted, the overall program has been influenced by changes that accompanied the election in 1995 of John Sweeney as President of the American Federation of Labor-Congress of Industrial Organizations (AFL-CIO). Sweeney's election brought a commitment to organizing and fostering labor-community alliances. The homecare and long-term care workers of Local 434B of the Service Employees International Union (SEIU), in Los Angeles, made an alliance with community groups to advance their job security and win increases in wages and benefits as well as recognition, respect, and dignity. In 2000-2001, the Scholars Program was based on in-depth research about lessons learned from that campaign.

Name of Scholars Project	Year	Description
Accidental Tourism	1991-92	Critique of L.A.'s tourism promotion strategy; proposed alternatives to bring economic benefits to working-class and minority communities.
Manufacturing L.A.'s Future	1992-93	Sectoral examination of apparel, electric bus, and manufacturing with recyclable resource industries to shape industrial policy to benefit working-class and minority communities.
Banking on Communities	1993-94	Examination of popular education as tool for addressing complex economic issues; bilingual participatory workshop on money and banking resulted.
Los Angeles Manufacturing Action Project	1994-95	Sectoral research in various manufacturing industries for 10 labor unions to develop strategy for upgrading wages and working conditions in L.A.'s Alameda Corridor.
Worker Ownership: A Strategy for Job Creation and Retention in Los Angeles	1995-96	Research on worker cooperatives and employee stock ownership plans to determine ways to bring these efforts to scale via a supportive infrastructure of education, technical assistance, and financing.
Learning for a Change: Experiences in Popular Education in Los Angeles	1996-97	Study of popular education and economic development techniques, and application of them in two places in the region in the form of (1) support and economic education for community experiencing plant closures; (2) welfare reform educational workshops for a local social service agency.
Banking on Blight: Redevelopment in Post-Proposition 13 California	1998-99	Critique of California's redevelopment policy through case studies of four cities; contribution to advancing more just and accountable economic development policy in L.A.
Models of L.A. Organizing for Social Justice: Pushing the Boundaries, Crossing the Isms.	1999-2000	Research on organizing methods; popular education materials produced around immigration; timeline of key immigration events.
Participatory Democracy and Coalition Building — Organizing for Social Change in L.A.'s Communities and Workplaces	2000-01	Lessons from SEIU Local 434B's campaign to win recognition as bargaining agent with County of Los Angeles appointed public authority; needs assessment and recommendations on housing, transportation, and training.
Connecting L.A.: Toward a Social and Economic Justice Landscape	2001-02	Mapping of residences of 150,000 low-wage workers in Los Angeles County; research of key campaigns and organizing opportunities.

Table 2. Project Topics by Year

Successes and Lessons Learned

The Scholars Program has wide-ranging benefits. Some are academic in nature. "The Community Scholars program provided me with a theoretical framework for understanding social change," one former Scholar noted (Perez 2000). Other benefits are purely practical, providing Scholars with tools to do their jobs better. From another former Scholar: "I learned to broaden my outlook on the various ways to obtain support for my ideas… and include those I would not ordinarily expect to side with my ideas" (Stavnezer 2000). On a broader level the program raises the consciousness of many participants. "It increased my awareness of the unequal distribution of resources," said one Scholar (Cannon 2000). "It opened my eyes to how much social change is actually needed," said another (Valencia 2000).

One of the program's most frequently cited benefits is the networking and relationship-building it fosters. These relationships, which tend to live on long after the program ends, contribute to the long-term advancement of the economic and social justice movement. Some Scholars come into the program already knowing each other. For example, the 2002-2003 class included three Scholars representing three different organizations that were founding members of the Multi-Ethnic Immigrant Workers Organizing Network (MIWON). Scholars may enter the program while working for one organization, only to move on to another, becoming work colleagues of another Scholar. Students find internships with the Scholars' organizations and in some cases are hired as staff.

Relationship-building serves another purpose as well: it helps make the program a safe space for the sharing of ideas and perspectives: "We talk about race, class, and gender, which are things that we need to talk about… The class and the program enable participants to learn from each other and to share experiences" (Jackson 2000). In the 2002-2003 class, a Scholar from a community development corporation involved in organizing neighborhood youth realized that the residents in his community also had identities as workers, and he came to appreciate the overlapping objectives in workers' and residents' community struggles. At a meeting of Scholars in 2003, when each was asked what they wanted from the program a common request was for learning about organizing methods and ways in which to sustain membership after initial recruitment. Three of the 10 class sessions for the following quarter included community and labor organizers, who worked with students and Scholars on exercises that included icebreakers and integrated ways of understanding similarities and differences regarding race, ethnicity, class, and gender.

Despite all these positives, the program is not without its challenges. One of them is geography. In a region as large as Los Angeles, the time required to get to a class at the UCLA campus can be a barrier. In response to the logistical challenges, some class meetings were moved to the community, making it easier for participants to attend. Scholars tend to be very engaged in many issues and activities, so meeting once a week can be very demanding, especially when it involves preparation time. Therefore, during the changeover of directors, in 1999, the program was restructured from three quarters to two quarters, in part to respond to the time-pressure issue. Attendance rose immediately, but the change meant sacrificing an introductory class that was an incubator for developing the class research topic. Another challenge is trying to make the program truly of the community. One former Scholar noted that the program is not community-friendly enough, since Scholars tend to be staff persons of organizations. "These are not truly community members," she stated, arguing that the program should be reaching down into the constituents of organizations (Portillo 2000). A related challenge is trying to bridge the divide between academia and the on-the-ground struggles for justice that Scholars are immersed in on a daily basis. One Scholar cited the difficulties of interpreting academic jargon and complicated university procedures (Brennan 2000). But when the bridge between the academy and practice is built, it can be among the most rewarding aspects of the program. There is also the constant challenge of trying to make the project useful to the work of the Scholars. This can be complicated by the broad array of fields from which Scholars hail. Picking and redefining projects, to the extent that it attempts to be democratic and inclusive, can be a time-consuming and difficult process. This becomes a frustrating experience for many Scholars, students, and faculty alike.

There are also the differing motivations among students and Scholars, and different expectations among all involved. Tension can arise when students, who are graded on their work, and Scholars, for whom the project is often secondary to their jobs, need to negotiate the terrain of their very different vantage points, time commitments, and levels of interest. While the bulk of the actual written parts of projects tend to fall more heavily on the students, the input of Scholars is critical, and in some instances Scholars assume as much responsibility for the final product as students. Furthermore, some project topics are especially difficult to research within the time frame of the two-quarter class, and others do not appear to relate directly to the immediate needs of a Scholar's organization.

But the program has been a success overall. One indicator of this is the number of Scholars who apply based on recommendations of colleagues who participated in the program or knew others who did. Another is the ongoing work with SEIU Local 434B, which has sponsored six to seven Scholars in the past two years. Perhaps the most powerful indicator of success is the social justice landscape of Los

Angeles today. The Scholars Program has directly influenced two organizations, the Los Angeles Alliance for a New Economy (LAANE) and Strategic Actions for a Just Economy (SAJE). As noted earlier, LAANE was an outgrowth of the TIDC and the client for the first Community Scholars project, and today is a leading and innovative resource for accountable economic development organizations in the region. SAJE was founded in response to the need, pointed to over a number of years by several Scholars classes, for a different kind of institution located in the community that would initiate and follow through on action research projects. Since its founding in 1996, SAJE has spearheaded innovative research and community development projects, including acting as facilitator for the Figueroa Corridor Coalition for Economic Justice (FCCEJ), a participatory planning process in which the community has negotiated for jobs, parks, housing, and health and safety benefits in the area adjacent to downtown Los Angeles.

Conclusion

For more than 20 years prior to the inception of the Scholars Program, the urban planning faculty at UCLA had been working with communities of the unrepresented. Not until 2002 did UCLA embark on a campaign to encourage university-wide involvement with such communities. As a result, the number of university initiatives that in some form or another involve work in the Los Angeles community has dramatically increased. Nonetheless, the Community Scholars Program remains unique, one of the few points of connection among social justice activists, students, and academics. As Carlos Porras, a Scholar in 1992-1993 and former executive director of Communities for a Better Environment (CBE), told the 2003 class, "I have come full circle. I was a Scholar, on the advisory committee, and now I am speaking to a Scholars class" (Porras 2003).

Notes

1. In 2003, the University of California at Berkeley Center for Labor Research and Education, in conjunction with the Department of Sociology, launched a Community Scholars Program. Their approach differs from the UCLA program and includes more attention to organizational capacity building. Older programs exist nationwide but to our knowledge, and with the exception of UC Berkeley, none brings students and Scholars together in the same classroom.
2. The Rockefeller Foundation awarded a grant of $25,000 in 1990-91 and extended this for the following year. The program received $10,000 from the ARCO Foundation in 1992. From 1992 to 1994, the California Community Foundation awarded a grant for $20,000. The Great

Western Bank awarded $3,000 in 1993. From 1999 to the present, the Harvey S. Perloff Foundation has provided $15,000 annually to pay for honoraria for visiting academics and practitioners, a teaching assistant, and production costs. The Lucie and Harry Lang Memorial Fund at the Center for Labor Research and Education contributes $10,000 for small stipends to Scholars to partially cover parking costs at UCLA and books. Additional money from the Institute of Labor and Employment (ILE) contributed to production costs of products from 2001 to 2003. A Community Outreach Partnership Grant (COPC) awarded by the U.S. Department of Housing and Urban Development also included some support to the program.

3. The time frame for a project has changed since the program's inception. Initially the program was the length of an academic year (three quarters, in the case of UCLA), with meetings held once a week. Given the difficulty Scholars had in attending once a week for three quarters, in 1999 the class time was shortened to two quarters, beginning in January in the winter quarter and ending in mid-June. The positive outcome of this change was that attendance immediately went up; the disadvantage was the lack of an introductory class that served as an incubation period in which the class could develop a research topic.

4. In 1994, restructuring at UCLA divided the School of Architecture and Urban Planning, with a Department of Urban Planning created in the School of Public Policy and Social Research. Faculty involved in Community Scholars were more engaged with the Center for Labor Research and Education, facilitated by a U.S. Department of Housing and Urban Development (HUD) grant for a Community Outreach Partnership Center (COPC). While an architectural faculty member was written into the grant, her subsequent departure from the renamed School of Architecture was not followed by a replacement. Other events contributing to greater collaboration with the Center for Labor Research and Education can be traced to interests of some faculty within urban planning. A reactivated labor movement raised questions about economic development that further heightened the need for community-based groups to understand those issues. Simultaneously, housing-based community groups and community development corporations were turning to economic development as housing money dried up and housing costs outpaced income. These events drew the Community Scholars Program closer to traditions of movement building in labor and civil rights.

References

Altenbaugh, R.J., and R. G. Paulston. (1978). "Work People's College: A Finnish Folk High School in the American Labor College Movement." *Paedagogica Historica. International Journal of the History of Education* 18: 2. As cited in Auvo Kostiainen (1980), *Work People's College: An American Immigrant Institution.* www.genealogia.fi/emi/art/article243e.htm. Accessed October 8, 2003.

Association for Community Design. (2003). *History of Association for Community Design.* www.communitydesign.org/rex/support_docs/History.pdf. Accessed October 12, 2003.

Bobo, K., K. Jackie, and S. Max. (2001). *Organizing for Social Change: Midwest Academy Manual for Activists.* 3rd edition. Santa Ana, CA: Seven Locks Press.

Brennan, C.N. (February 9, 2000). Personal interview.

Cannon, R. (February 7, 2000). Personal interview.

Communications for a Sustainable Future. (2000). www.csf.colorado.edu/sl/what-is-sl.html. Accessed October 1, 2003.

Freire, A. M. Araujo, and D. Macedo, eds. (1998). *The Paulo Freire Reader.* New York: Continuum Publishing Company.

Freire, P. (1973). *Education for Critical Consciousness.* New York: Continuum Publishing Company.

Jackson, R. (February 4, 2000).Personal interview.

Kohl, H. (2002). "Developing Teachers for Social Justice." *Radical Teacher* (65): 5-10.

Leavitt, J., and A. Yonder. (2003). "Local Organizing and Global Networking: The Case of the Huairou Commission." In *Memoria del IX seminario internacional: Derecho y espacio urbano,* edited by B. Alfonsin and E. Fernandes, pp. 209-215. Quito, Ecuador: Programa de Gestion Urbana.

Leavitt, J., and S. Saegert. (1990). *From Abandonment to Hope: Community-Households in Harlem.* New York: Columbia University Press.

McElroy, E. (n.d.). *The IMLR: Labor Education at Rutgers University,* 1931-1981. www.rci.rutgers.edu/~smlr/library. Rutgers School of Management and Labor Relations. Accessed October 12, 2003.

National Committee for Responsive Philanthropy. (1998). "Community-Based Research Gathers Momentum, Not Dust." *Responsive Philanthropy.* www.ncrp.org/articles/rp/commbasedres.htm. Accessed October 16, 2003.

Perez, R. (February 9, 2000). Personal interview.

Porras, C. (2003). Presentation to Community Scholars Class at UCLA.

Portillo, S. (February 2000). Personal interview.

Stavnezer, M. (February 9, 2000). Personal interview.

UCLA Joint Planning Studio. (1990). *Paths for Tomorrow: Nickerson Gardens, A Community Planning for Change.* School of Architecture and Urban Planning.

Valencia, A. (February 2000). Personal interview.

Ward, A. (1991). "Biculturalism and Community Design: A Model for Critical Design Education." In *Voices in Architectural Education: Cultural Politics and Pedagogy*, edited by T.A. Dutton, pp. 195-223. New York: Begin & Garvey.

Beyond Boundaries, Weaving Connections:
Reflections on the American Indian Housing Initiative

By David Riley, Michael Rios, Scott Wing, and Beth Workman[1]

The American Indian Housing Initiative (AIHI) integrates research and education about sustainable community building practices with hands-on interdisciplinary experiences for students, faculty, and design professionals. It focuses on the housing crises endemic to American Indian reservations and promotes economically and environmentally sustainable design strategies. The initiative was established in 1998 as a national collaboration involving Pennsylvania State University, the University of Washington, and Chief Dull Knife College of the Northern Cheyenne reservation in Montana.[2] Its academic program concentrates on students and faculty in the design disciplines of architecture, architectural engineering, and landscape architecture, but also includes students with diverse backgrounds in fields such as nutrition, biology, and art education. The yearlong, three-part service-learning course pivots around a summer design-build experience on tribal lands, where faculty and students join practitioners and the Northern Cheyenne community in the construction of housing, community facilities, and site installations. Projects to date include a demonstration home, an adult education center and courtyard, a community meeting hall, and three privately owned residences. Practitioners with backgrounds in architecture, historic preservation, art, landscape architecture, engineering, construction management, and various building trades join with students in the planning and construction of load-bearing straw bale buildings and associated landscapes.

The initiative was spurred by Boyer and Mitgang's *Building Community: A New Future for Architecture Education and Practice* (1996) and creates a collaborative, interdisciplinary, active learning environment linking students and practitioners across the country and across generations in a common pursuit of an ethical and culturally appropriate basis for work. Combining innovation in architectural and engineering design with projects of social consequence, the AIHI broadens participants' understanding of environmentally responsive technologies through research and the inclusion of an underrepresented population. It also aims to implement sustainable community development strategies through the technical assistance it provides to tribal organizations.

Housing Challenges: Marking Turf under the Big Sky

The Northern Cheyenne were severed from their nomadic building traditions after federal resettlement, a century ago, on a portion of their native lands on the upper plains of eastern Montana. Their housing, including much planned and built by the U.S. Department of Housing and Urban Development (HUD), is ill-suited to local needs, shoddily constructed, and inadequate. Statistics illuminate the housing crisis on tribal reservations:

• Only 25 percent of Native Americans have acceptable housing, the lowest proportion of any sector of the U.S. population (Gaffney 1997; U.S. Department of Housing and Urban Development 1994).

• More than 40 percent of homes in tribal areas are overcrowded and have serious physical deficiencies. In the United States as a whole, only 5.9 percent of households are overcrowded (National American Indian Housing Council 2002).

• The average lifespan of a Plains Indian is only 45 years (Indian Health Services 2002).

Federally subsidized housing programs addressing the tribal housing crisis have failed from a lack of education, commitment, tribal involvement, or acceptance. Short-lived and limited HUD housing programs often ignore the cultural and social values of tribes, use inefficient modular housing technologies, and import labor and materials into communities that already have capable labor and indigenous building materials.

Social Challenges: "Native" Identity and Youth

On the reservations, the social construction of youth identity can be doubly problematic: the increasing media depiction of youth as a "problem" is coupled with the fact that youth represent one of the most actively targeted consumer groups. Youth lack space to articulate their fears, desires, and identities. In the case of the Northern Cheyenne reservation, lack of agency is complicated by stereotypes of native identity as exotic "other" and the absence of Northern Cheyenne references in mainstream culture.

Not surprisingly, the social conditions of reservation youth continue to decline. *Native America at the New Millennium*, a report published by the Harvard Project on American Indian Economic Development (Henson et al. n.d.), identifies the challenges:

• Of the approximately 500,000 Indian children enrolled in primary and secondary level schools, over one-third will drop out; Indian children have the lowest educational attainment of all minority groups.

• Nationally, one in five Indian children between the ages of 12 and 17 uses illicit drugs, the highest rate for any ethnic group in that age class.

• Teen cigarette use stands at 180 percent of the national average, and the death rate of Indian youth (ages five to 24) from alcohol abuse is 17 times the comparable level for all races.

The confluence of so many economic, social, and health problems leaves Indian youth few opportunities to experience self-affirmation or become fully engaged members of the community. Gang activity and related violence are increasing as a result (Henson et al. n.d.).

An Alternative Approach: Working from the Inside Out

The AIHI and its main partner, Chief Dull Knife College, are committed to making local improvements and identifying culturally specific strategies with the potential for national application. Working from the inside out, the AIHI helps the tribe use the research, expertise, and technical assistance of faculty and design professionals in defining their own terms of sustainable development. To reduce dependency on federal programs, the AIHI explores alternative housing solutions through the application of regionally appropriate materials, "green design" strategies, and community-centered construction processes, creating community facilities and homes that reflect Northern Cheyenne culture, values, and visions of sustainability.

With the Northern Cheyenne Housing Authority the AIHI has started an apprenticeship program in which tribal members work with students, faculty, and practitioners to learn how to build with straw bale construction and other sustainable technologies. The long-term goal is for apprentices to apply their new skills to the construction of additional housing units, educating more community members in the process and working toward a model of community-built sustainable housing. A new community arts program, the Youth Restoration Art Project (YouthRAP), in partnership with the Northern Cheyenne Boys and Girls Club, aims to bring art back into the spaces of everyday life. Art was once a multifunctional force, variously meeting the personal, social, political, and spiritual needs of the Northern Cheyenne (Spang 2003). YouthRAP enables local youth to explore aspects of their own identity and the reservation landscape through site installations associated with AIHI projects. The program creates a space for dialogue about what it means to be a Northern Cheyenne, and gives participants skills in team-building and group dynamics, in addition to opportunities to learn about photography, digital media, and other art forms.

East and West Meet on the Northern Plains

The core of the AIHI is a collaboration between two major land-grant universities and a tribal college. This unique institutional relationship combines the resources of Penn State and the University of Washington along with the unique mission of Dull Knife College — a community-based, tribally controlled community college and land-grant institution that serves the Northern Cheyenne reservation and surrounding communities. The combined efforts of Penn State and the University of Washington, through a variety of external and internal grants to support teaching, research, and outreach, create the capacity needed to sustain intensive service-learning programs such as the AIHI. At Penn State, the initiative is supported through a number of colleges and departments that provide financial and human resources through existing programs and centers, including Penn State's Schreyer Honors College, Bowers Program for Excellence in Design and Construction of the Built Environment (an endowment that supports interdisciplinary programs in architecture, landscape architecture, and architectural engineering), and Hamer Center for Community Design Assistance (a research and outreach unit of the School of Architecture and Landscape Architecture). In addition, a multiyear National Science Foundation grant supports research through service-learning and provides resources for graduate student assistantships. At the University of Washington, the AIHI benefits from the BaSiC (Building Sustainable Communities) Initiative, a program of the College of Architecture and Urban Planning, which also supports similar projects in Africa, India, and Mexico.

The completion of several projects and the mutual learning gained through trial and error have built the trust and respect that define the AIHI. The results of this process testify to the emergence of a strong and resilient partnership. In the past two years, approximately $200,000 has been raised to support teaching and research at Penn State associated with AIHI projects and related programs. In addition, a memorandum of agreement signed in 2003 formalized the relationship among the three academic partners and made explicit the goals and objectives of the AIHI.

Three-Part Coursework: Prepare, Participate, Reflect

At Penn State, the AIHI coursework introduces students studying architecture, engineering, landscape architecture, and a range of other disciplines to emerging sustainable technologies, and applies them in a public context, introducing issues of ethics, cultural identity, economy, and politics. Students of all levels, from first-year to graduate, participate in the three parts of the course — spring, summer, and fall semesters sequentially — which provides an opportunity to apply and evaluate straw bale technology through design and construction on the Northern Cheyenne reservation. Past building projects include the construction of private and community-owned houses, a community center, and an adult education literacy center and courtyard. The course objectives are for students to (1) identify the effects of cross-cultural interaction and ethics as applied in housing and community development programs, (2) assess the application of appropriate technologies and community-built housing methods on a reservation, and (3) understand the attributes and limitations of straw bale building methods.

The course has three parts:

Part One (Spring), Preparation. Students review applications of straw bale construction with an emphasis on housing in marginalized communities. They review attributes and limitations of load-bearing straw bale technologies, including construction of a test wall to introduce building methods and evaluate the straw bale system. Students learn concepts of transcultural intervention and the effects of culture in the design of buildings and landscapes, with a specific focus on Native American culture. They also encounter community design and development concepts and explore links between housing and larger community issues. Students are introduced to project partners and Web-based tools for the collaborative exchange of design ideas with peers in a similar course at the University of Washington and with project advisors from the Northern Cheyenne tribe. Students and faculty consult with practitioners experienced in construction documentation, material specifications and ordering, and construction scheduling and management, in preparation for the summer phase. Given the range of interests and the time required for preparation, design of the summer's project is often led by an individual faculty member and a smaller group of students.

Part Two (Summer), Participatory Learning. The class travels to the Northern Cheyenne reservation to join construction of a straw bale building and smaller installation and renovation projects. They work alongside tribal members, alumni practitioners, and students from the companion course at the University of Washington. Lodging for students and faculty has ranged from sleeping in the classrooms of a local elementary school to pitching tents near project sites. Although projects typically take three to five weeks to complete, students work on-site for two full weeks. Smaller groups of faculty, students, and local partners begin with site preparation, before the rest of the students arrive, and often extend the work beyond the two weeks to complete a project. Students take part in workshop presentations, study circles, and other social and ceremonial activities with tribal members. The group visits completed projects to assess the performance of straw bale walls and the functionality of designs, based on inspection and post-occupancy interviews. Students must document their experiences through drawings, photographs, and writings, comment on the application and viability of sustainable building technology in the region, and plan projects for the following year.

Figure 1. Demonstration house for local housing authority (detail on right), constructed to highlight energy cost savings of straw bale technology

Part Three (Fall), Reflection and Recording. Students compare their expectations of the building process and on-site experience with their actual observations. Along with recording their experiences through photographic and video compilations and as-built drawings and models of the project outcome, they suggest improvement of the design, construction process, collaborative activities, and interaction with the tribal members, and they summarize the results of the project for an informational website. Small groups of faculty and students evaluate previous efforts and begin to plan for future projects, through dialogue with tribal partners. The fall semester also offers the opportunity for beginning the design of speculative projects to be considered in subsequent semesters. The course concludes with a public presentation of the yearlong effort to the university community.

Knowledge, Competencies, and Skills

Engagement with the Northern Cheyenne community offers knowledge and skills that differ from but complement classroom learning. The immersive experience of being on the reservation exposes students to a different life-world and helps them gain cultural competencies — tools necessary in understanding diverse perspectives and communicating across cultural, class, and racial differences. They are also exposed to the material conditions on the Northern Cheyenne reservation and gain a deeper understanding of the complex social and economic issues that define reservation life.

Students also gain first-hand knowledge of an emerging sustainable building technology. They apply concepts of sustainability to a real situation and acquire a multidimensional understanding of the tensions and tradeoffs among design options. Working in groups and collaborating with students in other disciplines enables them to develop communication and team problem-solving skills. The hands-on components of designing and building allow students to develop competencies in working within the physical constraints of material properties and gravity, as they negotiate intercultural sensitivity and the ethics of design and construction.

Expanded Visions of Design Practice and Education

The AIHI course series responds to the current rapid shift toward promoting the design and construction of buildings that are healthier for occupants, more energy-efficient, and less disruptive to the environment. Buildings and their construction processes in the United States alone account for one-sixth of the world's freshwater withdrawals, one-quarter of its wood harvest, and two-fifths of its material and energy flows (Roodman and Lenssen 1995). The need to minimize the environmental effects of buildings is evident, considering that 65.2 percent of total U.S. electricity consumption and more than 36 percent of total primary energy use relate directly to buildings and their construction (U.S. Department of Energy 2001). A widely accepted concept in green building design and construction is the shift away from linear and sequential design toward an integrated process allowing for greater system efficiencies. The roles and contributions of many disciplines must be recognized simultaneously in order to achieve success. An integrated design process requires new formulations, in which design and construction teams collaborate in a design environment. The AIHI course series prepares students from varied design disciplines to function productively within integrated green design teams.

The course series also provides a pedagogical hybrid of collaborative learning and public scholarship. In addition to developing skills and a research body in a specified field, students learn to appreciate the dynamics of integrative process, in which disciplinary skills inform a greater interdisciplinary effort. When the student's research in the lab informs the work carried out in the public realm, the borders of collaborative learning expand to include a real-life client and community.

The culturally rich and historically devastated context of the Northern Cheyenne community raises issues of ethics, culture, history, economy, politics, and race. Here, the learning becomes active and the research meaningful. The development and survival of the AIHI depends on the flexible working relationship of all colleagues involved, a relationship that is collaborative in its truest sense, a "co-laboring." The roles of participants are dynamic. For instance, a faculty member doing research on community nonprofit organizations may network with tribal advocacy groups on one day, and help design a communal space on the next. A graduate student in architecture might divide her time in Montana between meetings with tribal housing authority members to determine solutions to housing needs, working as a crew member on the construction site, and driving the student van on field trips to Medicine Wheel, a Wyoming rodeo, or a pow-wow at a nearby reservation. The vice president of the tribal college might work with a grant-writer on a budget for a proposal in one hour, and in the next be making a trip to provide more water jugs to the construction site. Essentially, each person has a fluid role, with success depending on the understanding that everyone is a key contributor to a greater effort and that leadership is collaboration.

In his book *Learning by Building: Design and Construction in Architectural Education* (1997: x-xi), William Carpenter explains the advantages of this type of public scholarship:

> With the recent focus on redesigning the way an architect learns, construction studios are an ideal vehicle to synthesize complex areas of knowledge... Construction studios offer a way to learn in a practical sense without sacrificing a high caliber of design... [and] can offer students the opportunity for cross-disciplinary approaches and projects that reach out to the community groups who are in need. Most of all, students learn the ability to communicate with teammates and actual clients... and [learn] that architecture is a collaborative effort and not an exercise in isolation. Both in school and in practice, the ethic of giving back to society can be encouraged.

As an ambitious pedagogical model, the AIHI course series seeks to enhance the quality and meaning of integrated research, education, and outreach in the greater academic community. The three-step process of experimentation, application, and assessment serves as a model for other programs in the university community that seek to integrate teaching and service and deploy valuable research results.

Building Civic Capacity through Community-Based Design

The AIHI brings issues of art, culture, and education to the fore to address the social dimension of sustainability. Recently developed programs, such as YouthRAP, enable the AIHI to apply an art-based approach through which Northern Cheyenne youth can communicate their world to others. Projects acknowledge diversity as a central element in community-based design, by exposing the fallacious stereotypes of native peoples and revealing the rich complexity of hybrid and transcultural identities. The material result, whether a small courtyard on a college campus or a photo exhibit by youth, establishes a discourse between native and non-native epistemologies, youth and adult realms.

YouthRAP will be adopted as an ongoing community arts and design program on the Northern Cheyenne reservation. Youth and students will explore issues of identity, landscape, and civic engagement while designing and constructing communal spaces on the reservation. Studies of design-based learning conducted by the National Endowment of the Arts have shown that design education programs engage many intelligences, create student-centered program development, and assist students in developing a variety of communication skills (Davis 1997). These studies have also demonstrated that students participating in design-based programs develop an increased sense of civic responsibility and community engagement. Students thus learn about community affairs, political issues, and the processes through which citizens become informed and effect change. Specific civic leadership skills include collaboration and conflict resolution, active listening, perspective taking, and public speaking and engagement with social institutions (Flanagan and Faison 2001).

Figure 2. Stones inscribed with words chosen by youth as a form of self-expression (detail on right) and placed in a courtyard symbolic of a Cheyenne campfire

Additionally, the AIHI program creates a framework that emphasizes interdisciplinary, collaborative, student-centered, engaged learning experiences. In 1998, representatives of the state educational agencies constituting the State Education and Environment Roundtable initiated a study to examine environment-based education to determine its effectiveness in improving learning and influencing the ability of students to garner the leadership and civic skills needed to be active citizens. After examining 40 programs from across the nation, the study's authors concluded that students engaged in place-based learning experiences outperform their peers in traditional programs, develop an interest in arts skills, mathematical concepts, scientific problem-solving, and civic processes, and develop analytical skills. They also think creatively, apply knowledge to complex community and natural systems, promote stronger group-work values, communication skills, and mutual respect, and have fewer disciplinary problems (Lieberman and Hoody 1998). Teachers report an increased enthusiasm and commitment among students, and greater opportunities to apply innovative instructional strategies. Few models exist that permit students to explore and learn through an integrative process such as YouthRAP.

Future of the AIHI and Public Scholarship

The AIHI's collaboration is challenged by geographical distance, since its lead collaborators are based in Pennsylvania and Washington, but it compensates through a collective sense of leadership. The AIHI has developed an identity separate from yet dependent upon the institutions it joins. Collaborators see in AIHI's grassroots, hands-on, straw-and-stucco nature the potential both to make learning active and research meaningful and to change lives. The program's search for productive working relationships actively addresses social and pedagogical priority, while benefiting all who participate. Public scholarship programs like the AIHI put "knowledge in the service of a more fully realized democracy" (Long 1997: 17), and, by rupturing the traditional insularity and privileged isolation of higher education, stretch the capability of traditional scholarship.

The AIHI advances a definition of public scholarship that is participatory and requires mutual engagement and collaboration, characteristics essential to creating new sites of knowledge centered on civic, social, and cultural issues. Thus, it addresses several goals in public scholarship and integrative learning:

- partnering across academic, institutional, and social boundaries
- engaging diverse perspectives in community-centered projects
- learning through process and participation
- collaborating and exchanging across cultures

Further, the initiative seeks to transcend traditional modes of education and recognizes that knowledge develops through negotiation: instead of being regarded as a predetermined product of experience, knowledge is the experience, it is the process.

Notes

1. Coauthors are listed in alphabetical order and share equal responsibility for this essay.
2. Program collaborators are David Riley, Michael Rios, and Scott Wing of Pennsylvania State University and Sergio Palleroni of the University of Washington.

References

Allen, W.R. (May 21, 1998). "W. Ron Allen, President, National Congress of American Indians, Senate Committee Oversight Hearing on the Unmet Health Care Needs in Indian Country." Testimony before the U.S. Senate.

Boyer, E., and L.D. Mitgang. (1996). *Building Community: A New Future for Architecture Education and Practice: A Special Report*. Princeton, NJ: Carnegie Foundation for the Advancement of Teaching.

Carpenter, W. (1997). *Learning by Building: Design and Construction in Architectural Education*. New York: Van Nostrand Reinhold.

Davis, M. (1997). "Design as the Catalyst for Learning." Alexandria, VA: Association for Supervision and Curriculum Development.

Flanagan, C., and N. Faiso. (2001). "Youth Civic Development: Implication of Research for Social Policy and Programs." *Social Policy Report: Giving Children and Youth Development Knowledge Away* 15(1).

Gaffney, S. (1997). "Profile of Native American Housing." Inspector General's Statement before the Committee on Indian Affairs and the Committee on Banking, Housing, and Urban Affairs, United States Senate.

Henson, E., J.B. Taylor et al. (n.d.). *Native America at the New Millennium*. Cambridge, MA: The Harvard Project on American Indian Economic Development. www.ksg.harvard.edu/hpaied/pubs/pub_004.htm. Accessed January 25, 2004.

Indian Health Services. (2002). *Statistical Database*. www.ihs.gov/NonMedicalPrograms/IHS_Stats/IHS_HQ_Publications.asp. Accessed December 1, 2002.

Lieberman, G.A., and L.L. Hoody. (1998). *Closing the Achievement Gap: Using the Environment as an Integrating Context for Learning*. San Diego, CA: State Education and Environment Roundtable.

Long, E. (1997). "Introduction: Engaging Sociology and Cultural Studies: Disciplinarity and Social Change." In *From Sociology to Cultural Studies*, edited by E. Long, pp. 1-32. Malden, MA: Blackwell Publishers.

National American Indian Housing Council. (2002). "Too Few Rooms: Residential Crowding in Native American Communities and Alaskan Native Villages." *Cooperative Agreement H-21257-RG with U.S. Department of Housing and Urban Development*. Washington, DC: U.S. Department of Housing and Urban Development.

Roodman, D., and N. Lenssen. (March 1995). "A Building Revolution: How Ecology and Health Concerns Are Transforming Construction." *Worldwatch Paper* 124.

Spang, B. (January 28, 2003). Personal interview.

U.S. Department of Energy, Energy Information Administration. (March 2001). *Monthly Energy Review.* Washington, DC: U.S. Department of Energy. http://tonto.eia.doe.gov/FTPROOT/multifuel/mer/00350103.pdf. Accessed January 27, 2004.

U.S. Department of Health and Human Services, Substance Abuse and Mental Health Services Administration, Office of Applied Studies. (2000). "Summary of Findings from the 1999 National Household Survey on Drug Abuse." Washington, DC: U.S. Department of Health and Human Services. www.samhsa.gov/oas/oasftp.htm. Accessed January 24, 2004.

U.S. Department of Housing and Urban Development. (1994). "Our Home: Buildings of the Land." In *HUD-1410-CPD. Energy-Efficiency Design Guide for Indian Housing.* Washington, DC: HUD Office of Native American Programs.

Shifting Ground:
Design as Civic Action and Community Building

By Paula Horrigan

Introduction

Practicing place-based design and planning that is local, participatory, and engaged with the community is the approach advocated by five State University of New York (SUNY) Network schools that are helping to spearhead the New York State Quality Communities Initiative (QCI). The QCI's main goal is identifying and fostering innovative urban design and planning projects. In 2000, a QCI task force was charged with studying community growth and ways of assisting with land development, preservation, and rehabilitation projects that promote economic development and environmental protection. The task force report (Donohue and Treadwell 2001) included 41 specific recommendations for rethinking how and when communities need help and imagining ways to maximize resources through cooperative and integrated processes. Recommendation 14 identified SUNY as an underused resource and led to forming SUNY Network, which I direct. The network consists of SUNY schools with departments, programs, and institutes dedicated to design and planning. They began meeting in late 2001 with the goal of repositioning their teaching, public scholarship, and outreach efforts to align with the QCI goals. (See the QCI website: www.dos.state.ny.us/qcp/qcp2.html.) SUNY Network faculty and students assist QCI communities by facilitating design visioning and preparing community-supported urban design proposals for state funding.

The North Side Neighborhood Visioning Project in Binghamton, New York, was the first SUNY Network project undertaken by faculty and students in the departments of Landscape Architecture at SUNY College of Environmental Science and Forestry (ESF) and Cornell University. It began in January 2002. Seven months later, North Side leaders would stand with city and state officials to recognize Binghamton as one of 12 state demonstration QCI cities. The North Side's agenda got to City Hall as a result of an academic service-learning design process involving student designers, faculty, and community members. This project offers a glimpse of service-learning's potential to shift ground in the academy and the community. It demonstrates how service-learning addresses mutual academic and community goals while fostering design as place making, civic action, and community building. The process and approach outlined in the following pages are part of an emerging methodology for undertaking projects between the SUNY Network and participating QCI communities.

The North Side Neighborhood Visioning Project demonstrates a move toward design as civic action and community building. It is about shifting design education's responsibility toward process and away from its usual product focus. It is about shifting educators toward adopting pedagogical methods and modes that help designers become engaged and reflective practitioner-citizens, sensitive to the exigencies of place and the complexity of communities. It is about shifting the academy toward public design scholarship. And it is about recognizing that the diverse and complex world of contested public and private space requires educational approaches and design practices that cultivate positive relationships between people and places.

Most importantly, this work is about shifting the "space" of design learning to the community. Only then can design be fully realized as civic action and community building. When the space of learning shifts from the academy to the community, the center of knowledge and inquiry shifts too. Knowledge is rediscovered in place, in a community's residents, institutions, patterns, and history. A letting go of rigid course structure and design methodology occurs, as participants — students, faculty, and community — are drawn into dynamic partnerships and engaged in steering and directing the course of action. The shift fosters democratic engagement, encouraging participants to become generators and producers of knowledge, not passive consumers. Planning and design processes and proposals begin to work closely with building community identity and local capacity. When the space of learning moves to the community, the designer is recast as a partner and co-learner, and the distance between "experts" and "clients" narrows. Finally, evaluation and reflection are transformed from endgame activities into ongoing shapers and indicators of a project's unfolding direction.

Place Theory as Guide

The North Side Neighborhood Visioning Project took a place-based approach. Embedded in such an approach are theories, concepts, and practices drawn from place making, phenomenology, service-learning, participatory community design, and action research. Place, as defined by geographer Edward Relph, means a concrete totality or environmental character (Relph 1976, 1993). Places are "indeterminate wholes," "impalpable territories of social activities and meanings projected into entire assemblages of buildings and spaces" (Relph 1993: 26). Place theory and practice recast the landscape architect as an insider, a member of the community. The act of design as place making becomes "the way we transform places in which we find ourselves into places in which we live" (Schneekloth and Shibley 1995). Place theory and practice relink design process and product. Resisting the appeal of perfection, they seek more humanistic rather than formalistic approaches to design.

Many landscape architects, architects, and planners have led in deriving the vocabulary and theory of place and the practice of place making (Hester 1993; Schneekloth and Shibley 1995; Arendt and Yaro 1990; Brown and Moorish 2000; Mugerauer 1994). Architect Robert Mugerauer calls place making a homecoming, a return to design as an act of cultivating relationships between things. It requires designers to act as "articulators" and advocates of ways of living, and to think reflectively while remaining critical, flexible, and sensitive to the unique circumstances of each context. It requires new ways of seeing and engaging relationships and belonging. To Wes Jackson, homecoming means "becoming native" (Jackson 1997) by being attentive, listening and reconnecting to the realities of place, things not readily taught and learned in the canons of design and design teaching.

Place theory informs asset-based community development, a community-driven process that mobilizes individual and community talents and skills. It builds on a community's successes and strengths, and focuses on the power of associations and community relationships. Asset-based development seeks to enable people to own the process of planning their community's future, while encouraging local government to be effective and responsive. It adheres to the idea that real change begins internally. This approach and framework are expressed in William Moorish and Catherine Brown's work with the Center for American Landscape and their book, *Planning to Stay*. Moorish and Brown advocate a process of community planning and design that begins with the individual and grows to embrace the whole. Such an act of community participation is a powerful strategy for change.

Educating Designers as Place Makers
To make places, designers must become sensitive to the attributes of place, distinguish what a place-based approach is, and understand how design processes and plans can enhance relationships between places and people. Design practitioners and educators are uniquely poised to lead place-based design that reinforces and enriches social, cultural, and environmental relationships. However, the on-campus design studio is not the best place to engage the real dynamics of a community context. In fact, it often works against place making by fostering a purely professional-expert approach. Using a "real" site as the basis of a studio problem offers an opportunity to examine conditions and even meet a client, but it often misses the nuances and

complexities of a place by favoring academic design learning goals over all else. Design challenges and discoveries are more narrowly limited by the critic's parameters and the discourse between faculty and students.

Academic service-learning, on the other hand, is uniquely suited to place-based design education. Combined with participatory design, service-learning has the potential to literally move the space of learning into the community, by engaging both academic and community partners as co-teachers and co-learners. Service-learning positions the young designers for direct encounters, and fosters an inquiry grounded in lived experience, phenomenology, contradiction, and direct encounter with multiple and conflicting meanings and interpretations. It exposes them to the complexities of places and enables them to understand how design process and product are reflective acts from which concepts and ideas emerge. Service-learning makes visible what is hidden in the on-campus studio setting. It advocates reflection and critical revision, dialogue and responsiveness.

Service-Learning at Cornell and ESF

Cheryl Doble and I have enjoyed a collaboration with students that grew naturally out of our commitment to academic service-learning as a pedagogy through which to discover the theories and practices of place making and community design. We have developed academic service-learning courses and curricula that interweave community design outreach with design instruction, practice, and public scholarship. For the past six years, my senior year studio, Experiential Community Design (LA 402), has been the academic locus for many participatory community design projects, including the North Side Neighborhood Project. At SUNY ESF, Doble's elective workshop course exposes students to the theory and practice of community visioning and sets the stage for longer-term planning and design initiatives in later studios. We encourage service-learning, while also engaging in participant action research (PAR), a flexible process that is evaluated and reconsidered over the project's duration as community needs develop and unfold (Barnsley and Ellis 2001).

Collaborating with Binghamton's North Side Community

Binghamton, New York, once a thriving business and manufacturing nexus for IBM and Endicott Johnson, has declined over the past few decades. Transportation planning, urban renewal, suburbanization, and shifting demographics have left the city's population near its 1900 level. The North Side's deteriorated housing stock, dwindling homeownership, and rising crime are all symptoms of its downward trend. But the North Side also offers advantages, including proximity to downtown and extensive, albeit inaccessible, frontage along the

Chenango River. These attributes are focal themes in the city's Comprehensive Plan and Local Waterfront Revitalization Plan (Saratoga Associates 2003; Smith and Company 2003).

While the city busied itself with plans, a North Side neighborhood alliance began growing into the North Side Communities of Shalom (NSCS), a "mission community" made up of residents affiliated with churches and other area organizations. Several North Siders joined a community-planning seminar sponsored by the National Communities of Shalom. The United Methodist Church began the Communities of Shalom initiative in 1992, after the Los Angeles riots, as a way of equipping residents of a neighborhood with the ideas and skills for local development. A six-month training course was developed to give clergy, community leaders, and residents skills in planning and leadership and knowledge for creating partnerships for Shalom development. More than 380 sites have received training in the United States and Africa (http://gbgm-umc.org/programs/shalom/).

The North Side Communities of Shalom received training from Jean-Pierre Duncan, coordinator of the Wyoming Conference United Methodist Church, Southern Tier of New York Communities of Shalom. Residents received information and strategies for identifying community assets and working on solving local problems. It was the Shalom training that sparked the search of the North Side Communities of Shalom for "a broad plan" of neighborhood revitalization that addressed "issues of community morale and confidence, as well as the condition of houses, opportunities for youth, and attraction of business."

For assistance, the NSCS reached out to university partners representing the New York State Quality Communities SUNY Network. When Doble and I met with our North Side community partner in January 2002, the community was ready to move. As Pastor Gary E. Doupe of the Centenary-Chenango Street United Methodist Church would later recall: "We had a sense of spiritual readiness. We were prepared as a result of the Shalom training and we were already developing our goals and mission." Doble and I talked about our service-learning and participatory design process, an approach that resonated with the community development approach championed by the Communities of Shalom. Recognizing threads of Paolo Freire's adult learning pedagogy in the service-learning and participatory partnership, Doupe and his Shalom group decided to work with the Cornell and ESF team. So began the North Side Community Visioning process described in the following pages.

Integrated Project Dimensions

True integration means a joining together, an enfolding of the academic and the community realm — a difficult task. The North Side Project demonstrated (1) integrated collaborative roles and responsibilities, (2) integrated processes (scoring, storytelling, matrix visioning, representing, and modeling), and (3) integrated outcomes.

Integrated Collaborative Roles and Responsibilities

How one enters the community and seeks to relate to it are the first conscious acts of service-learning and place making. Students must integrate with the community in a sensitive, open-minded, and responsible manner. They must be both invited and willing to enter as participants with those who have organized the initiative, in a context where actions may already have been set in motion.

It was important that the involvement of Cornell and ESF grow in a way that contributed to the directions and partnerships already established, and that the energy of our students not detract from the momentum. An important first step was to define the project as a collaboration. The three entities negotiated guiding principles that included explicit statements framing the project as a partnership of peers who would participate fully and openly and assume important roles and responsibilities. Partners also agreed that the project would be community-located and accessible, and would teach, practice, and model community design and visioning whenever possible. Finally, the process would be modeled as action research: revising, iterative, and nonlinear.

Faculty and the students in the introductory sessions of the course probed these principles and responsibilities, along with the theory and practice of place-based community design and service-learning. At both Cornell and ESF, classroom dynamics seek to underscore participation and reflective learning. This means that each meeting and session is interactive and participatory, shifting away from a traditional teacher-student model and toward a mentor-student and collective team-partnership model. The goal is to make visible and experientially cultivate approaches and attitudes that will be carried into the project with the community partner. My class, for example, devotes an initial period to developing a shared history, storyboard, and timeline that depict the history of community work, service, and creative enterprise. An empty timeline stretched across the room registers the earliest date of birth of the course participants and moves to the present. Each student has time to draw pictographs representing their lifetime experiences. Then the students retell the visual story to one another. Invariably, invisible attributes of the group come to the surface. This process recasts the relationship of individuals to the group, redistributes equity, introduces a participation tool, and exposes students to assets on which they can capitalize as their project moves from campus to community. Finally, an informal contract outlining student, faculty, and community responsibilities is reviewed and agreed upon by each participant.

Two joint Cornell-ESF workshops, held as team-building and dialogue sessions devoted to learning and practicing the participatory tools used in community meetings, along with the initial community meeting, led to the formation of four working groups of students and community collaborators. The groups met regularly, stayed in touch with each other, and worked together on North Side focus areas including the riverfront, shopping district, Liberty Street neighborhood, and vision statement. The students and community members brought different expertise and understanding to the groups.

The tasks of each working group emerged out of its dynamics, challenges, and goals. The Vision Group had to expand on a vision of social goals to incorporate physical conditions of the neighborhood. The Riverfront Group had to imagine new land-use and design opportunities on a derelict site that had always been considered dangerous. The Neighborhood Group had to identify a framework in a troubled neighborhood on which they could rebuild a vital residential community. The Commercial Group had to imagine the dynamics of integrating local needs with citywide economics, transportation, and recreational planning initiatives.

Integrated Processes

Scoring. A "process score" acted as a flexible and fluid tool or "participatory design methodology" for guiding the five-month project. Unlike a design program, the process score is a written document that is modified as the project unfolds. It situates the planning process within the community by being the first act of agreement and action that the partners design. Scoring, an approach advocated by landscape architect Lawrence Halprin, is a method for choreographing participant interaction and assessing environmental changes over time (Halprin 1970). Both terms — process and score — project a sense of action, flexibility, and openendedness. Place-based designers and planners emphasize the importance of a project's preparatory phase, when collaborators begin designing participatory approaches and meeting venues (King 1989; Schneekloth and Shibley 1995). Creating the process score is the first act of redistributing power and sharing leadership and responsibilities among project participants. In this way they acknowledge that the process will be open and unfolding, not fixed and prescriptive.

Partners contributed to writing and finalizing the process score. The North Side Shalom group offered space at churches for all planning meetings, including a Sunday dinner served by the host church. The dinner became a social ritual and provided an opportunity for participants to become acquainted. The Shalom group was sensitive to reaching out to all residents, especially those who were particularly underserved. Hosting each dinner and event at a different church became a way to make visible the community's assets, increase participation, and represent the neighborhood's diversity. In total, five community dinners, followed by breakout work sessions and group dialogues, were held during the project.

The process score created a temporal picture of how the project might unfold. It established the concept of working in smaller teams of students and community members, whose scope of work emerged from the group's dynamics and interests. The process score outlined methods that could be used to engage the community in seeing and comprehending their neighborhood. Visioning was used as an informing principle to encourage broad and integrated ways of thinking about problem solving.

Storytelling. A big challenge is the constraint of a semester-bound timeframe. Relationships and a "dialogic space," where teamwork, dialogue, and disagreement are all welcome, require time to grow and develop. Stories were chosen as a way of initiating and developing dialogic space (Schneekloth and Shibley 1995) among students, Shalom members, and residents. The students began by sharing stories uncovered through background research and community site visits. They used maps to present, for example, the "River Story," "Settlement Story," and "Canal Story." The stories and maps provided historic perspective and illustrated the dynamics influencing the North Side's physical change over time. While visible traces of some stories remain, others have been buried and forgotten. Community members were fascinated by the interrelationships among the different stories. Then community members shared and mapped their more personal stories of the neighborhood. This story and mapping process gave participants new perspectives on the neighborhood's identity, values, and hopes. The groups continued to use stories throughout the project. Residents conducted a walking tour of their neighborhood and recorded it with photo essays, while students shared success stories from other communities. The storytelling became more collaborative as students and community members began to construct narratives together. Storytelling was an effective way to share information without giving privilege to one group's expertise or understanding; it encouraged listening rather than debate and fostered true dialogue.

Matrix Visioning. When the North Side Project began, the Shalom group had already prepared an outline vision statement. Not surprisingly, they grounded it in social issues. One of the first tasks was to relate the Shalom vision to the spatial and physical condition of the

North Side. The Vision Group developed a large matrix to visualize and construct the relationships between their vision and the physical planning opportunities. Such a matrix approach is illustrated in Moorish and Brown's work (Moorish and Brown 2000). On the right side of the matrix, the Vision Group listed the objectives of the original vision statement, and across the top they listed the physical places that Shalom members identified as neighborhood attributes. Vision Group members then considered how each of these sites might play a part in realizing the original vision goals. The matrix enabled the community to consider their vision from a new perspective, coordinate the activities of the three other project teams, and gain an understanding of the interconnected nature of planning decisions. Such a shift in visualizing the interconnectedness of community issues was acknowledged in the reflection of a participant who exclaimed, "Now I get it, I'm seeing how these things are all interconnected." Groups working on riverfront, neighborhood, and commercial areas added detail to the matrix as their work progressed. The Vision Group then revised the matrix and refined their vision while focusing on specific action steps.

Representing. The Neighborhood Group had the largest participation by the Shalom members and faced seemingly the greatest challenge. The southernmost part of the North Side was once a vital residential neighborhood but had experienced falling investment and an increase in rental properties, absentee ownership, vacancy, and crime. The social fabric and physical condition were so discouraging that residents found it difficult to engage in physical planning. As part of the group's storytelling, the students began to share stories of the interwoven spatial and social dynamics constituting "healthy" neighborhoods. They then developed a visual diagram (circle graph) representing the totality of neighborhood dynamics and used it to inventory and evaluate the dynamics in the North Side. The study revealed that, in varying degrees, each of the elements constituting healthy neighborhoods was still present in the North Side, though some were weak or out of balance. This holistic, positive portrayal and understanding of the community's dynamics helped to catalyze ideas for actions that would strengthen, not remake or remodel, the neighborhood.

Modeling. Modeling helps understand potential changes and evaluate the impacts of alternatives. However, it's often difficult to engage community residents in the modeling process, for while they talk willingly about ideas that others model, they are often uncomfortable generating ideas themselves. In this particular project, storytelling actually facilitated the modeling process. The Riverfront and Commercial groups had been working separately for several meetings when they decided it was time to join and mutually consider the interrelationship between the riverfront and its surrounding development. They thought it would be helpful to use modeling as a way to develop a dialogue between the two groups, combine goals, and explore initial design and planning concepts and ideas. Before the modeling activity, the students shared several case studies of community riverfront projects that addressed many of the same opportunities identified by the Riverfront Group. After reviewing the case studies, group members gathered around a simple foam-core contour model over which an aerial photograph had been mounted. They modeled and discussed a range of ideas using simple but elegantly constructed model pieces. Two things seemed to contribute to the success of this process and quality of the discussion. First and probably most important, the discussion of the case studies planted the seeds of new ideas and initiated thinking beyond the ordinary. Second, the model elements were crafted with a level of detail that gave them visual and tactile interest. Once the group began handling the elements, the modeling process was well on its way.

Integrated Outcomes

Several results of the North Side Project testify to its success. It gave the North Side Shalom Group a greater role in planning their neighborhood's future and gained them an audience at City Hall. It helped to redirect resources and attention from city planning to the North Side, and led to an invitation to comment formally on the city's draft comprehensive plan. The North Side group was invited to submit a significant grant proposal, requesting continuation of their planning process and funds to undertake a community-based revitalization plan for the riverfront. This proposal was funded and the North Side began a second phase of the community design process with Cornell and ESF. Finally, at the July 2002 public announcement of Binghamton as a Quality Community, representatives of the North Side Shalom Group spoke on behalf of the North Side's commitment to neighborhood revitalization from the ground up and the inside out. The group was able to articulate a clear vision for undertaking long- and short-term, broad and small-scale approaches.

Through the North Side Project, Cornell and ESF students enjoyed a service-learning experience that allowed them to learn and practice a place-based community design approach. They learned how design and planning decisions affect people's lives, and they began to comprehend the reciprocity between process and product.

Integrated Evaluation and Reflection

Integrated evaluation and reflection support the "shifting ground" premise of this essay and underscore the need to continually reframe all aspects of the design process, in and outside the academy, as a set of "actions" that strengthen civic and community building for students, faculty, and residents.

The ESF workshop integrated three reflection experiences, and at Cornell, reflection included frequent roundtable discussions and an end-of-semester "reflection essay." Ongoing evaluation occurred through frequent contact and interaction between partners. Students, faculty, and community members engaged in shaping and framing the project's unfolding. Students were in direct contact with community partners through telephone, workshops, and meetings. Students sought to cultivate a cycle of inquiry and confirmation by creating a communication flow among ESF, Cornell, and the North Side. While this was difficult and cumbersome at times, it underscored the reflective act as an important aspect of the project and drew students into closer relationship with their community partners.

At ESF three evaluation exercises tracked the students' changes during the semester. One of the most marked changes was the shift from viewing the design as being for the critic to being for the community. At Cornell, frequent group reflection sessions drew out the critical incidents, questions, and concerns arising throughout the project. One of the biggest challenges for students was the nonlinear aspect of the process and redefining their perception of movement and momentum. The North Siders had the opposite concern, that things might move too fast. For both academic and community partners, a big challenge involved striking a balance between wholesale vision — the big ideas — and feasible and tangible action steps. The students addressed this concern in the vision plans and documents by representing both ends of the spectrum: they outlined goals, directives, and action steps alongside the grander visionary plans illustrating future redesign of the neighborhood.

Conclusion

The North Side Neighborhood Visioning Project offers an example of combined service-learning, place making, and participatory community design. Undertaking such a project is messy and nonlinear. The effort to interweave community dynamics with complex integrated teaching, service, and research goals generates unexpected challenges and situations. The results of the project are helping to shape future collaborations undertaken through the SUNY Network and the Quality Community Initiative, and to interconnect a set of dynamic actions and practices to foster change in both the community and the academy. It is this interconnected set of changes that takes place when the ground shifts, when design education combines with service-learning. The alignment of service-learning, public scholarship, and design research contributes to a larger community benefit, while it prepares students to be both citizens and professional practitioners, engaged in supporting interconnections between people and places.

Note

Cheryl Doble and I presented parts of this paper at the 2002 CELA annual conference held in Syracuse, New York, in September 2002, and at the Second Annual Quality Communities Conference in Albany, New York, in October 2003. Quotations by North Side Shalom participants come from meetings, discussions, and interviews.

References

Arendt, R., and R.D. Yaro. (1990). *Dealing with Change in the Connecticut River Valley: A Design Manual for Conservation and Development*. Amherst, MA: Lincoln Institute of Land Policy and the Environmental Law Foundation.

Barnsley, J., and D. Ellis. (2001). "Research for Change: Participatory Action Research for Community Groups." Originally published in 1992 by the Women's Research Centre, Vancouver, BC. Reprinted in *What Is Participatory Action Research and Why Does It Matter?* Saint Albans, VT: National Community Forestry Center, Northern Forest Region.

Brown, C., and W. Moorish. (2000). *Planning to Stay*. Minneapolis: Milkweed Press.

Donohue, M.O., and A.F. Treadwell. (2001). *Quality Communities Interagency Task Force Report*. Albany, NY.

Halprin, L. (1970). *The RSVP Cycles: Creative Processes in the Human Environment*. New York: G. Braziller.

Hester, R. (1993). "Sacred Structures and Everyday Life: A Return to Manteo, North Carolina." In *Dwelling, Seeing and Designing: Toward a Phenomenological Ecology*, edited by D. Seamon, pp. 271-297. Albany: SUNY Press.

Jackson, W. (1997). "Becoming Native to this Place." In *People, Land and Community*, edited by H. Hannum, pp. 153-167. New Haven: Yale University Press.

King, S. (1989). *Co-Design: A Process of Design Participation*. New York: Van Nostrand Reinhold.

Mugerauer, R., ed. (1994). *Interpretations on Behalf of Place*. Albany: SUNY Press.

Relph, E. (1993). "Modernity and the Reclamation of Place." In *Dwelling, Seeing and Designing: Toward a Phenomenological Ecology*, edited by D. Seamon, pp. 25-40. Albany: SUNY Press.

_____. (1976). *Place and Placelessness*. London: Pion.

Saratoga Associates. (2003). *City of Binghamton, NY Comprehensive Plan*. Saratoga Springs, NY.

Schneekloth, L.H., and R.G. Shibley. (1995). *Placemaking: The Art and Practice of Building Communities*. New York and Toronto: Wiley.

Smith, P.J., and Company. (2003). *Two Rivers: One Future. Draft Local Waterfront Revitalization Program for the City of Binghamton, NY*. Buffalo, NY.

Service-Learning as a Holistic Inquiry and Community Outreach Studios

By Joongsub Kim and James Abernethy

Current Trend: Two Prevailing Approaches

This essay discusses several models of holistic inquiry into the built environment that use collaborative and interdisciplinary strategies. Two such examples — a service-learning model and a human equity model — are considered here because they are most relevant to the goals of three community outreach programs of Lawrence Technological University in Michigan: the Detroit Studio, the Pontiac Studio, and a Habitat for Humanity (HFH) project.

The social value of service-learning has received much attention as a possible vehicle to assist in the revival of American community. Sociologist Robert Putnam (2000) and others argue that the ethical bond in American society, what Putnam calls generalized reciprocity, has somehow been lost. This leads to individual isolation and lack of interest in social or collective activity in its many forms. According to Putnam, we stop to help an elderly person change a tire on the road, not because we expect that person to return the favor but because we want to live in a world where that kind of behavior is commonplace. He sees the lack of social interaction, shared understanding of values, and social capital as dissolving a sense of common purpose and community in America.

The service-learning model has also been widely debated in architecture, urban planning, and related fields. Although its definitions vary, its supporters would agree that service-learning is at heart a form of experiential learning that employs service as its primary focus (Crews 1995). It is often referred to as an outgrowth of the Progressive educational philosophy of John Dewey, who advocated for a close interaction of knowledge and skills with experience as key to learning (Ehrlich 1996). The argument is that students require direct involvement with problem solving, not abstractly examining such problems in social isolation by reviewing academic concepts in "the great books." By integrating community service projects with academic learning, lessons in citizenship and social responsibility can be merged with traditional academic knowledge. Service-learning as a pedagogy links community service and academic study and enables each to strengthen the other. Learning starts with problems and continues with the application of increasingly complex ideas and sophisticated skills to more complicated problems (Ehrlich 1996).

Kraft and Krug (1994) observe that a service-learning program offers educational experiences through which students learn and develop by actively participating in carefully organized experiences that meet community needs. Coordinating such service in collaboration with the community and schools enhances what is taught by extending learning beyond the classroom This fosters a sense of caring for others with greater needs. Forester's central thesis (1999) is that citizen participation in complex issues like the quality of housing and urban design often provokes anger among stakeholders and power plays by many. Community designers, planners, and architects can be instruments of social equity by helping disadvantaged communities maintain democratic principles to overcome inequities and private-sector manipulation of resources by special interest groups (Mayo 1990).

Many scholars in architecture have been concerned about education as an agent of socialization, and some of them have contributed essays in several recent publications and reports about architectural education as part of a debate about alternative approaches to teaching a design studio. One such approach pertains to human equity. Arguably, a study by Boyer and Mitgang (1996) best advances the human equity model. Proponents urge faculty to engage in teaching architecture as a socially embedded discipline and practice, and to foster an atmosphere of collaboration and respect in their classrooms. Boyer and Mitgang contend that the curricular and design sequences should foster a climate of caring for human needs by including more frequent contact with clients and communities and by placing greater emphasis on environmental and behavioral design elements. Building to meet human needs means helping architecture students become effective teachers and listeners who are able to translate the concerns of clients and communities into caring design.

A recent report, *The Redesign of Studio Culture*, by the American Institute of Architecture Students (AIAS 2002) recognizes the design studio as both a challenge and a venue, with the potential for increasing awareness of human equity issues. It calls for change throughout its detailed critique of current practices, emphasizing the need for more diversity in architectural education. In addition to issues of race and gender, architectural education too often ignores other underrepresented groups, the authors argue, when in fact we should be seeking acceptance of all individuals regardless of gender, race, creed, religion, sexuality, socioeconomic background, or physical disability. Consequently, exposure to people with whom we may be less familiar helps strengthen the discipline through a better understanding of how to design for everyone.

The ideas underlying both the service-learning and human equity models, which are closely related to each other, are comparable to the concepts that support the community-based facilities at the Detroit

Studio and the Pontiac Studio, as well as the HFH project in Pontiac. The studios, along with organizations such as Adaptive Environments, advocate for more human-centered curricula and improved access for people who need it the most in schools of architecture (see www.adoptiveenvironments.org). They also favor a holistic view of design that does not separate human health, environmental health, and social justice, and they highlight the essential or vital connections that must be made to create inclusive, healthy, and sustainable neighborhoods or communities. The increasing separation of populations or societies by race and income and the struggle to end environmental racism and gender discrimination are all interrelated community-building challenges and tasks. Such models or approaches also emphasize teaching the goals and techniques of inclusive or universal design in design school programs.

Community design centers or design-build studios housed typically in colleges or schools of architecture have been developed in part on the basis of a human equity model or a service-learning model. They have grown in number, yet rigorous empirical study of their effectiveness is rare, as the 2003 study by Hou and Rios and other research suggests. This paper lays the foundation for a social-scientific assessment of our community-based studios or projects.

Introduction to Three Programs

Service-learning as a holistic inquiry into the built environment uses community-based, interdisciplinary, and collaborative strategies, as well as social-scientific methods, in a design studio or in a building construction project. Working with residents and community agencies in low-income neighborhoods through architectural design studios or design-build projects challenges instructors, students, and other stakeholders to overcome limited resources, such as low resident participation or funding and lack of facilities for community meetings or presentations, as well as communication difficulties (e.g., between student architects and laypersons) and cultural differences (e.g., white suburban students versus black urban residents). Moreover, teaching white students the value of a community-based approach while building a long-term, professional working relationship with poor residents of color imposes an extra pedagogical challenge.

Working with instructors from several disciplines, students collaborate with residents of poor neighborhoods at either the Detroit Studio or the Pontiac Studio. During a typical semester, the studios offer a junior-level course that consists of three distinctive but related components: architecture, urban design, and building systems. An architecture instructor takes the lead, coordinating the three components regarding major studio activities (e.g., joint review sessions, community presentations). The HFH project represents approximately 10 percent of the student grade for the building systems course, which is taken concurrently with the design projects at the Detroit Studio or the Pontiac Studio. The HFH project is nested within the building systems course, but the HFH undertaking and the studios are distinct programs.

Each studio's location is an important factor, given the interdisciplinary and collaborative structure of the studio and its typical project content — for example, design of a church in a poor urban area. Each studio is located a short drive from poor urban neighborhoods in Detroit or Pontiac. Each has community-based satellite facilities of the College of Architecture and Design, serving as outreach studios and community learning labs to engage the community and diverse stakeholders in any given project. The HFH involvement adds a community-building construction experience to complement the design emphasis of the studios. HFH projects are located in underserved neighborhoods in Pontiac. Our role has been to partner with the client (HFH) to explore design and construction alternatives that offer improvements in resource conservation and sustainability.

For the last three years, almost the entire junior class (about 120 architecture students) has committed eight hours to the HFH project. Most students are encouraged to sign up for two different four-hour periods so that they can participate in different portions of the construction process. Our approximately 1000 hours represent about one-half of the volunteer hours necessary to build a house. The student activity concludes with individual reports of their activities, comparing the construction systems used at HFH with those most commonly observed in local construction. In general, Lawrence Tech's commitment to build the major part of 1200-square-foot houses in Pontiac begins with spring and summer meetings with HFH officials, full-time and adjunct teaching colleagues, and the house designer. The course facilitator participates in the official groundbreaking event and students participate in the final house dedication ceremonies. Our construction involves a weekend presence over a three-month period, ending just before Thanksgiving. The house completion is accomplished by other volunteers during the winter months.

The Detroit Studio, in particular, receives project proposals from community organizations or residents who are interested in collaboration. All of the projects are located in underserved areas of Detroit. Proposals are reviewed by the studio's coordinating faculty and its advisory committee.

Theoretical Constructs and Strategies for a Holistic Inquiry

The projects address the concerns and ideals described earlier in the works by Boyer and Mitgang and others, but specific models proposed by other scholars provide a theoretical underpinning and practical tools. We will discuss the five models below.

Conversation

Schneekloth and Shibley, proposing the place-making model (1995), argue that place making embodies a set of tasks performed to support practice: creating an open space for dialogue about place and place making through good relationships with constituencies or stakeholders; seeking the dialectical work of confirmation and interrogation; and facilitating the framing of action. Such place making can be realized in part through a conversation-based, "constructive" design process to promote more active community participation. Frequent informal but personalized "desk crits," for example, at the Detroit Studio and the Pontiac Studio emulate intense conversational place making. Regarding the HFH undertaking, selected students and the HFH team are constantly engaged in conversation as issues arise daily at the construction site.

Social Learning

Dogan and Zimring, seeking to demonstrate the social-learning benefit of interaction with clients, argue that the relationship between programming and design is interactive (2002). Programmatic issues and design issues should be clarified together. Accordingly, during this interactive process both client and architect assume significant responsibilities, and clients have the potential to play crucial roles in design. The interactive model suggests that the architect-experts should facilitate the opportunity for clients to play a co-partner role in identifying challenges and opportunities that the project presents and in developing or evaluating design alternatives. Such an interactive process offers the opportunity for each party to learn from the other's perspectives in diverse social settings. Frequent informative meetings and focus-group sessions with the studio clients and other stakeholders at the Detroit Studio or the Pontiac Studio, as well as constant on-site interaction among the students, the HFH client, and the house designer, provide ample opportunity for rich social learning.

Negotiation

The approach taken in Day's consensus design model (2002) posits negotiation as an essential component of successful consensus building. Day contends that when professionals design places for people, many things obvious to the residents are overlooked; when places are designed by laypersons, the design can suffer from a lowest-common-de-nominator effect; when places are designed by both together, conflict often ensues. However, as the author argues, co-design is not doomed to conflict or banality if it is managed correctly. Consensus design teaches us how to reach agreement within a specific time frame with diverse groups of people. Negotiation is one such approach to facilitate consensus. Consensus design can involve people in meaningfully shaping where they live and work. Constructive negotiation can help stakeholders to see opportunities and challenges that each other's environments present, to recognize the constraints within which they have to work, to live together but differently, and to maintain stable and healthy relationships among different parties. Day argues that consensus can influence social stability, personal health, and building longevity, all of which in turn affect environmental costs. In various reviews at the Detroit Studio and the Pontiac Studio sessions, both formal and informal, all participants are challenged to engage in negotiation concerning design decisions. Similarly, HFH project participants are often involved in negotiation regarding the selection of building materials in terms of budget and construction timing.

Figure 1. Distribution of survey questionnaire and contact with residents, Community Theatre Design and Urban and Cultural Regeneration Project in Detroit

Deliberative Design and Practices

Forester, in *The Deliberative Practitioner* (1999), contends that citizen participation in such complex issues as the quality of the environment, housing, and urban design often provokes anger among stakeholders and power plays by many — as well as appeals to rational argument. Forester shows how skillful deliberative practices can facilitate practical and timely participatory planning processes. He draws on law, philosophy, literature, political science, and planning to explore the challenges and possibilities of deliberative practice. Forester's ideas are relevant to architecture since the design and construction context is often fraught with differences, conflicts, and inequalities. A design and building process can shape opinion and create value, transforming not just material conditions but human relationships. Forester's theory demonstrates the significance of public deliberations that give space to plural voices and strengthen democratic practices. He argues that adversarial situations are not predetermining. In the context of design or construction solutions, they can be negotiated toward collaborative action. Deliberative design and practices should use a process of learning together to craft strategies toward greater community good. Specific examples that promote deliberative design and practices, such as group decision making, workshops, or design charrettes undertaken at the Detroit Studio, or through the HFH involvement, are discussed later (Figures 1, 2, 3, and 4).

Environment and Behavior Perspective

Boyer and Mitgang emphasize environment and behavior in design education and practice (1996). Canter's "place" model is one such example of a social-scientific perspective. He proposes that place consists of physical attributes, people's behavior, and people's meaning (1977). This suggests that an inquiry into a place requires an understanding of its characteristics (e.g., the condition of buildings) and of the people who use it (e.g., activities, demographic information). Given the poverty of the neighborhoods we work with at the Detroit Studio, for example, this would require us to better understand the unique needs of the subgroups within any given place. Such investigation would often require a social-scientific approach, such as a survey. In Detroit or Pontiac, within an audience that is primarily African American, the subgroups often include children and older people as well as people of all ages with disabilities. Similarly, the Lawrence Tech team, in its collaboration with HFH, considers demographic, social, and economic factors in deciding, for example, appropriate building materials through behavioral, observational, and precedent studies.

Drawing upon these findings, we have created a design/research studio or a building construction project using interdisciplinary, community-based, and collaborative approaches to architecture and urban issues. Furthermore, we have explored architectural design or construction conceived as a set of "deliberative" practices. To this end, the Detroit Studio, the Pontiac Studio, and the HFH project focus on the use of architectural design or construction as a tool to promote social learning, negotiation, conversation, and community building. All of these constructs — conversation (a dialogue on common goals), social learning (sharing community perspectives), negotiation (for group consensus), and deliberative practices (fostering participation for creating community value) — promote community building during the planning, design, and construction of the built environment.

Any given project area becomes a living laboratory for exploring fresh perspectives in community design or building construction, for fostering healthy cultural reform, and for revitalizing the urban environment. The studio or the project serves as a civic design forum for debating contemporary design paradigms, developing arguments for new urban theories, and testing theories. To accomplish this the Detroit and Pontiac studios — in addition to including the typical focus-group sessions, charrettes, neighborhood presentations, crits, and workshops — engage in social-scientific research (interviews, a survey, observational studies, post-occupancy evaluation, and archival research). Research activities include testing hypotheses, evaluating existing facilities, conducting feasibility studies, and formulating design principles. Social-scientific research is also used to evaluate student work and studio outcomes, for example, by testing a design hypothesis through a community survey.

Figure 2. Deliberative design with students and stakeholders, Quinn AME Church Design and Neighborhood Revitalization Project at Detroit Studio

Documentation of studio outcomes involves not just the final product but also the process: what steps we take, how we arrive at consensus, how we resolve conflicts or differences of opinion in design, what disagreements we have, and how we use disagreement to promote consensus. Studio publications include, in general, students' design and planning works; outcomes of community-based activities (e.g., meetings with residents, community design charrettes), field trips, and site visits; and information on interviews, surveys, and other research tasks. Readers of studio publications would be able to use such process-based information as a practical, precedent-setting educational resource. In the case of the HFH project, selected students shadow the HFH house leader, documenting the key activities of the day. This graphic and written commentary is intended to assist house leaders in the production of safe, efficient, and accurate results in greatly expanded HFH construction in the future.

Once the semester begins, the students gain direct contact with the studio clients and other stakeholders through site tours, interviews, the survey, meetings, presentations, focus-group sessions, design charrettes, desk crits, and the public reception of the final project. Some meetings and interviews are initiated or coordinated by the students themselves. Also, the studio activities are shared with the entire university via the Detroit Studio's website (www3.1tu.edu/detroitstudio, currently being renovated) or the university's sites. The focus-group sessions and a community charrette provide additional special occasions when other students and instructors are welcome to participate.

Specific Processes and Approaches

Understanding the Needs of the Subgroups within a Target Area

The following is an overview of a multifaceted system that we incorporated into the two studios and the HFH involvement to address this issue effectively. For example, regarding the current project at the Detroit Studio ("Community Theatre as a Catalyst for Urban and Cultural Regeneration in Poor Areas of Detroit"), the students have been conducting site, local, and regional analyses of our project area. One of the main goals of the analysis is improved understanding of key demographic characteristics. The class and the Detroit Repertory Theatre (our studio client) met several times to compare notes regarding the findings of research by students and the theater. This was to benefit from one another's perspectives and to capture a reasonably accurate demographic picture of the project area. In the Lodge/Linwood Area Community Design project, this was done in collaboration with students in an urban planning class from our neighboring university and the studio clients.

The second component of the multifaceted approach is using the initial findings of the demographic analysis as a base from which to reach out to local community organizations. With the assistance of block organizations and other groups, we attempt to identify and understand the unique needs of the subgroups within the target area. Regarding the Southwest Detroit Neighborhood Urban Design project, in the spring 2003 term, the class had a number of meetings at the studio with some of these organizations regarding the needs and concerns of the subgroups and the community at large. In some of the projects at the Detroit Studio, a series of workshop mini-sessions was held with city planners, developers of public housing, economic and business development agencies, transportation providers and traffic planners, and other representatives of municipal services. The sessions enabled community leaders to gather and exchange information about agency services and public approval. This aided in developing a greater public awareness about the groups' plans for community redevelopment activities. Students enjoyed ample social-learning opportunities to interact with all participating community groups.

In the Lodge/Linwood Area Community Design project, community leaders representing nonprofit groups and local neighborhood block clubs formed a steering committee whose purpose was to be the primary contact group to facilitate resident involvement and to identify the needs of subgroups. In the HFH project, the students interact with our client (HFH) and the house designer to facilitate social-learning opportunities in which all participants debate types of construction materials and systems so as not to delay the project or strain the limited budget. Our role has been to bridge the gap between our client and the house designer, to suggest the use of various construction materials and systems that will fit the needs of the target residents. These two approaches offer social-learning opportunities through which studio participants can enrich their views on the characteristics of the target community.

The third component is conducting in-depth interviews with representative samples of each of the subgroups regarding their needs. We developed the interview questions for the Community Theatre and Urban and Cultural Regeneration project and for the Southwest Detroit Neighborhood Urban Design project at the Detroit Studio in collaboration with the students, the client, and other organizations based on the outcomes of the second component above. Our students and we conducted the interviews.

The fourth component is using social-scientific methods to explore the needs of the subgroups. Regarding the Quinn AME Church and Neighborhood Revitalization project, the Community Theatre and Urban and Cultural Regeneration project, and the Southwest Detroit Neighborhood Urban Design project at the Detroit Studio, an effort was already underway by us to develop a questionnaire survey in the beginning of the semester. The main goal was to reach the larger population in the target area, especially groups who were underrepresented or reluctant to participate in the in-depth interview sessions mentioned above. Moreover, the conversational and qualitative nature of interviews supported the quantitative data of the survey. The preliminary questionnaire was developed on the basis of additional fieldwork and interviews with the client group and other stakeholders. The students, the client, and the community groups reviewed the draft survey. We had multiple pretests in the beginning of the semester. The studio conducted follow-up interviews with some of the survey participants who were willing to be interviewed.

Approach to Review of Students' Work

The following describes the philosophy and process used for the implementation of the holistic assessment of the students' projects at the two studios. A holistic assessment approach incorporates various measures that are inclusive, balanced, and multidimensional. A studio acts both as a community outreach agency and a learning lab to engage the community and diverse stakeholders in a given semester's project. Both aspects provide ample opportunity for participants to assess the students' work according to an approach that is interdisciplinary, process- and product-based, incremental and comprehensive, formal and informal, theoretical and practical, and architectural and social-scientific.

Figure 3. Design charrette with community, Lodge/Linwood Community Design Project at Detroit Studio

For example, in the case of the Southwest Detroit Neighborhood Urban Design project, we did not completely reject the typical, traditional review process where students publicly present their work to expert juries/critics for their comments. Rather, the studio invited the critics to the public arena where their views, points of focus, and review approaches were contested and contrasted with the views of other stakeholders such as the studio clients, local community organizations, and local officials. This public forum exposed disagreements, conflicts, and miscommunications, and all assessing parties had to learn how to reconcile differences among participants of diverse backgrounds and between theory and practice. Participants learned how to arrive at a timely consensus about a successful or desirable response to the issues that the target community and the client group faced.

The key lay in promoting each participant's ability to manage differences, democratic decision-making, and collective agreement through various review and deliberative processes. These approaches promoted ample opportunities for rich social learning, deliberative practice, and negotiation.

Also incorporated into the schedule throughout the semester are numerous less formal or progress reviews, such as weekly assignment progress reviews, a pre-final review, and individual desk crits — where students have more informal, casual, or conversational but nevertheless focused and personalized attention and input from design-expert critics and laypeople (e.g., studio clients) as well as municipal officials. Arguably, this type of informal review in a non-threatening atmosphere also respects those introverted students who do not always perform well in a traditional review process. Moreover, such casual/conversational, individual-based reviews can benefit nontraditional student groups in the diverse student mix at the Detroit Studio.

For the HFH project, the house designs have suggested features, materials, and systems that exceed code and HFH minimums. Negotiations with HFH, material suppliers, and the house designer sometimes result in tradeoffs. Judging how best to understand these tradeoffs figures in the examination topics as part of the student's progress review and the project review. In our most recent project, for example, suggestions to use more energy-efficient (and costly) wall and roof framing and insulation were adopted. Recommendations for the use of framing systems that use fewer resources were rejected, though, in order to control budgets and construction timing and to assure adequate student volunteer supervision by trained personnel. The students are aware of these negotiations as they build using the selected systems and materials.

Figure 4. Deliberative practices with students, Habitat For Humanity officials, instructors, and residents, in Pontiac

Community-based design charrettes and focus-group sessions provide invaluable venues for testing the students' design hypotheses and reviewing preliminary design alternatives through hands-on, collective exercises and thematic group discussion in the class and with various participating groups. Moreover, the survey of the studio participants suggests that these events help promote community-building efforts.

On the whole, grading is based on the combined assessment scores of students' work as judged by all participating reviewers — design experts, studio client, local community organizations, and us. Reviewers use the questionnaire to document their comments or grades for each review. Overall student progress is aggregated and incorporated into the publication of the final studio projects. This is one way to ensure the documentation of the process through which studio progress is made.

In the Southwest Detroit Neighborhood Urban Design project and the Quinn AME Church Design and Neighborhood Revitalization project, the survey questionnaire and interviews were used to assess the overall outcomes of the studio at the Detroit Studio after the semester was completed. This was used in turn to assess the studio from the viewpoint of the clients, other stakeholders, and guest critics.

Conclusion

Students, studio clients, community residents, guest critics, and other stakeholders have participated in a survey and interviews since fall 2002. Based on 45 completed survey questionnaires, which included both closed- and open-ended questions, more than 95 percent of respondents reported that the studio experience was positive in various respects. The benefits included gaining real-life experience, learning from diverse perspectives, experiencing a sense of community, promoting community building, learning from various disciplines, building working relationships with stakeholders, and networking — to name just a few. These findings were corroborated by 20 qualitative interview findings. Respondents frequently commented to the effect that the studio taught them how to work with people who were different from them in terms of age, race, or educational background. "I learned that reality out there is messy," is a typical comment; "things take so much time and effort... being inclusive and collaborative is so important. ..." The few comments on negative aspects of the experience mentioned disagreements, working on group projects where diverse stakeholders had strong voices on every issue, and not being able to make decisions in an expeditious manner because so many people participated in the project.

Most respondents agreed that the approach taken at the Detroit Studio and the Pontiac Studio gave them an invaluable opportunity to experience place making in a holistic way. The outcomes of the interviews and the survey of participants in this interdisciplinary and collaborative studio demonstrate the considerable benefits of learning from people who represent diverse professional and disciplinary fields. The studio activities promote a better understanding of the cultural, political, and economic fabric that shapes urban design or community design. This in turn helps students understand how design becomes meaningful for a community or neighborhood and how theory and practice are woven into a holistic view of and inquiry into the large-scale built environment.

Acknowledgments

We would like to thank Professor Daniel Faoro of Lawrence Technological University for his contribution to our paper.

References

Adaptive Environments. (July 2003). *Access to Design Professions.* www.adaptiveenviron-ments.org. Accessed July 31, 2003.

AIAS. (2002). *The Redesign of Studio Culture: A Report of the AIAS Studio Culture Task Force.* Washington, DC: The American Institute of Architecture Students.

Boyer, E., and L. Mitgang. (1996). *Building Community: A New Future for Architecture Education and Practice.* Princeton, NJ: Carnegie Foundation for the Advancement of Teaching.

Canter, D. (1977). *The Psychology of Place.* London: Architectural Press.

Crews, R. (1995). *What Is Service-Learning? University of Colorado at Boulder Service-Learning Handbook.* 1st ed. Boulder, CO: University of Colorado at Boulder.

Day, C. (2003). *Consensus Design: Socially Inclusive Process.* Oxford: Architectural Press.

Dogan, F., and C. Zimring. (September 2003). "Interaction of Programming and Design: The First Unitarian Congregation of Rochester and Louis I. Kahn." *Journal of Architectural Education* 56 (1): 47-56.

Ehrlich, T. (1996). "Foreword." In *Service-Learning in Higher Education: Concepts and Practices,* edited by Barbara Jacoby et al., pp. xi-xii. San Francisco: Jossey-Bass.

Forester, J. (1999). *The Deliberative Practitioner: Encouraging Participatory Planning Processes.* Cambridge: MIT Press.

Hou, J., and M. Rios. (September 2003). "Community-Driven Place Making: The Social Practice of Participatory Design in the Making of Union Point Park." *Journal of Architectural Education* 57 (1): 19-27.

Kraft, R., and J. Krug. (1994). "Review of Research and Evaluation on Service-Learning in Public and Higher Education." In *Building Community: Service Learning in the Academic Disciplines,* edited by R. Kraft and M. Swadener, pp. 129-141. Denver, CO: Colorado Campus Compact.

Mayo, J. (Autumn 1990). "Book Review: Planning of the Face of Power by J. Forester." *Journal of Architectural Education* 7 (3): 258-260.

Putnam, R. (2000). *Bowling Alone: The Collapse and Revival of American Community.* New York: Simon and Schuster.

Schneekloth, L., and R. Shibley. (1995). *Placemaking: The Art and Practice of Building Communities.* New York: Wiley.

Reflection and Reciprocity in Interdisciplinary Design Service-Learning

By Keith Diaz Moore and David Wang

In 1996, Barbara Jacoby suggested that "reflection and reciprocity are key concepts of service-learning" (p. 5). Reflection refers to the opportunities to make learned understandings explicit, while reciprocity is twofold in nature, suggesting (1) a sense of equilibrium with both the community and students viewed as learners and teachers and (2) an interaction that balances the different agendas of these groups. Also in 1996, the Interdisciplinary Design Institute of Washington State University (WSU) at Spokane was founded with the explicit mission "to advance knowledge to enhance the quality of people's lives in the built and natural environment... through interdisciplinary instruction, research, and service among design, construction and allied disciplines." Instituting interdisciplinary expectations within the learning setting necessarily challenges the assumptions of language and approach found in the different disciplines (Diaz Moore 2003). The implementation of service-learning has shown significant merit in transcending disciplinary boundaries while simultaneously posing substantial challenges to students, teachers, and the institution.

Although the concepts of reflection and reciprocity as defined by Jacoby remain internal to the service-learning activity, this essay extends the connotations of these terms by using them to structure a reflective evaluation of the interdisciplinary service-learning activities at the Interdisciplinary Design Institute. The focus of the following program evaluation is consistent with these key aspects of service-learning — an attempt at practicing what service-learning preaches. The chapter focuses on the two primary activities of service-learning at the institute, namely, community design and construction charrettes and interdisciplinary design studios. It evaluates the program of service-learning with a focus on both reflection and reciprocity. Reflection refers to a critical consideration of the purposes and action-taking of the various human systems engaged in the service-learning experience. Reciprocity refers to the balance in exchange found in the relationships among students, faculty, institute, and community, here discussed in terms of social trust (Toole 2002). The discussion emphasizes the lessons learned from engaging in service-learning for seven years.

Context

The Interdisciplinary Design Institute involves students and faculty of the School of Architecture and Construction Management (SOACM) and the programs of Interior Design and Landscape Architecture of WSU. An urban branch campus in Spokane is home to the institute. The campus has local control over administration, including budgets, but its academic affairs, such as teaching assignments and promotion and tenure, are run from the main campus in Pullman. This situation creates conflict for both faculty members and the organizational leadership, in particular with regard to investment in and rewards for service-learning endeavors. It demands collaboration between the two campuses in order for effective decision-making and program implementation to occur. The flip side is that faculty are torn, with their mission and resources (salary, assistantships, software) coming from the institute but their teaching responsibilities and tenure and promotion criteria coming from their academic department in Pullman. They find themselves serving two masters who are likely to have quite different visions about the faculty's role and purpose. These varying expectations also limit the ability of the administrations in Spokane and Pullman to facilitate their differing visions.

This situation is quite unsettling for students too. Undergraduates from the three different academic units, having completed three years of their programs in Pullman, are transplanted to the Interdisciplinary Design Institute in Spokane for their senior year of instruction. Students find themselves in a new context, with a new cohort of colleagues and unfamiliar faculty, engaging in a paradigm-challenging mode of instruction, namely, interdisciplinary service-learning.

The institute's geographical location offers enormous opportunities for meaningful community engagement. Spokane is a city of approximately 180,000 residents, with almost one half million people in the corridor from Spokane to Coeur D'Alene, Idaho. In Spokane, one out of every eight residents, one of four preschool children, and nearly one out of four elderly residents live in poverty (One Spokane 2003). Add the many social ills related to poverty and Spokane is a city in critical condition.

What Spokane lacks in economic capital it offsets with a large reservoir of social capital — "the networks, norms, and social trust that facilitate coordination and cooperation for mutual benefit" (Putnam 1995: 67). Faculty members from the institute are able to quickly find impressive networks of individuals working to address various areas of social concern. This positions the Design Institute in an urban setting that can benefit from service-learning and also has assets that can be leveraged in service-learning efforts.

These are precisely the conditions under which the land-grant-university idea of providing education and research in service to society was meant to be applied. However, the land-grant idea is just that — a set of beliefs about the social role of the university (Bonnen 1998). WSU's vision (Washington State University 2003) heavily emphasizes education and research while casting "engagement" into an eventuality: "Washington State University offers a premier undergraduate experience, conducts and stimulates world-class research, graduate and professional education, scholarship and arts, and provides an exemplary working and learning environment that fosters engagement."

This vision does not embrace outreach to the degree found at some other land-grant universities, and endorses a rather traditional conceptualization of the university as an ivory tower repository of knowledge by focusing on its own environment in isolation from its context. Thus, while WSU is a land-grant university, it does not emphasize the outreach aspects often associated with the land-grant mission, but rather aligns itself more as a research university. Although Spokane is ripe for engagement, both cognitive and structural barriers associated with the university and the branch campus provide challenges to those interested in engaging in service-learning.

Service-Learning Components at the Institute

Jacoby (1996: 5) defines service-learning as "a form of experiential education in which students engage in activities that address human and community needs together with structured opportunities intentionally designed to promote student learning and development. Reflection and reciprocity are key concepts of service-learning."

At the Interdisciplinary Design Institute, service-learning occurs mainly through charrettes and studio projects. A community-oriented design and construction charrette, in which interdisciplinary teams work intensively for three days developing a schematic design proposal for a given problem, takes place during the first week of every fall semester. Semester-long design studio projects are often structured as problem-based service-learning experiences involving interdisciplinary teams. These efforts are described more fully below, each description briefly addressing the core service-learning issues of reflection and reciprocity.

**Figure 1. Charrette projects being judged on the Friday morning
of Charrette Week. The director of the Mayor's Office of
Economic Development comments on the feasibility of Team
5's proposal as students look on.**

Community Design and Construction Charrettes

At the beginning of each academic year, instruction at the Interdisciplinary Design Institute commences with a community design and
construction charrette. The concept of the charrette, stemming from a
tradition at the L'Ecole des Beaux-Arts in France, has, in design education, come to mean a project of short duration with a strict deadline.
The community design and construction charrette is confined to a few
hectic days in which the students are given their project on a Tuesday
and are judged the following Friday morning by community representatives, design professionals, and some faculty. Each team is limited
to one 30 by 40 inch posterboard (Figure 1). However, our version of a
charrette adds extra dimensions by engaging the community for the
purposes of service and participatory learning.

Figure 2. U.S. Senator Patty Murray speaking at the 2003 Gateway to the City of Spokane project, just after the 2003 charrette. She has been involved with WSU representatives and Spokane civic leaders to procure funding for revitalization of this area.

The charrettes only address projects that are on the agenda of an actual privately owned organization, public company, or governmental agency having a key stake in Spokane's built environment. Interested organizations need first to provide the necessary financial support for the charrette effort and then work with WSU design faculty to develop a design program. As an example, the fall 2003 charrette targeted a Gateway to the City of Spokane, involving architectural-landscape-sculptural elements to give focus to the city's downtown and a proposed university district. The reality of this project is evidenced by concerted efforts to acquire funding for improvements to the university district (Figure 2). Sponsors of the charrette included AVISTA (the utility company of eastern Washington), the Downtown Spokane Partnership (an umbrella organization working on growth management), and the Mayor's Office of the City of Spokane, as well as a local art store.

Students from the disciplines of architecture, landscape architecture, interior design, and construction management are assigned to interdisciplinary teams. The 2003 charrette consisted of 22 teams, numbering approximately 150 students. This format is itself a kind of community learning. It is the philosophical position of the Design Institute that design instruction is best delivered "in community," that is, when the educational content "simulates" the actual business environment. This concept of simulating the production of actual designs in group settings adds another important layer to the meaning of reflection. Jacoby posits that reflection entails "stepping back and pondering" a service-learning experience for the purpose of abstracting general principles (Jacoby 1996: 285-286). This largely diachronic view of reflection suggests that much of the learning takes place after the event itself, through class discussions and journal articles written by faculty. In this regard, students have few opportunities for reflection, limited to a series of surveys by one charrette faculty member (Septelka 2000). We posit however, that the charrette *process* necessarily demands "reflection-in-action," a concept championed by Donald Schön's *The Reflective Practitioner* (Schön 1983) and the literature in action research (Susman 1983), yet seemingly overlooked by Jacoby's definition. If this is viewed as meaningful reflection, then the entire charrette process is rich with reflection opportunities. Of course, reflection-in-action is often simply asserted and then assumed to occur in design activities, but the challenge remains to document it explicitly.

The charrettes serve as opportunities for reciprocal learning, which Jacoby defines as a learning context where participant labels (e.g., teacher, client, professional) are subordinated to a joint collaboration in which all are considered "colleagues" (Jacoby 1996: 36). Charrette efforts over the years have consistently found that the student designs — although clearly stated as proposals for the purpose of design education and not for actual construction — often inform subsequent "implementation" designs. Because the sponsors are aware of the academic nature of the effort, they are freed from having to commit to any particular design or idea and are able to sample a wide range of possibilities. This freedom allows clients to embrace a spirit of collaboration in the design process and to be open to challenging their own assumptions, just as their projects similarly challenge the students. For the students, because they need to address clients as opposed to only faculty, their role is stretched in the sense that what they say will be evaluated by the client as coming from a design professional. In the charrette process the various roles of the real world are reciprocated even as ideas for a real project are shared.

Interdisciplinary Design Studios

The interdisciplinary undergraduate studios that take a service-learning approach have typically adopted problem-based service-learning (PBSL), a method that engages students working in teams to solve real-life, community-based problems (Heffernan 2001). In the more successful PBSL projects, community groups approach an individual faculty member to assist in exploring a particular design issue. For example, the Easter Seals Society wanted to develop a national network of intergenerational day centers and asked the lead author to have a studio explore the design implications of the architectural program they had developed. The project proved to be of interest not only to Easter Seals, as the client, but also to the design community who, through the Architects for Health Panel, provided funding and volunteered their professional time to assist in the educational experience.

Figure 3. Design professionals and community clients collaborate with students in developing their designs.

This project provided numerous opportunities for student reflection. Students gained understanding of one of the user groups by spending a day in a wheelchair and developing a slide presentation reflecting upon their experiences. Students participated in a symposium with panels involving national and local experts in gerontology, childcare, developmental disabilities, and healthcare design. They discussed the needs of the various user groups and effective strategies for meeting those needs and facilitating a successful environment. Students were able to engage in dialogue with community representatives as well as experts through an email Listserv. Finally, students worked in teams to develop design proposals. Volunteers from the design and care-providing communities were assigned to the teams as co-investigators (Figure 3). In the final assignment, students were asked to document and critique both their designs and their process; reflective questions were provided to stimulate the task. These inter-actions provided opportunities for students to reflect upon their un-derlying assumptions and values and assess any changes needed to promote efficacious practice, a process often referred to as double-loop learning (Argyris 1976).

For most students, PBSL design projects result in a formative learn-ing experience, as is reflected in the following comments:

> *I learned different languages & perspectives on design — that used by my [architectural and interior design] teammates as well as of our clients and of design professionals. This helped us elevate the project to another level we otherwise would not have achieved.*

> *I learned the importance of respecting different experiences/backgrounds as their perceptions can really inform a better design. [And] communication is the key to working as a team.*

Other PBSL studios have not received as positive commentary. Typically community clients seek "discounted" professional services. These types of projects are often accepted by the institute and given to faculty members to enact because their revenue-generating char-acteristics preempt the pedagogical intention. When service-learn-ing is viewed solely through the lens of "academic entrepreneurship," the balanced reciprocity between service and learning is often com-promised, resulting in less than desirable learning experiences for students, and often less than the desired commodity for the commu-nity client.

Reflection and Reciprocity in Program Assessment

Both the charrettes and the PBSL interdisciplinary studios constitute the majority of service-learning efforts at the Interdisciplinary Design Institute. In this section we will consider the service-learning efforts through Jacoby's (1996) elements of reflection and reciprocity. First we reflect upon the land-grant-university purposes of service, teaching, and research. With "social trust" as a focus, we then consider reciproc-ity (Toole 2002).

Reflection on Service
The Interdisciplinary Design Institute engages in community-oriented projects that have wide-ranging impacts on the Spokane community, a community hungry for environmental design assistance in many

arenas. The poor and elderly are populations for whom service-learning provides a great potential benefit. This benefit is reciprocal. The community gains a better understanding of the environmental needs of these marginalized groups, while the students have the opportunity to learn about important issues involving alternative perspectives on environmental experience.

The service to community from the charrette and the Interdisciplinary Studios may be assessed as largely positive, but the learning outcomes are more uneven. Much of the service-learning at the institute takes the form of what Sigmon (1994) refers to as "SERVICE-learning," where the service agenda is primary to the learning outcomes. This happens when the activity is done purely for the benefit that may come from community engagement (e.g., public awareness, community learning). Faculty members see themselves as facilitating the rendering of a service useful to the community, and assume learning will simply occur through that activity. Other projects of the institute are of the type Sigmon labels "service learning," where the two activities are viewed as completely separate endeavors. Few if any opportunities for reflection are extended to students during their service activities. These projects are often efforts to raise external funds to support the project as well as other institute endeavors. Part of the drive to engage in such entrepreneurial activities derives from the fact that faculty must show service as a generator of grants or contracts in order to count toward tenure and promotion.

Reflection on Teaching/Learning

One primary area of needed improvement in service-learning projects is in balancing the service and learning outcomes. Several factors limit the degree to which positive learning outcomes are achieved in these activities. First, both the interdisciplinary and service-learning aspects that students confront in these studios are not chosen by the students but rather are imposed by the curriculum. Additionally, the desired learning outcomes are typically quite nebulous, and may not even refer to the service-learning character of the course. Finally, these new challenges take place in a context unfamiliar to the students. The conditions diverge from their preceding educational experience, which has been traditional, disciplinary-based design education, and constitute a challenge that many students are simply not excited about nor prepared to confront during their senior year. This affects the degree of investment many students have toward service-learning activities. Quite simply, many students may not know what they are in for, do not know how they are going to be assessed, do not know the faculty or the community or many of the students with whom they need to work, and arrive with less than a full commitment to or knowledge of interdisciplinary service-learning.

Reflection on Research

Similarly, institute faculty have missed the opportunity to document the innovative nature of these endeavors and, more importantly, to learn from them. Most faculty inquiry on interdisciplinarity has focused largely on its theoretical aspects (Ndubisi 2003), but the grounded experiences of the past few years raise significant questions regarding those theoretical exercises. Three factors largely account for this lack of inquiry. First, as a faculty, the institute's instructors do not reflect a shared sense of vision or commitment to service-learning. Those who are engaged in service-learning invest a tremendous amount of time and effort to ensure that service-learning experiences occur, and do so essentially on their own and without support. Time spent on structuring the service-learning activities leaves less time for reflection. Second, the service-learning faculty have such divergent interests that there is no informal support network even among themselves. Third, the context within which these activities occur makes inquiry much less palatable to faculty. The ambiguity regarding the intention of the studio, its place in the various curricula, the lack of explicit support for service-learning in organizational missions and priorities, and finally the lack of endorsement from the faculty on the main campus for both interdisciplinarity and service-learning all create a precarious situation in which to cast one's effort in creative scholarship.

Reciprocity in Key Relationships

Reciprocity is really about the nature of the relationship between the server and the served. In order to have true reciprocity, the community needs to define the need or problem the academy will address, and the valuation of the knowledge of both server (the students and faculty) and served (the community) must be equal. Toole (2002) points out that such reciprocity can occur only when there is social trust between the involved parties. Service-learning demands working in ambiguity, creating a clean dialogical space where communication salient to the local condition can emerge (Giroux 1992). In order to engage in such an ambiguous activity with another, trust becomes essential. The reciprocity that exists in the key relationships between students and faculty and students and community can be addressed in terms of trust.

Reciprocity in the Student-Faculty Relationship

One of the core relationships in service-learning is that between students and faculty members, all of whom are engaged with the community in this educational experience. The activity asks students to engage in service to the real-world community and interact with people whom they have never met, and, as discussed above, to do so under very uncertain circumstances. Students, therefore, need to believe that their instructor is both competent and benevolent, has the ability to assist in facilitating the problem-solving activity, and cares about each student's well-being. The instructor needs to be available to students and create an atmosphere that favors open dialogue.

From students, open and honest communications with the faculty member (as well as other classmates) are essential. Additionally, because service-learning projects are by definition more uncertain and fluid than traditional academic projects, students must be dedicated to the service and learning intentions of the class. That is why clear course objectives are particularly essential in nontraditional educational activities such as service-learning. Students need to buy in to the underlying purposes of the project. If they do not, or if those purposes are unclear, the conditions are ripe for confusion and the loss of trust.

Reciprocity in the Student-Community Relationship

Reciprocity between students and community depends upon the specific service-learning experience. For those experiences characterized above as most successful, the reciprocity in service and in learning was significant. To illustrate, consider the Intergenerational Wellness Center for the Easter Seals Society. Easter Seals approached the lead author about pursuing the design implications of a prototype program they had developed for this kind of place. They volunteered their time and expertise to work with students and be sure that all parties understood the program and its intentions. Students provided a design service that Easter Seals simply did not have in-house and could not afford to buy. While understanding that student designs are theoretical in nature and not meant for construction, Easter Seals still gained insight into what those places could look like and some of the environmental parameters within which such a facility would need to be designed. Easter Seals learned about the criticality of the physical environment in therapeutic settings, and students learned about the environmental needs of various specialized user groups, such as the aged and those with developmental disabilities. Both parties also learned about the design process.

Students emerging from successful service-learning experiences grow a great deal, not only academically but to a greater extent personally. One of the telling successes is that the last three presidents of the campus student association have all come through a service-learning studio. Typically, because of the time constraints associated with design education, student leadership is not exhibited from the design disciplines; but here, these service-learning experiences are fundamental in altering the students' views on the importance of leadership and activism. As one sign of this increased civic engagement, two service-learning "graduates" are now serving on the city of Spokane's Design Review Committee. Such growth in civic leadership is more likely to manifest itself years down the road, so the greatest successes of the studio are likely still to come.

Discussion

Service-learning at the Interdisciplinary Design Institute has met with a certain degree of success, with projects such as the University District and the Easter Seals Society serving as exemplars. As a pedagogical strategy, there is little doubt that service-learning, because of its involvement of community stakeholders, demands the dropping of disciplinary barriers and enables the creation of a shared language among all participants, thereby facilitating interdisciplinarity. While engaging in service-learning to facilitate interdisciplinary dialogue makes great pedagogical sense, enacting such activities at the institute requires a special effort by faculty. A faculty member must be active in the community in order for such service-learning opportunities to arise. This requires time that the institution, again, would implicitly prefer be spent on scholarship. The interdisciplinary dimension of these activities makes these teaching situations more complex by fundamentally challenging the disciplinary presumptions (Giroux 1992). This can easily become a precarious situation in departmental dynamics, inasmuch as faculty members engaged in interdisciplinary activity are by definition challenging their own disciplines. Furthermore, there is no question that the emphasis on entrepreneurship placed upon faculty to fund such initiatives affects the project type and meaningfulness of the learning experience. Finally, the financial constraints of the branch campus often burden Design Institute faculty members with teaching overloads in comparison to their Pullman colleagues, who are not challenged by interdisciplinarity.

Together these factors create a situation in which resource use conflicts with the interdisciplinary intentions of the Design Institute. Design Institute faculty, with their teaching overloads, have less time to engage in research and service, yet need to engage in more service-related activities to facilitate the service-learning pedagogy. Simultaneously, they are encouraged to seek funding for these endeavors to offset the resource shortfall of the branch campus, which requires even more time for solicitation, nurturing of the relationship, and similar activities. Thus faculty are engaged in a highly demanding activity in a context where mission, curricula, tenure, and promotion criteria all fail to even mention either service-learning or interdisciplinarity in any meaningful way. No wonder some interdisciplinary service-learning efforts have proven disappointing for both community clients and for students. This context makes success the least likely of outcomes.

We suggest that clear and open communication regarding the reflective and reciprocal aspects of both service and learning needs to occur among students, faculty, community members, and the university administration. First, it is imperative that faculty carefully craft reflection opportunities in the service-learning activity, rather than assuming that the experience itself will lead to educational growth. The rationale is simple: each design program places great emphasis on the quality of education that their students receive, and thus if positive outcomes emerge and can be substantiated, the situation may slowly evolve toward greater acceptance and perhaps even support for this revolutionary approach to design education. Having students emerge viewing design as an act of social responsibility and civic leadership is perhaps the most palpable outcome from these efforts. Leaders already have emerged from these experiences, as referred to above, suggesting that the activities do encourage greater civic engagement. This was one of the mandates for architecture from the so-called Boyer Report, *Building Community: A New Future for Architecture Education and Practice* (Boyer and Mitgang 1996), and the interdisciplinary service-learning occurring at the Interdisciplinary Design Institute could easily be seen as a beacon in this regard.

While some students experience a staggering growth in the civic and moral dimensions of their education, others less confident in their disciplines or mature in their personalities are ill-equipped to engage meaningfully with the robust educational opportunities presented within interdisciplinary service-learning. For the excellent student, this studio is often a springboard to another level in design thinking, but for the struggling student, the challenges are too significant to overcome. Is the disparity an acceptable trade-off? From a curricular standpoint this observation begs the question as to which students should be asked to engage in the activity. Perhaps interdisciplinary service-learning cannot be viewed as one size that fits all.

An emerging suggestion to facilitate curricular coherence, ease the risk factor for faculty, and enhance student buy-in is to identify a single social issue as the fulcrum on which to structure all service-learning activities in a given semester. This would necessitate team building among faculty and linking such activities as the design and construction charrette and the fall interdisciplinary studios. Faculty could rotate the lead role, easing the burden of coordination, and the community clients would see greater development and understanding of their issues. The curriculum for the semester could be integrated by embracing a shared problem focus, likely increasing both student and faculty buy-in to the service-learning and interdisciplinary aspects, and probably enhancing the learning outcomes.

Still, such radical suggestions could only be offered after developing clear and compelling learning outcomes, and, in the case of interdisciplinary service-learning, the outcomes may best be expressed in terms of qualitative long-term outcomes such as civic leadership. Yet it is uncertain if such an effort could succeed, given that the institutional leadership is fractured and the institute and university have missions weak in regard to community service. A lack of purpose at the Interdisciplinary Design Institute casts service-learning, as an alternative pedagogical approach, in a dubious context. Without a clear mission that embraces service-learning, and institutional action that would support these initiatives in both word and deed, faculty will continue to explore this pedagogy at their own peril. The question is, for how long and to what end?

Acknowledgments

This essay benefited greatly from the initial blind reviews facilitated by the review team and by subsequent reviews from Mary Hardin and Corky Poster. Additionally, we would like to thank our faculty colleagues at Washington State University for supporting our efforts to engage in an honest and open reflection upon the state of interdisciplinary service-learning at the Interdisciplinary Design Institute.

References

Argyris, C. (1976). *Increasing Leadership Effectiveness*. New York: Wiley.

Bonnen, J. (1998). "The Land-Grant Idea and the Evolving Outreach University." In *University-Community Collaborations for the Twenty-First Century: Outreach to Scholarship for Youth and Families*, edited by R. Lerner and L.A. Simon, pp. 25-72. New York: Garland.

Boyer, E., and L. Mitgang. (1996). *Building Community: A New Future for Architecture Education and Practice*. Princeton, NJ: Carnegie Foundation for the Advancement of Teaching.

Diaz Moore, K. (2003). "Overcoming Disciplinary Boundaries: Weaving a Discourse of Place-Making in an Interdisciplinary Studio." *In Weaving: Constructing and Construing the Material World as Tapestry (Proceedings of the 2003 ACSA Central Regional Meeting)*, edited by P. Harwood, p.10. Muncie, IN: Ball State University.

Giroux, H. (1992). *Border Crossings: Cultural Workers and the Politics of Education*. New York: Routledge.

Heffernan, K. (2001). *Fundamentals of Service-Learning Course Construction*. Providence, RI: Campus Compact.

Jacoby, B. (1996). "Service-Learning in Today's Higher Education." In *Service-Learning in Higher Education: Concepts and Practices*, edited by B. Jacoby, pp. 3-25. San Francisco: Jossey-Bass.

Ndubisi, F. (October 2003). "Facilitating Collaborative Learning among Design and Planning Disciplines: Opportunities and Challenges." Presentation at the Council of Educators in Landscape Architecture Annual Conference, New Orleans.

One Spokane. (2003). *Key Poverty Indicators.* Retrieved November 1, 2003, from www.onespokane.org/_docs/keypovertystats4-10-02.pdf.

Putnam, R. (1995). "Bowling Alone: America's Declining Social Capital." *Journal of Democracy* 6(1): 65-78.

Schön, D. (1983). *The Reflective Practitioner: How Professionals Think in Action.* New York: Basic Books.

Septelka, D. (May 2000). "The Charrette Process as a Model for Teaching Multidisiplinary Collaboration." In *Proceedings of CIB W89: International Conference on Building Education and Research*, pp. 35-44. Atlanta: Georgia Institute of Technology College of Architecture and Clemson University.

Sigmon, R. (1994). *Linking Services with Learning.* Washington, DC: Council of Independent Colleges.

Susman, G. (1983). "Action Research." In *Beyond Method: Strategies for Social Research*, edited by G. Morgan, pp. 95-113. Newbury Park, CA: Sage Publications.

Toole, J. (2002). "Civil Society, Social Trust, and the Implementation of Service-Learning." In *Service-Learning: The Essence of the Pedagogy*, edited by A. Furco and S. Billig, pp. 53-81. Greenwich, CT: Information Age Publishing.

Washington State University. (2003). *2002-2007 Strategic Plan.* Retrieved December 23, 2003, from www.wsu.edu/StrategicPlanning/strategic-plan.html.

Service-Learning in Texas Colonias

By Anne Beamish

Introduction

Service-learning and community outreach projects have become increasingly common in K-12 schools, as well as in higher education, in a wide range of fields including public health, social work, education, technical writing, and psychology. Service-learning was a term coined in the late 1960s to describe "the accomplishment of tasks that meet genuine human needs in combination with conscious educational growth" (Stanton, Giles, and Cruz 1999). Sometimes called experiential learning, community-based education, or field experience, service-learning differs from volunteerism because of its intentional focus on rigorous academic experience (O'Grady 2000: 6-7).

For the liberal arts, which have depended mainly on lecturing as the primary teaching method, incorporating service-learning into teaching is a radical departure, but for the design and planning professions, which have long incorporated experiential learning into their curricula, the step to service-learning is a much smaller one (Forsyth et al. 2000: 244). Learning-by-doing has been one of the foundations of design and planning pedagogy, and the number of service-learning projects in landscape architecture, architecture, and planning curricula has been increasing (Forsyth et al. 1999; Forsyth et al. 2000; Haque et al. 2000; Winterbottom 2003). And though the shift between practical learning-by-doing and service-learning may be a less dramatic one, there are still significant issues to consider.

The Community and Regional Planning Program at the University of Texas at Austin aims to provide students in the two-year master's program with an education as challenging, relevant, and "real-world" as possible. It does this not only by teaching the skills and knowledge they will need as planners but by giving them a glimpse into the types of projects and work that their future professional work may hold.

All second-year students in the Community and Regional Planning Program are required to take the Physical Planning Workshop, which gives them experience working in interdisciplinary teams and developing physical planning and design solutions in real-world situations. The goal is not to turn the students into designers but rather to help them become more versatile planners and more effective partners with the design professions. Students learn to deal with the many and often conflicting needs of client, site, and context, as well as the complexities of design and the design process. Most of the students come to the class with no design background, and therefore this class is often the first and sometimes the only experience they have with physical design. (Though we strive to make the workshop realistic, not all the projects involve service-learning.)

Each year we choose a different site and project. In fall 2002, the students were asked to design a community open space or park for a *colonia* — a very low-income community located on the Texas-Mexico border. The experience of this class highlights both the successes and challenges of service-learning for teaching design to planning students. This paper will describe the project, discuss the conditions that worked for and against it, and conclude with the lessons learned for successful implementation of future projects.

The Project

Colonias are very low-income rural communities, located along the U.S.-Mexico border, with living conditions that are often compared to those of developing countries. For example, Starr County, where the project was located, is the third poorest county in the United States with an average annual family income of $12,000. Twenty-three percent of residents are farmworkers and 75 percent have less than a ninth-grade education. Over 70 percent of residents live below the poverty line. Though two-thirds of the residents are American citizens (not illegal immigrants as is often assumed), they lack access to education and work opportunities (Davidhizar and Bechtel 1999; Office of Strategic Management, Research, and Development 1988).

Colonias are unregulated subdivisions on private land outside city limits that typically lack water, sewerage, electricity, paved roads, and other basic services. In the past, developers would sell lots for low sums of money and offer contracts for deeds. Residents would then place trailers, construct manufactured homes, or engage in self-build on the lots (Ward and Carew 2001). Most colonias are plagued by substandard housing, inadequate plumbing and sewage disposal systems, and limited access to clean water, resulting in a number of severe public health problems (Davidhizar and Bechtel 1999).

As the location for the second-year Physical Planning Workshop, we selected Mike's, a colonia of 300 households in Starr County, 14 miles east of Rio Grande City, that was apparently named after the son of the rancher who originally divided and sold the land. The site was a long, narrow, empty two-acre lot that flooded moderately several times a year. Because of its location in a flood plain, the land was unusable for housing, but the community was interested in using it as some type of park, recreational area, or common open space.

There were three main reasons for choosing this location and site. First, the fact that it was located in a colonia was very attractive because of the unusual and extreme conditions that exist there — most

Texans are aware only vaguely, if at all, that colonias exist and very few ever visit or experience them first hand. For planning students, who are generally very politically aware and sensitive to equity issues, it was highly likely that they would be excited at the opportunity of working in this community.

Second, the project was relatively modest. The site was rather small and the program was comprehensible, making it more accessible to students with no design experience. In addition, the project was very likely to be implemented. The opportunity to design a project that would actually be built would clearly be a motivating force for the students.

And last, but most importantly, the project and site were chosen because we would be collaborating with the Community Resource Group (CRG), a nonprofit organization that had been working on the Texas-Mexico border for many years to improve water, sanitation, housing, transportation, and access to small loans. Based in Austin, they had an office in Rio Grande City and had worked closely with the community for several years. It was CRG that actually held the two-acre piece of land.[1] They were making it available as a park because it was unusable for housing and because the residents had long expressed an interest in having a common space in the settlement. The assistance of CRG was invaluable. They served as a resource for the workshop, acted as liaison with the community, and participated in reviews and discussions during the semester. It would have been nearly impossible to bring a large group of students (many of whom did not speak Spanish) to a community such as Mike's without their active support.

Class Organization

The Physical Planning Workshop is a required course, and therefore the class size of 27 students was rather large. Initially the students were divided into five teams, each responsible for undertaking the site inventory and basic research for one of the following categories: physical environment, natural/biological environment, social environment, park design, and user needs.

The Physical Environment Team was charged with studying and reporting on geology, climate, surface water, drainage, and possible flood-control strategies, as well as creating a survey of the site. The Natural Environment Team catalogued the soils and vegetation and researched native plants in the region. The Social Environment Team investigated the demographic, social, cultural, economic, and historical backgrounds to the site and region. The Park Design and Implementation Team looked at existing parks and community open spaces in the area, examples of parks and park design in the region and elsewhere, and possible funding sources for the community. Finally, the Users Needs Team met with community members to assess their requirements, possible uses of the site, existing land use surrounding the site, and overall goals of the community.

Early in the semester, the entire class of 27 took the six-hour drive from Austin down to Rio Grande City and Mike's for a three-day field trip. There, students undertook their site inventories, collected data, met with the community, contacted local government officials, and generally became familiar with the community, the site, and the area. Each team wrote a summary of their findings and shared it with classmates.

**Figure 1. Students Camelia Suarez and Mark Mazzola
of the Physical Environment Team surveying the two-acre site**

Once the data was collected, compiled, and summarized, the students were redistributed into six design teams for the second half of the semester. Every design team included at last one member from each of the inventory teams in order to ensure presence of an "expert" in each subject. The design teams were responsible for first developing design concepts and then producing a realistic and detailed physical design and plan for the park, taking into consideration community needs, climate, appropriate technologies and materials, native plants and landscaping, drainage, implementation, local resources, and the community's limited budget.

While the students were working on their proposals in Austin, several guest speakers came from Starr County to speak to the students about the conditions, challenges, and issues faced by residents in the valley. A second field trip took place near the end of the semester, with two members from each of the six design teams traveling to Rio Grande City and Mike's to present their work to the County Commissioner and community members.

Figure 2. Student Danielle White of the Users Needs Team working with community members to record their desires and wishes for the park

The objective of the project was not to have one of the six team proposals chosen or declared the winner. Instead, the intention was to offer the community a range of possibilities to consider, combine, and adapt — and this is exactly what they did. The community is using the six design proposals as the basis for developing their own version, which will be built in phases as funds become available. There was clearly not enough time to build the park during the semester, but a VISTA volunteer working with CRG took on the project and is working with the community and the County Commissioner to secure funding and begin implementing some aspects of the designs.

Each team's final design was unique, but with many overlapping approaches and features. All teams took the approach that a significant part of their design would be self-built by the community and emphasize low-cost maintenance. They proposed phasing the design so that features could be built as funding became available. And all proposed to use water-conserving native plants in the landscaping and make the park accessible and attractive to all age groups. In addition, some of the teams emphasized aspects such as celebrating local culture, using the park for income-generation, promoting health in the community, and flood mitigation.

All of the teams proposed children's playgrounds, and most included basketball courts and multi-use playing fields. A couple of teams proposed an extreme bicycle park and a "zip-line" (a tightly stretched steel cable, down which the rider glides while grasping a handle attached to a trolley). All included a performance area or stage for the frequent shows, plays, and music produced and enjoyed by the community. The proposals also all incorporated community gardens, community art, picnic areas, and a pavilion for the frequent family and community gatherings. In addition, some teams proposed a water feature, plaza, contemplative garden, community center, or market area.

The community members were interested in all the designs and the proposed features. At first they had difficulty, however, articulating their vision because of their limited experience with parks in general and because there were so few examples in the area. They were familiar with children's playgrounds, but were not sure what other features could legitimately be included in a community park. The students' proposals greatly increased their range and apparently legitimized their wish list of features. Although none of the teams included exactly the desired combination, community members were able to select from the proposals the features that they most hoped for in their future park: a stage for community shows and entertainment, a covered market area where vendors could sell produce and homemade products, a community garden, a playground for the children, a playing field, a basketball court, a picnic area, shaded seating, and a community center.

Successes

Certainly, from one perspective, working in the colonia was an overwhelming success. The students' work was intended to offer a range of possibilities to consider, combine, and adapt, which the community is doing. Residents, in conjunction with CRG and the County Commissioner, are raising funds to build the first phase of their park. In addition, the project was recognized by the Central Texas and Texas state chapters of the American Planning Association (APA) and won the 2003 best student project awards.

We were very fortunate to work with CRG, an organization that had a solid relationship with the community in Mike's, as well as with other colonias in the valley, and who shared their experience, knowledge, and insight with the students. Their support of the project legitimized the project in the eyes of the community and enabled the students to become quickly knowledgeable about the community and involved with the issues it faced.

The pedagogical intention was to give students experience working in a real-world situation, on a scale that they could manage, and introduce them to design and the design process — goals that the project met. The size and scale of the project were appropriate for the students, given that none had a design background. Initially, they were frustrated at the small size of the site, but they soon appreciated how much effort it takes to plan and design even a small space. A park or community space was a good program choice because all the students had some kind of personal experience with parks. Planning students come from a wide range of backgrounds, but all are familiar with a variety of parks, community gardens, and public spaces, and therefore can build on that strength and familiarity. Because there was enough of the unknown in this class (an unfamiliar community and no experience with design), a program with which they were comfortable was very helpful.

**Figure 3. Students of the Users Needs Team discussing
the community's ideas for a future park in Mike's**

As expected, the students were highly motivated by working with a real client on a real project that was likely to be implemented in some form. The opportunity of working in a colonia caused them to work harder and push themselves more than with an academic exercise.

The combination of working with an expert and dedicated local community group, choosing a project that was appropriate in size and scale, and locating it in a community that excited and motivated the students all helped the quality of the proposals. Though the students came to the class with no design background, their work was thoughtful, responsive, realistic, and often creative. They displayed a high level of maturity and insight, which allowed them to succeed in an unfamiliar environment and less than ideal working conditions. They also demonstrated enormous respect and sensitivity to the community's needs and resources.

An additional, and admittedly somewhat unexpected, bonus of using a service-learning project for teaching design to planning students was that it helped overcome their bias against design. Planning students often stereotype design as simply the ability to draw well, or at most a process of making something "look good," and they often assume that design is irrelevant to issues such as poverty and social inequity. This project, which forced students to consider many conflicting demands and needs, made them realize not only how demanding design is, but also the important role physical design can play in supporting the aspirations and sustainability of communities. Simply put, working in a very low-income community made physical design accessible and acceptable to students who previously might have held less than positive views or attitudes about its value or worth.

Challenges

There are many challenges to service-learning, well described in Forsyth et al. (1999, 2000), including increased faculty responsibility and work load, pre-professional work, scheduling difficulties with the academic calendar, and creating unrealistic hopes for the community. The challenges certainly applied to an extent, but in this particular case four major pedagogical and administrative challenges took precedence and became serious obstacles to future service-based projects: lack of a design background on the part of the students, inadequate class time and credit hours, excessive administrative and logistical demands, and lack of financial support from the university administration.

The first challenge, the lack of design experience on the part of the students, can be a problem, as noted by Forsyth et al. (2000: 237), because the pre-professional quality of the students' work can burden a community with low-quality product. Fortunately it was not a problem in this case, mostly because of the relatively simple and straightforward program and because the work proposed by the students was always couched in terms of offering a range of ideas to the community for their consideration and as a means of prompting discussion, rather than giving an answer to their problem.[2]

The lack of design experience is not unique to a service-learning project. Any practical design project would have posed the same or a similar challenge, but the service-learning project seemed to exacerbate the problem because the students took it far more seriously than an academic exercise. In addition, because they had no experience with design, designers, or the design process, the students often had wildly unrealistic expectations and assumptions about the amount of time and effort required to gain design and drawing skills, and were consequently quickly frustrated. For example, most planning students are skeptical about their ability or potential to draw, having convinced themselves years ago that they have no talent in this area. We invited a talented landscape architect and experienced instructor as a guest lecturer to demonstrate quick drawing techniques. Initially the students were thrilled because he managed to convince them that they could indeed draw, but when their first attempts were not quite as polished as his, they quickly became irritated at the gap between their ability and their aspirations.

Figure 4. Students Christina Lowery and Christopher Frye presenting their team's proposal to community members

The ambiguous and iterative nature of design was also a challenge to many of the students, most of whom had liberal arts backgrounds. Since their previous education had trained them to look for and expect the "correct" answer, they initially approached design in a similar manner. They hoped for a formula that would deliver the correct answer or at least a straightforward, step-by-step process that would allow them to arrive at the right solution. Realizing that there could be multiple answers and paths to a successful design was initially confusing and very frustrating.

The demands of designing a community park for Mike's pushed the students outside their comfort zone, and in the process created a certain amount of anxiety. However, their frustration can also be seen in a very positive light because it demonstrated that they cared deeply about succeeding and producing a successful and professional design proposal for the community. Again, a lack of design experience would be a challenge for any project, but the service-learning aspect of the problem heightened the stakes for the planning students and increased their fear of failure.

Many of these concerns and much of the frustration caused by a lack of skills could have been addressed and simply alleviated with more class time. However, the workshop only met for three hours per week (compared with the normal architecture or design studio of 12-15 hours),[3] which meant that we were expecting students with no background or experience in design or familiarity with the community to produce fairly professional proposals in a fraction of the time allotted to design students — obviously an ambitious and (in hindsight) perhaps unrealistic expectation. In spite of the limited time for the workshop, the students met the challenge by putting in an extraordinary amount of extra work and effort, and succeeded in producing very convincing work. Nevertheless, it would have been fairer and less stressful to increase the number of class hours, as well as to increase the number of credit hours to a level that more closely reflected the time and effort required in the class. An alternative would have been to scale back the project to better fit the assigned credit hours, but the students would still have had to spend time learning basic design skills, which is time-consuming in its own right, and any project would have to be so simple as to be unrealistic, uninteresting to the students, and not very useful to a community.

The third major challenge was one of geography — a simple problem but not easily overcome. The colonias are located along the Texas-Mexico border in the Rio Grande Valley, and Austin is a six-hour drive away. The sheer distance limited the number of trips we could make during the semester and created logistical challenges. In addition, the organizational work involved with taking 27 students on a field trip entailed arranging accommodation, van rentals, transportation, insurance waivers, and health insurance, and collecting money, assigning volunteer drivers, and coordinating room-mates, all of which took up an inordinate amount of time and created an additional administrative burden for the instructor and teaching assistant.[4]

Finally, one of the most disappointing aspects of the project was the lack of practical and financial support from the university. In spite of repeated statements by the highest levels of the administration about the importance and necessity of working with colonias along the border, no funding was earmarked for this type of work, and the students had to shoulder most of the costs themselves. Several of the senior planning faculty did contribute funds to support the second trip to Rio Grande City, and made it possible for two students from each design team to present their final work to the County Commissioner and the community. The extra burden of having to pay for field trips for a required class created a sour note in an otherwise exciting and fairly positive (albeit demanding) experience. The students thought having to pay extra for a required class was unfair, and interpreted the lack of funding and support as a lack of interest in their work and effort. Obviously, if the class had been an elective, paying for the field trips would have been much less of an issue.

Lessons Learned

As the class instructor, I learned an enormous amount about using service-learning as a means of teaching introductory physical design to planning students. I'm convinced that service-learning and community-outreach projects offer an extraordinary teaching and learning opportunity. They motivate students, especially those who are already engaged, to go to great lengths to succeed. In spite of all the frustrations and challenges, they create an educational experience that is far more vivid and memorable than many of their other classes. Service-learning also does what a good educational experience does best — it pushes students outside of their normal lives and assumptions, to experience and explore a much wider world.

I also came to understand that service-learning holds a special role in teaching design to planning students and that it requires a delicate balance. On one hand, a community-based project is an extraordinarily useful entry point to get planning students interested in design. On the other hand, because it can be so real and so meaningful to them, it can create an extra level of stress because of their limited skills and experience.[5] I certainly intend to continue to incorporate service-learning projects in the future, but they will not happen every year for every class. The class will always have realistic and practical projects, but the service-learning and community projects will be very carefully selected to meet the needs of the students as well as the community.

Service-learning in Texas colonias offers a particularly rich and challenging educational opportunity because they are such unusual communities in terms of land ownership and the level of poverty. Few Texans know this part of the state and the conditions in which the residents live. These communities deserve far more attention and assistance from fellow Texans and have an enormous amount to offer and teach us. As useful and rewarding as working with communities in the Rio Grande Valley can be, however, the physical distance between them and Austin limits our access. In the future, we will restrict site selection to the city itself or to sites within an hour's drive. This will allow students to visit the site (and client) much more frequently and require less organizational work. Clearly this reduces the range of projects, and unfortunately it excludes any work in the colonias. I would repeat a project on the Texas-Mexico border only if we had adequate funding and support or if the class was an elective.

Learning about physical design requires the student to practice design and experience the iterative process that leads to an appropriate solution. This takes time and, combined with a community-based project, requires significantly more than the average three-hour-per-week class. The class and credit hours for any service-learning project should be increased to reflect the time needed and the effort invested by the students, compared to other planning classes. Expecting students with no design background to produce fairly professional work with only three hours of class time per week, and awarding only three credit hours, is not only unrealistic but unfair.

Longer-term follow-up between students and the community is also needed. Students and residents invest a great deal of time and energy in the project, and it is disappointing and unsatisfying when the project abruptly ends or the students disappear at the end of the semester. Not many service-learning projects can fit gracefully into a 14-week-semester schedule. Scaling down the scope of the project is one solution, but continuing it over more than one semester would be more advantageous and realistic.

For reduced frustration on the part of students, service-based courses are probably best limited to electives. However, one has to question whether minimizing frustration, though completely understandable, should be the driving force behind making this choice. If service-learning is a valuable educational experience, and teaching the skills needed to work in communities is an important goal, should it not be a goal for all students, not just those who actively seek it out?

If service-learning is deemed valuable, funding and active support by the university are absolutely essential. Not only would they alleviate or reduce the financial burden on the students (in a sense charging an additional fee for a required class) but they would also emphasize that the university has a responsibility and role in working with disadvantaged communities and considers it an important part of education.

Finally, working with an active and engaged community organization is essential for successful service-learning, particularly in the colonias. They can quickly introduce the students to the problem and its context, act as the liaison between the students and the community, and continue contact after the end of the semester. Any future project involving colonias would have to be done in conjunction with CRG or a similar organization.

Summary

The idea of using service-learning for teaching design to planning students is attractive, and having a project located in a very low-income community such as a Texas colonia is an even more exciting proposition. However, the potential pitfalls are many, and an instructor needs to be exceedingly sensitive to the needs of the community and the students. Consequently, educators need to ask themselves two fundamental questions — *can* they, and more importantly *should* they, undertake a service-learning project?

Whether one can run an effective service-learning project is often more a question of practicalities. Can the students gain these skills in the time frame of the class — usually a single semester? Do they have the background to accomplish the task? If not, can they learn in the allotted time? Can the class meet with the community as often as is necessary to learn from them and gain their trust? Is it logistically possible to have a positive educational experience and produce a useful product for the community given the resources?

The question of whether the students *should* undertake a service-learning project is much more profound and difficult to answer. It is an issue of ethics rather than logistics. Ought pre-professional students be involved in producing what should be professional products for any group, especially very low-income communities? Are students being involved simply because the community cannot afford professionals, or do the students offer something unique and important? Is it fair to put that kind of pressure on students who do not yet have the training or skills, but who take their charge and responsibility to the community extremely seriously? What happens if they do not produce high-quality results despite their best effort? Is it fair to burden the community with less than professional results? Do the community and students have realistic expectations about their roles, the process, and the product? Will the community feel used and abandoned by the university and students who disappear once the semester is over?

Pre-professional students and communities can work together on projects that are mutually beneficial, where students gain new skills and insight into communities very different from their own, and communities can gain enormously from the energy and ideas of the students. But the circumstances under which this can happen are unfortunately much rarer than we as educators would like. The case of service-learning in Texas colonias was an experiment — an experiment that was ambitious, challenging, and ultimately both successful and rewarding, but one that will not be repeated without significant changes in the future.

Acknowledgments

Peg McCoy, Rebecca Lightsey, and David Peterson of CRG offered extraordinary support, insight, and enthusiasm for the project. Anu Parmar, the teaching assistant for the class, was invaluable. The residents of Mike's and the staff of CRG in Rio Grande City welcomed us and taught us a great deal. Dean Fritz Steiner, Bob Paterson, and Terry Kahn provided financial support for the second field trip.

Notes

1. In the 1980s and early 1990s, two developers sold more than 2,500 under-serviced lots to nearly 2,000 families in Starr County. They sold the land using a "contract for deed" with very small down payments and small monthly payments toward ownership. Unlike mortgages, contracts for deed give buyers no deed or guarantee to their property upon purchase. Many buyers were promised that they would receive a deed upon full payment, and often that promise was broken. In 1995, Texas sued the developers for violations including failing to provide water and sewerage and fraudulently selling lots. It asked CRG to become the legal receiver for the 16 colonias and sort out the practical and legal problems on the land claimed by the 2,000 families (Community Resource Group 2001).

2. There was one challenge that we did not face when working with planning students in a disadvantaged community. Design students (architecture and landscape architecture) often need to learn to appreciate low-income communities, and they can overuse design jargon or use visual communication that is overly sophisticated and specialized (Forsyth et al. 1999: 176). The planning students did not have a design background and therefore did not have to undo those aspects of their training. And, unlike the traditional design students, planning students usually thrive on community-based work in disadvantaged

communities since this interest is often the motivating factor that prompts them to enter the profession. Forsyth et al. (2000: 246) state that "a significant minority of design students are frustrated by the poverty of the location rather than excited by their potential to help." Fortunately, this is not true at all of planning students.

3. At the University of Texas at Austin, all planning classes are three credits and meet for three hours per week, while the architecture studios meet for 15 hours per week and are worth six credits. The students in the Physical Planning Workshop also significantly exceeded the amount of homework hours that were expected for other planning classes.

4. As stated in Forsyth et al. (1999: 176-177), community-based projects significantly increase the demands on the faculty with preparation and follow-up, since the academic year does not overlap neatly with real projects. That was also true in this project because a fairly lengthy final report was written after the end of semester. Though much of the text was written by the students, it still required extensive editing, additional writing, layout, and production, all undertaken by the instructor. It was an extra burden but not a major obstacle.

5. The class also offered insight into teaching design to planning students. The process of design is very different from most of their previous experience or education. For those trained in design, the unknown or ambiguous nature of the problem and search for a solution are part of the challenge and excitement. For planning students, this can be uncomfortable and upsetting. It was clear that more time was needed to explain the process of design, acknowledge their difficulty and discomfort, and let them know that their struggle and feelings of frustration were shared by all designers.

References

Community Resource Group. (2001). *CRG's Land Title Work: Clearing Titles in Texas Colonias*. Available on CRG's website at www.crg.org/tcr_land.htm. Accessed November 11, 2003.

Davidhizar, R., and G. Bechtel. (1999). "Health and Quality of Life within Colonias Settlements along the United States and Mexico Border." *Public Health Nursing* 16(4): 301-306.

Forsyth, A., H. Lu, and P. McGirr. (Fall 1999). "Inside the Service Learning Studio in Urban Design." *Landscape Journal* 18 (2): 166-178.

_____. (2000). "Service Learning in an Urban Context: Implications for Planning and Design Education." *Journal of Architectural and Planning Research* 17 (3): 236-259.

Haque, M., L. Tain, and B. Vander Mey. (2000). "Horticulture, Planning and Landscape

Architecture, and Sociology." In *Service-Learning across the Curriculum: Case Applications in Higher Education*, edited by Steven J. Madden, pp. 23-38. Lanham MD: University Press of America.

Office of Strategic Management, Research and Development. (1988). *Colonias Factbook Summary*. (Available from the Texas Department of Human Services, Office of Strategic Management. Research, and Development, P.O Box 2960. Austin, TX 78769.)

O'Grady, C. (2000). "Integrating Service-Learning and Multicultural Education: An Overview." In *Integrating Service Learning and Multicultural Education in Colleges and Universities*, edited by Carolyn R. O'Grady, pp. 1-19. Mahwah NJ: Lawrence Erlbaum Associates.

Stanton, T., D.E. Giles, Jr., and N. Cruz. (1999). *Service-Learning: A Movement's Pioneers Reflect on Its Origins, Practice, and Future*. San Francisco: Jossey-Bass.

Ward, P., and J. Carew. (2001). "Tracking Land Ownership in Self-Help Homestead Subdivisions in the United States: The Case of Texas 'Colonias.'" *Land Use Policy* 18: 165-178.

Winterbottom, D. (April 2003). "Building to Learn." *Landscape Architecture* 93(4): 72.

The Electric Greening of North Hollywood:
A Case Study in Environmental Design Education Through Service-Learning

By Julie A. Dercle

Introduction

"Turn poison into medicine," says the old Zen directive. Doing so requires transforming an identified environmental contaminant into a cure for improving the quality of life. That spirit drives problem solving in the design and planning fields. It also supports the American Planning Association's definition of urban planning: "Furthering the welfare of people and their communities by creating convenient, equitable, healthful, efficient, and attractive environments for present and future generations." Toward that end, in fall 2002, my students in the Department of Urban Studies and Planning (URBS) at California State University, Northridge (CSUN), began to collaborate on a community-based project aimed at recycling land for community revitalization, environmental protection, and equal recreational opportunity in the Los Angeles Basin. With the support of the university's Center for Community Service-Learning, they became actively engaged in the Electric Greening Project, converting urban brownfields into developable land, a partial remedy for LA's affordable-housing crisis and thirst for green space. The project became an ongoing partnership with the Los Angeles office of Volunteers of America (VOA), a national, nonprofit faith-based organization. An offshoot of the Salvation Army, VOA addresses social issues by providing local human-service programs and opportunities for individuals and communities through a force of about 30,000 volunteers. It is also one of the nation's leading providers of affordable housing.

This case study is an overview of the Electric Greening Project in North Hollywood, a suburban Los Angeles community in the San Fernando Valley, located in the northwestern part of the city. It describes California State University's commitment to and funding for community-based courses, the department's actions to develop community service across its curriculum in conjunction with the university's Center for Community Service-Learning, and the role of the environmental design educator in involving planning students in the process of civic engagement as preparation for professional life. Finally, it provides a model for building a core of service-learning courses to deliver a continuum of service.

Service-Learning at Northridge

The Electric Greening Project began in July 2002, when Volunteers of America, Los Angeles (VOALA), approached the Center for Community Service-Learning with a request for assistance on a project located about 10 miles from campus. To place the project in context, a brief history follows of service-learning at CSUN and the 23-campus California State University (CSU) system, the nation's largest system of higher education.

CSUN is the only CSU campus located in LA's sprawling San Fernando Valley, an edge city home to 1.9 million residents. Had the valley's bid for secession from Los Angeles been successful in 2003, it would have produced the nation's sixth largest city. CSUN opened in 1958 at the valley's northernmost tip. In 1994, the campus made headlines when the massive Northridge earthquake destroyed or damaged most of its facilities, and has since undergone extensive rebuilding. Over the years, the number of students has climbed, mirroring the growth of the San Fernando Valley. By fall 2002, CSUN's enrollment of 33,579 students was the third highest in the CSU system (after CSU Long Beach and CSU San Diego).

Since the first CSU campus was founded in 1857, faculty, students, and administrators have partnered with local communities. By 2002-2003, CSU offered 1,659 courses with recognized service-learning components, more than 100 of them on the Northridge campus alone, largely resulting from system-wide efforts begun in the late 1990s to identify and promote community-based courses. In 1997, representatives from across the CSU system developed a Strategic Plan for Community Service Learning. Northridge president Blenda Wilson, who had joined Campus Compact, a national organization of college presidents committed to supporting service-learning and civic engagement on their campuses, appointed journalism professor Maureen Rubin and political science professor Stella Theodoulou (now dean of the College of Social and Behavioral Sciences) to represent the campus. Following the meeting, Rubin began to recruit professors informally to the new pedagogy, create partnerships with community organizations, and write grant proposals that would bring in funds to support faculty development to integrate service into curricula. In 1998, the center received its first grant, $2,500 from California Campus Compact to develop service-learning courses in science, engineering, architecture, mathematics, and computer science (SEAMS). A two-page story in the *Los Angeles Times* celebrated the grant and CSUN's new efforts in academically linked community service. The positive publicity, faculty support, and community response led President Wilson to give the center $10,000, providing 10 professors with $1,000 each to develop new service-learning courses. Rubin was soon given reassigned time equivalent to half of her teaching load to direct the effort through CSUN's new Center for Community Service-Learning.

The following year, the system-wide Office of Service Learning was created in the chancellor's office to provide leadership and coordination among the campuses. In April 1999, Governor Gray Davis called for a community service requirement for all students enrolled in the state's institutions of higher learning. In March 2000, the CSU Board of Trustees passed a landmark resolution requiring each campus president to ensure student opportunities. Six months later, Governor Davis authorized $2.2 million in the state budget for four consecutive years to develop new service-learning courses and create or expand service-learning offices on all CSU campuses. CSUN's center received $105,000 to support infrastructure and curriculum development activities, which continue through differing grant opportunities. By 2003-2004, its operating budget, funded through the Governor's office and CSUN's Office of Academic Affairs, exceeded $186,000. Since the center began in 1998, Rubin has raised over $1.3 million in additional funds through grants from other sources to support specific service-learning projects. The center's philosophy is best summed up in the *Community Partner Guide to Service-Learning & Volunteerism:*

> *Physicists use the term* vacuum *to describe an empty space, existing without contact to the outside world. CSUN borrows this term to emphasize its belief that education does not happen in a vacuum; a university could not survive without constant interactions and interconnections with its environment. (p. 3)*

At the department level, Urban Studies and Planning did not operate in a vacuum. It had been civically engaged long before the term became associated with community-based pedagogy. In July 2002, after 30 years as an interdisciplinary program of CSUN's College of Social and Behavioral Sciences, URBS became a full-fledged academic department, the only undergraduate planning degree program in the Los Angeles area. About a month prior to achieving departmental status, URBS was selected as one of nine academic departments from across the system to participate in CSU's second annual Engaged Department Institute, offered by Campus Compact and the Chancellor's Office of Community Service-Learning. Five faculty members, including me, and a representative of one of the community partners attended the institute held in San Francisco.

Professor W. Tim Dagodag, the longtime URBS Program Coordinator who became the founding department chair, is a professional planner and geographer. Early on, he worked to institute URBS's philosophy as a community resource and inspired other faculty to follow suit, supporting their efforts in developing courses with community-based assignments and conducting nonprofit advisory work. Graduation requirements for URBS majors included completion of both community-based fieldwork and professional, paid internships that placed students in government agencies as well as community-based organizations. In February 2001, the Educational Policy Committee of CSUN's Faculty Senate approved criteria for listing courses in the university catalogue and schedule of classes with an official CS (community service-learning) designation. URBS became committed to working toward obtaining the designation for all of its offerings. The curriculum was built on two tracks. One was geared toward public sector employment. The other was geared toward community service in LA's multiethnic urban setting, fostered through shared faculty positions with the departments of Pan-African Studies, Chicano/Chicana Studies, and Asian American Studies. In May 2002, in a special presentation to CSU trustee Roberta Achtenberg and CSUN president Jolene Koester, URBS unveiled its mission statement: "To prepare students as rational and critical thinkers and provide them with the skills necessary to enter professional planning fields to improve the quality of life in urban communities." The nascent department also listed as its first priority "community service and outreach," becoming the first on the Northridge campus to revise its faculty retention, tenure, and promotion guidelines to require community service. Accordingly, all full-time and most part-time faculty members in URBS emphasized community-based work, teaming with a number of community partners whether or not their courses were officially designated as CS or they received support through the center. Thus, the academy committed to Boyer's ideal of a "vigorous partnership in the active search for answers to our most pressing" problems (Boyer 1990).

Course Description

In July 2002, when URBS achieved departmental status, VOALA's project manager, Brian White, approached the center's Maureen Rubin. White had obtained funds from Proposition K, LA's bond initiative for parks, to develop a half-acre of gardening plots at the organization's vast apartment complex in North Hollywood, consisting of 475 units affordable to lower-income residents. He was seeking design assistance to expand the gardens on an adjacent site used as an above ground electrical transmission right of way and was negotiating its lease with LA's Department of Water and Power (DWP), its owner. The university was in a unique position to provide VOALA with ideas and additional energy for expanding its "electric" greening project. The center served as the catalyst when Rubin arranged for me to meet with Brian White. A $1,500 Faculty Curriculum Development Grant from the center enabled the three of us to craft a syllabus that met the center's community service-learning definition and the approved content for URBS 440, the upper-division, community-based urban design course I teach, which is required for all department majors. Entitled "Greening North Hollywood: Introduction to Environmental Design through Service-Learning," the fall 2002 course had objectives that included the following:

• To understand the nature of the environmental design process: identify the types of knowledge, information, variables, issues, and stakeholders involved and demonstrate their applicability to a practical, community experience.
• To understand the regulatory context for planning: from zoning to community "visions" and specific requirements for the North Hollywood project site.
• To identify the issues that affect the quality of life in North Hollywood and Southern California in general.
• To study, appreciate, and evaluate the latest trends in community development from the three e's of sustainability — economics, environment, and equity — to the New Urbanism's emphasis on diversity, regionalism, and transit-oriented development, and apply these to North Hollywood as a case study.
• To think creatively and invent tangible ways to improve the quality of life.
• To begin a lifelong commitment to civic engagement.
• To engage in and reflect upon a service-learning experience that combines academic study with practical experience and civic engagement.

Designing the Electric Greening Site

The North Hollywood site was part of a 20-mile-long right of way as wide as a football field that cut through working-class neighborhoods like an ugly scar. It was one of several created in the 1920s when land in the San Fernando Valley was still cheap, well before LA's post-World War II population boom turned farmlands into housing tracts. Diagonally shaped, the approximately 25-acre site was relatively flat, on stable, mostly clay soil, and enjoyed the valley's moderate Mediterranean climate. It was also barren except for 10 electrical transmission towers, whose high voltage lines emitted a pervasive buzzing sound. Additional noise came from traffic along Victory Boulevard, a major arterial with commercial uses, and Burbank Airport. Although the site was enclosed along the perimeter by chain-link fencing, several breaches led to makeshift paths frequently littered by trespassers.

Los Angeles had zoned the site PF-1VL (Public Facilities, Vacant Lot). This designation precluded the development of permanent structures as well as temporary ones exceeding 10 feet in height, but permitted parking, storage, and agricultural uses such as field crops, gardens, and nurseries. Use of the site was also subject to the "Guidelines for Nursery, Landscape, Greenbelt, and Agricultural Purposes (Transmission Line Rights of Way)" issued by the DWP (Rev. 02/12/02).

Surrounding the site were parcels zoned R-1 and R-3, consisting of single-family and multi-family homes respectively, including VOALA's housing complex and its Maud Booth Family Center, named after the VOA's cofounder. Fair Avenue Elementary School, a Los Angeles Unified School District (LAUSD) K-12 facility, bordered the site's northeast portion. According to 2000 Census tract information, the adjacent community consisted of predominantly low- and moderate-income families with median earnings of $37,679 per year, with 15.5 percent living below poverty level. Approximately 60 percent of the residents were of Latino descent, with half of the total households containing family members under the age of 18. The closest city-owned recreational facility, the 6.5-acre Victory-Vineland Recreation Center, was not within walking distance.

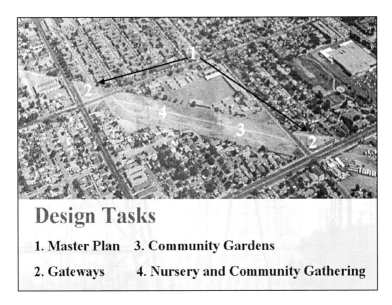

Figure 1. Design tasks

Prior to the start of class, Brian White and I identified four interrelated design tasks for developing the site. These included a Master Plan to identify major pathways and link the remaining tasks, in addition to more detailed plans for:

• Gateways at each end of the site to serve as major entrances, the northwestern one approximately 32,000 sq. ft., the southeastern, 34,000 sq. ft.

• Community Gardens south of Fair Avenue Elementary School for children and their families to participate in educational botanical and gardening-related activities

• Nursery and Community Gathering with enough space for vocational education, a farmer's market, and community get-togethers

Twenty-six URBS students completed the 15-week course, working in teams of two to four members, two teams for each of the four design tasks. Most of the planning students had had little drawing and drafting experience and even less exposure to the history and theory of architecture and urban design. To overcome these deficiencies and reduce redundancy among the teams in collecting site information, a spirit of non-competitiveness, sharing, and team building was fostered. For example, one of the Master Plan teams conducted a preliminary door-to-door survey, in Spanish and English, of residents within a five-minute walk of the site to confirm safety needs and desired recreational opportunities for adults and children, then distributed the results. More experienced students were enlisted to help teach less-prepared ones. This shortened the time needed for novices to learn techniques prior to tackling a design submittal. To supplement their drawing skills, students were also encouraged to experiment with computer-based resources, producing drawings from general landscaping programs, manipulating their original digital photographs, and collecting and transforming digital materials from other sources.

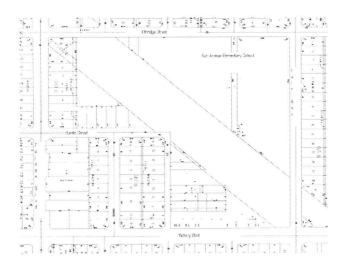

Figure 2. North Hollywood site

Forty-five percent of the course grade was based on scores for individual tasks. These included an assignment demonstrating basic drafting and measuring skills; a midterm exam on assigned readings, class lectures, and discussions emphasizing design history and theory; and a written field trip report on a site in Southern California selected as a high-quality example of public space, which students also presented orally, highlighting the formal and material aspects important for teams to consider in their designs. Thus, the class built an inventory of places to learn from and visit while preparing their submittals. The team proposal made up the remaining 55 percent of the course grade, with each member receiving the same score to encourage a sense of team spirit, commitment, and responsibility such as they would encounter in professional life. At the end of the semester, teams submitted their proposals to the client in the form of PowerPoint presentations and printed brochures. They included a statement of philosophy, reflecting their community-based experience and understanding of the course content, and a recommended design scheme using site plans, illustrations, and specifications for both hardscaping and landscaping materials based on their regulatory analysis (including local, state, and DWP requirements) and qualitative and quantitative analyses of the site.

From the outset, I found the class responded more seriously to this project than to the purely academic exercises I had assigned in other semesters. The students' work might lead to a demonstration project for VOALA and the DWP, a "greenprint" for other communities to redevelop underused lands, and a showcase to garner public support for future expansion and undergrounding efforts. With the possibility of implementation, the final schemes needed to be cost-effective with respect to future maintenance and take policing into account. Keeping the outcome in mind, the class generated a list of parameters, agreeing that each team would adopt the following sustainable design standards:

• Landscaping specifications shall emphasize native and drought-tolerant plants.
• Changes to site topography shall be minimal; designs shall not require extensive excavating, grading, and berming except to ensure safety.
• Designs shall not include extensive artificial water features, such as manufactured streams, rivers, or lakes.
• Safety of the greenway users and privacy and well-being of neighboring residents are very important; care shall be given to ensure adequate on-site lighting and the buffering or screening of adjacent properties from public use.

• There shall be no on-site parking other than that required by DWP for access to and maintenance of their facilities.

• Uses shall reflect the culture, needs, and desires of the community.

In discussion with VOALA, the students also determined the following additional considerations for the four design tasks:

1. Master Plan: overall scheme embodying a unique project *vision*

2. Gateways: highly visible from the public right of way; mostly landscaping; aesthetic treatment to create a public image for the entire project; passive recreational uses only; protection of neighboring residential properties

3. Community Gardens: small, productive plots with accessory facilities (e.g., composting and cleaning areas); pathways and entrances to connect with Fair Avenue Elementary School and the community

4. Nursery and Community Gathering: flexible, educational/vocational area adjacent to larger community plots; access for farm and nursery vehicles; shell or other structure for community uses

Tackling the Towers

In striving for environmental quality, students learned the process of design. Through their proposed schemes, they could transform context variables, or the *givens* of a complex problem, into desired performance outcomes that might lead to a satisfactory resolution. One of the Gateways teams wrote the following mission statement in its final brochure, describing the desired outcome for its proposed scheme:

> *To learn to live in harmony with the Earth on a genuinely sustainable basis begins with the smallest community projects. We seek to promote the beautification of abandoned and underutilized grounds as a holistic approach to urban decay. By eliminating negative physical characteristics and renewing the setting, we hope to foster a relationship between nature and humankind. A relationship that will yield as a final result the improvement in the quality of life for the surrounding community.*

Another team wrote, "Our goal is to create a beautiful and viable green space for community cohesion, growth, and prosperity." Increasing a sense of community pride by improving the site's aesthetics, removing or reducing its real or perceived environmental hazards, and providing access to nature for social, recreational, and educational opportunities — from gardening to gathering to bird watching — all figured into the design equation. To achieve the desired outcome, each team also adopted a philosophical attitude toward the electrical transmission towers. Eight of the towers run in pairs through the central portion of the site, with one on each of the Gateways, creating a dismal vista of jumbled poles and wires.

Figure 3. Towers

One team wrote about its initial dismay:

Shocking, surprising and disappointing are just a few of the reactions that our group had on our first visit to the North Hollywood site. Even though we had seen a video of the site, nothing could have prepared us for our initial reaction.... Everything from the enormously loud power structures that sit throughout the park to the near vegetation-less land, it was overwhelming in the beginning.

There seemed to be only two ways to deal with the towers aesthetically. One was to celebrate them as Art Deco sculpture (they were designed in the 1920s), symbolic of modern times, a metaphor for the industrialization that sparked LA's growth. As one team wrote, "The power lines present a unique feature from the site. Upon initial observation they create an obtrusive and noisy feature for the neighborhood. Instead of seeing them as a problem it is best to celebrate them for their uniqueness."

The alternative was to minimize the site's visual pollution through diversionary landscaping and the noise through the use of water features and textured pathways. One of the teams investigated yet a third approach: removing the need for the towers by burying the lines. According to the DWP, the cost would run approximately $40 million per mile, which seemed prohibitive without further investigation. The community surveys had revealed that although attitudes toward site redevelopment were generally positive, some residents worried about health risks associated with exposure to electromagnetic fields (EMFs) from the high-voltage lines. Teachers at Fair Avenue voiced concern about the children.

The class raised several important questions. While the answers are too lengthy to discuss here, these became the basis for further research:

1. How much underused public land is there in the San Fernando Valley and the City of Los Angeles?
2. How dangerous to human health is exposure to EMFs from high-voltage power lines?
3. How will brownfield clean up and conversion affect property values in the adjacent community and the amount of affordable housing available there?

From raising these issues, students became aware of the "organized complexity," in Jane Jacobs' terms, of the urban environment (Jacobs 1961). They learned that planning problems, as Weber and Rittel defined them, are characteristically "wicked" (Weber and Rittel 1973). With this theoretical understanding and considering an array of scenarios, the class decided the preferred choice was burying the powerlines, which would require a political and community effort beyond the scope of the course. Nonetheless, the Electric Greening Project would serve to publicize the poor use of a public site in a city starved for available land, an important first step toward converting brownfields to more green and sustainable uses.

Course Outcomes

Throughout the course, VOALA was available to students for consultation, site visits, and comments on interim schemes, which created a working partnership. The center handled risk-management issues and conducted pre- and post-course tests assessing students' satisfaction with their experience and attitudinal changes toward civic engagement, future careers, and personal development. The students reported high course satisfaction from having been given the opportunity to work on a "real" as opposed to an "academic" project. Their sense of empowerment from the experience may have contributed to the very high scores given in their formal Student Evaluation of Faculty at the end of the semester, which rated the course and the instructor. Out of a possible score of 5 points for more than a dozen variables, the total median score was 4.5. One student wrote anonymously, "Participation with a real life client (VOALA) served as an invaluable lesson." Another wrote, "One of the best classes I have ever taken in terms of applying what's learned in the classroom to the real world. Great class!" The professional, imaginative submittals by students with little prior design experience reflected an infectious enthusiasm for community building. The eight schemes submitted also produced scores of fresh ideas for the client. Presentations of the students' work to the community, its leaders, and local agencies highlighted some of them, including a unifying "dry" riverbed using native stone and plants, and a layout for the community gardens area based on Spanish and Baroque patterns.

As a result of the course, the Electric Greening Project gained momentum locally and on campus. Commitments for future muscle and materials came from many sources, including LA County's Master Gardeners, the Los Angeles Conservation Corps, and a number of business and environmental organizations. URBS 440 had included many nontraditional students who were either returning to school after having established careers or were considering changing careers to urban planning. One of the students had attended Fair Avenue Elementary School and was a Los Angeles fire commissioner. Another ran several city programs in the San Fernando Valley through the mayor's office. They were able to facilitate meetings with the City Council District to expedite VOALA's lease of the land from the DWP.

The following semester, in spring 2003, several of the students enrolled in my URBS 450 course, "Urban Issues," the capstone senior seminar. I offered them the opportunity to continue working on the Electric Greening Project; they all accepted. One team reviewed the submittals from the fall course, working with Brian White to synthesize the best ideas into a final site plan for the DWP's approval. Another team continued developing the community survey. A third conducted research on conversion of electrical transmission line rights of way in other parts of the country as well as health risks associated with EMF exposure.

Figure 4. Gardening

During that same semester, the center in cooperation with the LAUSD successfully responded to a request for proposals from the César E. Chávez Day of Service and Learning section of the Governor's Office on Service and Volunteerism (GO SERV) . The proposal, "César E. Chávez : Living His Legacy through Reading and Seeding," was funded for $110,000. It would engage four CSUN departments, including URBS, in an innovative community-serving program involving K-12 students in supporting the Department of Education's statewide service-learning goals. In fall 2003, I received a second Faculty Curriculum Development Grant from the center to revise my syllabus for URBS 150, "The Urban Scene," a general-education introductory course open to the entire student body and required for all URBS majors. I would teach my three sections of URBS 150 as service-learning courses to implement the GO SERV grant.

By that time, the DWP had agreed to lease VOALA a five-acre section of the original site. The plans were again revised and more than 125 students in my URBS 150 classes were given the opportunity to work with VOALA and the students and teachers at Fair Avenue Elementary on the "seeding" portion of the grant. This implemented the César E. Chávez Memorial Gardens, the name given to the first section of the Electric Greening Project developed from ideas generated by the URBS 440 class the year before. Each participating URBS 150 student fulfilled a 20-hour community-service work requirement through a combination of aiding Fair Avenue's teachers, participating in several work days on the site, or staffing the Community Fair and Celebration held in the local shopping mall. To complete the course, students discussed and reflected upon their experiences in work journals. Their candid writings revealed that although some of them lived in the area they had no previous experience with community work. Many had never known the satisfaction that gardening brings. Most expressed pride and pleasure, asking to continue their involvement beyond the semester and their coursework. The faculty and teaching assistants learned about the difficulties in coordinating and scheduling service-learning experiences and the amount of time and record keeping required. By the end of the semester, everyone understood the amount of time, labor, commitment, and political clout needed to remediate public land, especially the slow, tedious process of gaining approvals from a public agency.

Conclusion

Faculty who take on a community-based project meaningful to students and the community partner must commit themselves beyond semester-long time frames and incorporate service into their professional and civic agendas. Through our support of the Electric Greening

Project, Maureen Rubin and I became advocates for VOALA's and the community's goals. We have presented the project at the request of City Council members, state legislators, and the Economic Alliance of the San Fernando Valley. We have served as panelists at professional and academic meetings, including the national Brownfields 2003 Conference co-sponsored by the U.S. Environmental Protection Agency and the International City Managers Association. Indeed, service-learning instruction and opportunities benefited from an engaged university and department, but the fundamental task was to keep students motivated so they would engage themselves as stakeholders in the solutions to their community's problems. That meant more than structuring an environmental design course that was problem-based. Students had to be part of the project's evolution and be given opportunities to continue their work.

In fall 2002, urban design students developed site plans for the Electric Greening Project, but the same design problem could not be repeated each semester and stimulate the same level of excitement. It had to be real and current, so instruction and learning would need to grow and evolve. URBS seniors, in spring 2003, continued to conduct related research and strengthen their relationship with the community. The following fall, one of them became the teaching and research assistant for my three sections of the URBS 150 course, coordinating the service-learning experience of students new to urban planning. As development and the DWP's review of the plans continued, students and the community took on further ownership. The "official" groundbreaking scheduled for spring 2004 was delayed until early 2005, pending DWP's approvals, but with every expectation that the transformation of the blighting right of way into a community greenway would exceed the DWP's limited plans for using the land as shipping-container and recreational-vehicle parking and storage. In the interim, in spring 2004, a new crop of graduating seniors worked with a new, community-based organization dedicated to burying the powerlines, the Electric Greening Operation, or E-Go. For their capstone project, the students imagined the possibilities once the valley's power lines were gone, generating comprehensive plans for affordable housing and mixed uses linked to transit and greenspace on the old rights of way. Building upon the experience of previous URBS students, they evolved further ways to "turn poison into medicine."

References

Boyer, E.L. (1990). *Scholarship Reconsidered: Priorities of the Professoriate.* Princeton, NJ: Carnegie Foundation for the Advancement of Teaching.

Center for Community Service-Learning. (2003). *Community Partner Guide to Service-Learning & Volunteerism.* Northridge, CA: California State University.

CSU Office of the Chancellor, Department of Community Service-Learning. (2002). *Annual Report of Community Service Learning in the CSU, 2001/2002.* Long Beach, CA: California State University.

_____. (2002). *Facts 2002/2003, Facts on Community Service-Learning in the California State University.* Long Beach, CA: California State University.

Jacobs, J. (1961). *The Death and Life of American Cities.* New York: Random House.

Rittel, H.W.J., and M.W. Webber. (1973). "Dilemmas in a General Theory of Planning." *Policy Sciences* 4: 155-169.

Funded Planning and Design Studios:
Master of Infrastructure Planning Program at NJIT's New Jersey School of Architecture

By Darius Sollohub

For the past five years, the Master of Infrastructure Planning (MIP) Program in the New Jersey School of Architecture at New Jersey Institute of Technology (NJIT) has offered studio courses that conduct research, planning, and design for community-based clients and public agencies. Increasingly, the program undertakes this work in an interdisciplinary capacity, in conjunction with private entities and other units at NJIT and other academic institutions. The clients vary from neighborhood groups, institutions, and governments to regional and state agencies. In the face of university budget cutbacks, the program is notable for its success in generating external funding to the benefit of all involved. Because of each project's broad scope, the MIP studio is often coordinated with teams of students and faculty, from other schools at NJIT and other institutions, through courses and research collaborations. These teams simulate the conditions of professional planning and design practice. The MIP program targets the end-user locality but also addresses issues of regional smart growth and sustainable practices. By focusing on what universities do best — teaching and research — the program bridges a growing divide between agencies and communities. Its inclusionary approach demystifies and depoliticizes planning and design policy so that communities can absorb and adopt the outcomes as their own. This essay examines three projects, describes the program's background and structure, and discusses the challenges and successes of an interdisciplinary methodology that combines research, teaching, practice, and community service.

Case Studies

MIP research has focused on infrastructure-related projects at different scales in which service-based planning and design make up the core. These projects are a form of applied research that address an important and emerging need in the planning and design process in New Jersey, complementing the efforts of state agencies in advancing smart growth and sustainable development practices. Each project offers recommendations based on student work that has had significant impact. The three projects described below treat infrastructure as a fundamental driver of development with a strong emphasis on transportation, arguably the most critical issue of development. In different ways, they each involve aspects of the transit-village concept: compact, mixed-use, walkable communities centered on a transit station, where residents, workers, visitors, and shoppers are invited to drive their cars less and ride mass transit more. These villages extend roughly a quarter mile, a five-minute walking distance, from a transit station. They contribute to urban regeneration at a regional scale by embracing goals related to urban design, neighborhood cohesion, social diversity, conservation, public safety, and community revitalization (Bernick and Cervero 1997).

Riverside Transit Village Project

The Riverside Transit Village Project began in 1999 in anticipation of the impact of light-rail service on Riverside, a community in southern New Jersey. It was initiated by the New Jersey Department of Transportation (NJDOT) Systems planning director, William Beetle, in response to community criticism of the Southern New Jersey Light Rail system, a $1 billion project that had become highly politicized after residents felt they had been excluded from the decision-making process.[1] The light-rail system had been promoted as a balance to public investments made in the northern part of the state. Despite low ridership projections, the system was built with little input from the affected communities and without federal funding. When the Riverside governing body sought to redevelop a 32-acre former factory site next to the proposed light-rail train station, local skepticism impeded it. Director Beetle turned to NJIT to help resolve these difficulties. The MIP program achieved this through extensive outreach, using design proposals to explain the benefits of light rail to Riverside.

The project was carried out in two successive studios. I taught the first studio, which assessed local and regional conditions. Of primary importance were contamination and floodplain issues and the array of existing and potential transit, vehicular, bicycle, and pedestrian mobility networks affecting the site. Residential and mixed-use development were also at issue. The project team polled local high school students, whose views regarding Riverside's future surprised the governing body and were particularly useful in formulating design strategies. The studio culminated in three alternative development concepts that tailored different aspects of the transit village to Riverside.

Working with community leaders, MIP Program Director Tony Santos taught the second studio, which incorporated elements of the three alternatives into a comprehensive urban design framework for development. The proposal featured a new multi-modal arterial street acting as the neighborhood's spine and linking the downtown to the waterfront, or as the studio motto had it, putting "the river back in Riverside." It incorporated historical structures and the planned station, and presented options for various uses, including retail, commercial, housing, and open space. Students used two large physical models in addition to digital presentations to describe the results of the entire process to community groups at two transportation conferences and to the County Freeholders, whose support gave the project a strong boost. Subsequently, the final report became indispensable in redevelopment planning and in preparing requests for proposals for private developers. A private development project under review by the borough contains many features of the original NJIT proposal intact (MIP Program: Riverside 2002).

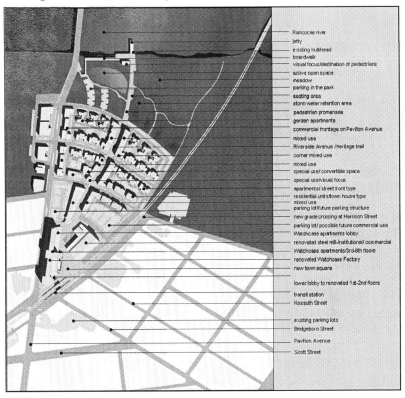

Rancocas river
jetty
existing bulkhead
boardwalk
visual focus/destination of pedestrians
active open space
meadow
parking in the park
seating area
storm water retention area
pedestrian promenade
garden apartments
commercial frontage on Pavilion Avenue
mixed use
Riverside Avenue /heritage trail
corner mixed use
mixed use
special use/ convertible space
special use/visual focus
apartments/ street front type
residential units/town house type
mixed use
parking lot/future parking structure
new grade crossing at Harrison Street
parking lot/ possible future commercial use
Watchcase apartments lobby
renovated steel mill-institutional/ commercial
Watchcase apartments/3rd-8th floors
renovated Watchcase Factory
new town square

lower lobby to renovated 1st-2nd floors

transit station
Kossuth Street

existing parking lots
Bridgeboro Street

Pavilion Avenue

Scott Street

Figure 1. Riverside Transit Village project: annotated plan of urban design framework

E-Stations: Physical and Virtual Mobility for the Inner City

The e-station project developed the prototype of an advanced form of bus station for inner-city low-income communities.[2] E-stations employ an intelligent transportation system that announces a bus's arrival, so that station users can wait indoors in comfort and security instead of anxiously waiting at the curb, frustrated as others stream by in cars. And while they wait, they could be introduced to the Internet, to which low-income urban residents often lack access. In this way, e-stations could help bridge the digital divide.

The project brought together faculty and students of infrastructure planning, architecture, biometrics, computer science, transportation engineering, and management. The classroom settings included infrastructure planning and architecture studios, management courses, and a community service course at NJIT's Small Business Institute. Faculty members taught seminars, led focus groups, and coordinated the overall effort. In addition, numerous individuals outside the university contributed, including agency and local government officials, community developers, information technology specialists, architects, engineers, construction professionals, and business people. The project was steered by a core group consisting of Santos, NJIT professor Karen Franck (an environmental psychologist), and me.

The project began in fall 2000 with an infrastructure planning studio, taught by me, that developed the e-station concept according to different transportation, information, and social networks. These networks were described in an evolving Web-based document that functioned as the primary work and reference tool for the project and was used to explain the project at numerous public presentations. Working with the steering group and the project's community partners, the studio ultimately identified a site for the prototype in a Newark neighborhood where a community development organization was proposing a 50,000-square-foot supermarket. From a transit point of view, the site was ideal, with 34,000 passengers on five bus lines passing daily. Members of the community were canvassed in a focus group programmed by a management class and organized by faculty and students.

Two comprehensive architectural design studios were involved. These courses required that projects integrate engineering, constructability, and regulatory aspects. The first, taught at the graduate level by Santos, ran concurrently with the infrastructure planning studio, thus breaking with the conventional sequence of research, planning, and design. Instead, the design studio acted as a conceptual probe, identifying architectural issues that might cross-pollinate research and planning in the infrastructure studio. Projects were developed at two sites, one adjacent to Newark's second and less used train station and the other at the supermarket site eventually selected. Both studios were closely integrated, with students attending their counterparts' reviews. The specifics of functional program and architectural design parameters evolved during the first semester. In spring 2001, I taught the second comprehensive studio, given at the advanced undergraduate level. This design studio focused on the supermarket site and assumed that the e-station design would be located next to the market's entrance. Student projects were critiqued by the steering group and guided by construction professionals on structural, mechanical, curtain-wall, waterproofing, furniture, and equipment issues. Five of the prototypes were included in the final report, one of which was the subject of a cost analysis by the project's construction management partner.

Figure 2. E-Station: prototype interior view — Ersela Kripa, designer (Federal Highway Administration 2003)

Concurrently, a student team in the Small Business Institute of the NJIT School of Management developed a business plan for operating the e-station as a public-private partnership. Under the plan, the e-station would be owned by a nonprofit community-based organization that would lease space to one or more businesses already operating in Newark. The business component would act as a catalyst for development along the supermarket frontage, eventually making the e-station self-sustaining and profitable. The student team identified public funding for initial operations from various city, state, and national programs. They included the Community Technology Center Network (CTCnet), a nonprofit organization that coordinates technology in poor communities, and One Stop, a New Jersey program geared toward computer training and workforce deployment.

Community endorsements and financial support notwithstanding, the e-station project has been affected by local politics and the economic downturn. As part of a program to disseminate profits from New Jersey's casinos, it was earmarked for seed funding of almost $300,000, roughly a third of its development budget. Those funds, however, were subsequently diverted from the neighborhoods to higher-profile downtown projects. Funding support from industry also contracted after the collapse of the dot-com bubble. Because of these setbacks, the project is now dormant. On a positive note, the supermarket project has received $400,000 in funding, proof that momentum still exists in the neighborhood. The team is hopeful that when the political and financial climate changes and supplementary support is secured, the project can resume with construction of an e-station prototype (Federal Highway Administration 2003).

Jersey City Bayside Development Project

This project represents the first collaboration involving the program, other institutions, and a professional firm. In spring 2003, the MIP program, joined by Rutgers University's Bloustein School of Planning and Public Policy and the Geosciences Department at New Jersey City University (NJCU), coordinated efforts with a planning and urban design firm, Anton Nelessen and Associates (ANA) of Princeton.[3] The consortium researched, planned, and designed alternative development proposals for the southwestern part of Jersey City. The area has two focal points: the NJCU campus and the terminus for a recently completed light-rail system. Santos taught an infrastructure studio at NJIT; I, as a visiting professor, co-taught a transportation studio at Rutgers with Martin Robins, the executive director of the Voorhees Transportation Institute; and William Montgomery taught a geographic information systems (GIS) course at NJCU. The work of the academic team and ANA was closely coordinated, each making regular presentations to the sponsor's steering committee. The teams interacted with one another and benefited mutually from the collaboration: the work of ANA relied upon an extensive database of land-use and building information, photographic surveys, computer models, and development scenarios produced as coursework, while students and faculty participated in several design charrettes and presentations directed by ANA staff. Though the academic and professional teams made separate public presentations, the work was consistent overall. Differences were considered as variations or alternatives rather than oppositions.

The academic work differed in scope, focus, and geographic extent. NJCU coordinated production of the GIS map, which incorporated computer data from the NJIT survey. The Rutgers studio, which met three hours per week, focused on the one-quarter-mile-radius transit-village circle surrounding the light-rail terminus. It also conducted a broad analysis of past and projected transit and economic development in Jersey City, which has seen explosive growth along its formerly industrial Hudson River waterfront but not on its western, Hackensack River side. The NJIT studio, which met 10 hours per week, was involved in work of greater scope, its two-square-mile study area slightly exceeding that of ANA. The studio developed the transit-village concept proposed by Rutgers, planned expansion alternatives and redevelopment alternatives for NJCU and the surrounding neighborhoods, and presented a comprehensive urban design framework for the Route 440 corridor, a strip highway that traverses the western portion of the site.

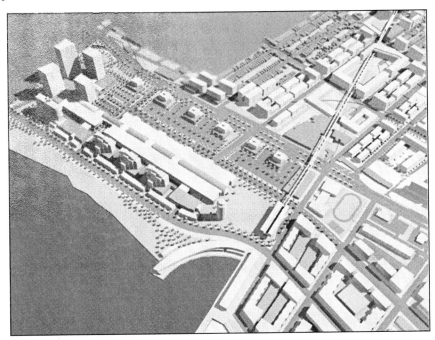

Figure 3. Jersey City Bayside Development Project: aerial view showing proposed development on Hackensack waterfront and new light-rail terminus (NJIT 2004)

The combination of professional and academic efforts operating in tandem in the Jersey City project has generated the most significant results of the MIP program to date. To maintain momentum, the original steering committee continues to hold regular meetings. Articulating a design strategy, the process affirmed the university's intention to buy an industrial site, doubling its acreage, for which ANA is now the master planner. The city's Board of Education is planning an early-learning center adjacent to the light-rail station, consistent with transit-village planning ideas, and is considering similar siting strategies for other school facilities. These decisions required some convincing by the academic team. The analysis of economic development and future ridership gave NJCU an appreciation for how light rail could benefit the campus and caused it to shift the thrust of expansion toward the station, enacting measures to enhance the pedestrian connection to it, and beginning negotiations with NJ Transit to incorporate a transit pass into student use fees. NJCU concluded that greater transit use by commuting students would lessen the demand for on-campus parking and free up space for classrooms and dormitories.

The most exciting prospect is the conversion of Route 440 to an urban boulevard, a project brought to the attention of NJDOT by the academic team and now atop the list of candidates for a pilot program. This development has renewed interest in the development of the Hackensack waterfront and expanding the light rail, a prospect that the studios studied in three alternative proposals. Arguably, some aspects of the project might have been advanced by a professional undertaking, but the academic collaboration allowed for the expanded scope, integrated data, comprehensive documentation, emerging knowledge, and invention that created the project's great synergy and momentum (MIP Program: Jersey City 2004).

Structure

The MIP program continues a university-based tradition of interdisciplinary planning that stresses collaboration between the academy and the profession. Developed at the School of Architecture at NJIT by Santos and launched in 1996 under Dean Urs Gauchat with me as associate director, the program has its roots in the social-science-based Chicago School and New Deal planning initiatives. In the 1950s and 60s, the tradition blossomed into an interdepartmental urban design program at the University of Pennsylvania under G. Holmes Perkins and coordinated by David Crane. This interdisciplinary manifestation of the Philadelphia School integrated architecture, landscape architecture, and city planning, and included Louis Kahn, Ian McHarg, Britton Harris, Edmund Bacon, and Melvin Weber. The approach was later brought to Boston under reform mayor John Collins through the Boston Redevelopment Authority (BRA), administered by Edward Logue and directed by Crane. A highpoint was the program's collaboration in 1967/1968 with the Bedford-Stuyvesant Corporation, sponsored by Senator Robert F. Kennedy, to redevelop a large area of Brooklyn. Multidisciplinary planning of this kind was undermined by the dismantling of federal funding mechanisms for urban development in the early 70s. Santos, who studied and worked with Crane and participated in the Bedford-Stuyvesant studio, provides a direct link to these earlier educational models.

When the MIP program was conceived several decades later, it was inspired by the educational ideas of the University of Pennsylvania program while responding to changed historical circumstances. In the program's five-year review, Santos (2002) described the academic climate in which it emerged:

> The need for such a program at the regional, national and international level was recognized by NJIT in the early 1990's. The emphasis on physical planning and urban design in urban and regional planning degree programs had decreased noticeably in the previous twenty years. The curricula of most planning programs were predominantly based on the social sciences and oriented towards non-physical aspects of the environment, and none of those that retained a physical orientation stressed the interdisciplinary relationship with infrastructure engineering and technology. Urban design, on the other hand, had tended to become an extension of the traditional design professions of architecture and landscape architecture.

The program was created in a period when architectural education in general was being re-examined. A 1996 Carnegie Foundation study recommended that architecture expand its scope and re-engage with allied disciplines (Boyer and Mitgang 1996). The study cited a previous call for re-engagement between the design academy and the profession (Schön 1983, 1987). Subsequent feminist criticism of training students to be "master builders" — solitary, heroic designers — argued for a pedagogy stressing teamwork, interdisciplinarity, consensus, and a keener awareness of community needs (Weisman 1996; Sara 2001). Responding to the same issues, MIP pedagogy seeks similar goals: cross-disciplinary engagement; a planning and design method that stresses collaboration, communication, and stakeholder involvement; and the integration of planning and design research, practice, teaching, and service in the form of community-based projects.

NJIT's course catalogue describes the methodology as focusing on "the natural environment and on public space, roads, transportation, services and utilities as interacting physical and spatial systems, as well as on parks, schools, housing and civic institutions of all kinds.... Capitalizing on NJIT's multidisciplinary resources and location at the center of the nation's greatest regional concentration of urban infrastructure, the MIP program incorporates applied research and realistic problem solving in its curriculum ..." (NJIT 2002). The program focuses on the interrelationships among elements to develop holistic strategies for integrally planned and designed infrastructure systems. It postulates that infrastructure is the fundamental framework for physical planning and design. In doing so, the program transcends the traditional identification of different infrastructure components with separate professional disciplines. Instead, it stresses a unified, coordinated approach that prioritizes the quality of the overall built environment over the efficiency of any one part. The program prompts students to take a leading and coordinating role in resolving and synthesizing the many, often conflicting elements of infrastructure and deal more effectively with the critical problems of development. The MIP program seeks to restore planners and designers as decision makers at the center of the infrastructure planning and design process.

The MIP studio is the primary engine of research, planning, and design. With 12 to 18 students from various disciplines including architecture, planning, engineering, environmental policy, and management, the studio simulates a professional planning and design practice, with bona fide clients and deliverables. Each studio is divided into three to five teams, which re-group several times during a semester. The studio critic directs team assignments to ensure a balance of backgrounds and skills. Team environments instill collaborative and coordinating skills essential to practice at the scale of infrastructure, where discipline-specific jargon is either eliminated or precisely defined. Working in teams, students learn new skills beyond their specialty. Recent studios have been coordinated with courses from other departments and other institutions, making collaborative skills essential. In addition to MIP students, studios typically include students of the Urban Systems (Ph.D.), Master of Architecture (M.Arch.), and Bachelor of Architecture (B.Arch.) programs.

Semesters are usually divided into three phases punctuated by presentations to interdisciplinary faculty, agency representatives, and community members. Teams are reconstituted for each phase. The first, a research and documentation phase, is devoted to a comprehensive assessment of issues. Students inspect the site and conduct interviews, surveys, and focus groups with the community. The project is placed in the context of prior and ongoing studies, applicable theories, and relevant precedents. Professionals and academics familiar with the issues give seminars at this time. The second phase sorts out the amassed information, searching for relationships — patterns, linkages, overlaps, and contradictions — that only become apparent when viewed holistically. Based on prioritizing variables, the teams develop planning strategies and lay the foundation for design development during the final portion of the semester. Alternative design propositions in this last phase might focus on urban form, streetscape, landscape, typology, and specific building design. At semester's end, a summary, synthetic digital presentation corresponds to the final review. As each project requires, subsequent presentations are given at town meetings, conferences, hearings, or other venues in which student participation is extracurricular and voluntary. The final project report chronicles the entire undertaking and makes recommendations for implementation.

Rather than desk-side critiques, MIP studios make extensive use of projected digital graphics, which are reviewed during each class in a seminar format. Even if the interval between classes is short, an effective division of labor within teams allows substantial revisions to be made. The regular use of a digital format prepares students for presenting effectively to other disciplines, agencies, and stakeholders. Presentations are limited to 30 minutes, forcing students to refine description and use animation to display information graphically. To emphasize collaborative structure, several students give scripted and rehearsed verbal presentations, closely coordinated with visual materials on the screen.

In team studios, it is difficult to assess an individual student's contribution when grading. To address this problem, a system in which students submit evaluations of their work and that of their team members has been introduced. These confidential statements are submitted via email upon completion of each phase. Typically, they confirm the sense already held by the instructor, but in dysfunctional situations they are effective in uncovering the reasons and identifying incompatibilities. Grades are based on performance in each of the phases and on personal development throughout the semester.

Though MIP projects are conducted through the medium of studio courses, they are structured along the lines of externally funded research projects in engineering and the sciences at NJIT. Principal investigators lead the effort and are responsible for the deliverables. In other departments, however, coursework is seldom, if ever, directly involved; staff, paid research assistants, or thesis students normally conduct tasks not performed by the principal investigator. While the MIP program's methodology still applies regardless of external support, funding has expanded the scope and increased the quality of deliverables, a fact recognized by sponsors. External support has ranged between $30,000 and $60,000 per semester in the form of grants or contracts. These generally break down as summer pay for student researchers and faculty (40 percent), graduate assistant tuition and stipend (20 percent), expenses and printing (30 percent), and university overhead (10 percent).

Results

With planning support cut statewide due to budget constraints, the MIP program is often challenged to clarify its relationship to the profession. The program stresses that while the studio brings a project to a high level of resolution and its methods simulate practice, it never preempts practice. It does not use free student labor to undercut the profession; rather, the program argues the contrary: that it launches projects that would not have been initiated otherwise, projects that professional planners and designers can take further toward implementation. MIP projects are often political hot potatoes like Riverside, research-based initiatives like e-stations, or too complex to undertake conventionally like Jersey City, where Nelessen and Associates produced a solution liberally using student work (MIP material is never proprietary). Without the academic component, the Jersey City project would not have had such an ambitious scope.

Institutional constraints would in any case prevent academic programs like MIP from competing professionally. Given the inflexibility of an academic schedule, projects so intertwined with coursework cannot respond to the rapid pace of the marketplace. At a university, the clock chimes figuratively at the beginning and end of each semester. If the schedule accelerates or slips, as it almost always does in professional work, complications result. A course cannot ramp up and add students as a professional office can add staff. If the schedule slips, such that deliverables are impossible to complete by semester's end, it is extremely difficult to keep students working after the course is over. These and other institutional constraints make more schedule-neutral projects, such as politically complicated or research-directed ones, natural subjects for MIP studios.

The MIP method provides many opportunities for students to acquire knowledge and skills, often independently of faculty. A notable example of this phenomenon is in computing. In MIP studios, students develop computer skills well beyond what they had when they set out. This is remarkable given that the program offers no formal computer training beyond a course in GIS. Some students who enter the studio with little computer literacy emerge capable of advanced website development. When work goals are shared, knowledge is exchanged more freely. In a team environment, it is far more effective to ask teammates how to execute a computer command than it is to consult a manual or use the Help function. The rapid development of computer skills is also attributable to the constant use of digital media in an iterative process, analogous to the beta-testing method of continual refinement in the computer software industry. In MIP studios, students discover new ways to use software, often ahead of both faculty and the design profession. To be regarded as industry pacesetters can be powerfully motivating for them.

Achieving excellence in collaborative design is a continuous challenge. When the heroic, solo designer is replaced by the consensus-driven team, the mediocrity of compromise and the stigma of design by committee constantly threaten. Students become aware that very little design today is solitary and that collaboration is a necessary condition of professional work. A group following effective methods and well-researched principles is better suited to respond to the fragmented and often contradictory needs of today's society. In an iterative process, having to regularly argue the merits of design to the ever enlarging ring of critics — one's team, the studio, the greater community — is not a compromise but a process of refinement and an exercise in leadership.

The notion that infrastructure is a common denominator of design, especially when expressed in an open and respectful environment, leads to a renewed engagement between architecture and planning. Most curricula in schools of architecture still default to the modern canon and regard "new urbanist" or postmodern design strategies as reactionary or even heretical. Planning programs, especially those that advocate smart growth, tend toward the opposite, often defaulting to new urbanist tendencies with their reliance on familiar, traditional imagery. The MIP program recognizes the excellent smart growth examples of European modernist infrastructure and attempts to reconcile those with the deep subconscious chord that new urbanism strikes with many American communities. An interdisciplinary, team-based environment in an MIP studio reduces planning and design problems to basic elements. The result is an entirely new strategy, developed from indivisible conditions that yield physical spatial combinations, where style is more an appropriate choice than an ideological precondition.

Perhaps the greatest added value of the program, which comes as an unexpected surprise, is the effectiveness students have in catalyzing the development process. Since students act as a community's primary contact, regularly presenting work in a thoughtful and professional manner, they ultimately earn a community's trust. The community knows that oversight of the students' work by academics, professionals, and agency representatives ensures the accuracy of information and a methodological rigor. On the other hand, professionals are often seen as allied with development or political interests, while academics themselves are regarded as impractical. In New Jersey, where the libertarian tradition of home rule prevails, communities often view agency officials with suspicion if not outright contempt. In contrast, students carry no ulterior motive and are perceived as earnest seekers of the public good. The sense of empowerment and license not only stimulates but often provides a tactical and strategic edge.

Robin Murray is the deputy director of the New Jersey Office of Smart Growth (formerly the Office of State Planning). Murray recognizes (2004) that the methodology of the MIP program can mediate between the agency and divergent community stakeholders, between policy and application. In this capacity, students become teachers, in a casual, non-threatening manner, educating a community about alternative ideas. For a local governing body, a state-funded and student-driven project is free of political liability. Any local agendas can be discussed impartially by the students and moved forward, abandoned, or commingled without local reprisal. If, for some reason, political or otherwise, a community officially rejects a plan, it can simply declare that it is student work or merely theoretical. Because it is student work in the form of multiple solutions reached by teams, its authorship is not singular and proprietary. A solution can be crafted by a host community from different parts of alternative proposals. The result is not the consultant's or the agency's plan. It can readily become the mayor's, the town council's, or simply the town's plan. In many instances over the last five years, MIP recommendations that were endorsed and advanced helped to catalyze the development of projects and forge new partnerships within the community and among the academy, government agencies, and the profession.

The service-based Master of Infrastructure Planning Program has created a productive new interface between public agencies and municipalities and professionals, successfully mediating among them in synergistic ways, as the three projects discussed above demonstrate. External funding has given the program the autonomy and freedom to evolve into this new role. Its interdisciplinary basis allows it to combine forces with other academic units of NJIT and other institutions, and carry out complex and innovative projects, all incorporating team-based coursework. In doing so, it has overcome some of the barriers between different disciplines involved in the formation of the built environment and continues to promote unified smart-growth strategies and sustainable planning and design principles.

Notes

1. The project received $53,000 in funding from the NJDOT and an additional $3,000 from the New Jersey Casino Reinvestment Development Authority.
2. The e-station project was funded by the NJDOT ($50,000), the National Center for Transportation and Industrial Productivity ($50,000), and the New Jersey Casino Reinvestment Development Authority ($10,000).
3. NJCU, the city of Jersey City, and the Jersey City Board of Education funded the professional planning component. The academic component was funded by New Jersey Transit ($25,000) and NJCU ($8,250), with matching funds ($8,250) from NJIT's Urban Lab (funded by the New Jersey Casino Reinvestment Development Authority).

References

Bernick, M., and R. Cervero. (1997). *Transit Villages in the 21st Century*. New York: McGraw-Hill.

Boyer, E.L., and L.D. Mitgang. (1996). *Building Community: A New Future for Architecture Education and Practice*. Princeton, NJ: Carnegie Foundation for the Advancement of

Teaching.

Federal Highway Administration. (2003). *E-Stations for Newark: Final Report,* FHWA-NJ-2002-009. Washington, DC: U.S. Department of Transportation.

Master of Infrastructure Planning Program. (2004). *Jersey City — Bayside Project: Final Report.* Newark, NJ: New Jersey Institute of Technology.

Master of Infrastructure Planning Program. (2002). *Riverside Transit Village Project: Final Report.* Newark, NJ: New Jersey Institute of Technology.

Murray, R. (January 2004). Personal communication.

NJIT. (2002). *Course Catalog.* Newark, NJ: New Jersey Institute of Technology.

Santos, T. (February 2002). "History of the Program." In *Master of Infrastructure Planning Program Review Report,* 2.1. Newark, NJ: New Jersey Institute of Technology.

_____. (October 2002). Personal communication.

Sara, R. (2001). "Feminising Architectural Education?" Paper presented at the Centre for Education in the Built Environment Conference, Cardiff, Wales, August 2001.

Schön, D. (1987). "Educating the Reflective Practitioner." Paper presented at American Educational Research Association Annual Meeting, Washington, DC. Available at http://educ.queensu.ca/~russellt/howteach/schon87.htm. Accessed January 10, 2004.

_____. (1983). *The Reflective Practitioner.* New York: Basic Books.

Weisman, L. K. (1996). "Diversity by Design: Feminist Reflections on the Future of Architectural Education and Practice." In *The Sex of Architecture,* edited by D. Agrest, P. Conway, and L. Weisman, pp. 273-286. New York: Harry N. Abrams.

Community Life and Places of Death

By Umit Yilmaz and Daniel J. Nadenicek

Introduction

In *Sense of History: The Place of the Past in American Life*, David Glassberg has argued that "places loom large not only in our personal recollections but also in the collective memory of our communities" (2001: 19). Clemson University's involvement in a Greenville, South Carolina, service-learning project supports that assertion. Two cemeteries, intertwined with history at the heart of this Southern town, reflect the segregated past of Southern society. Even though the cemeteries have been undermined by the placement of major roads and have become vulnerable due to other forces of change, they remain important physical remnants of heritage.

This essay reports on a master plan project for those two historic cemeteries — Springwood and Richland — undertaken by faculty and students from the Clemson University Department of Planning and Landscape Architecture. Through the project students directly engaged the community in proposing a design (and historical treatment), suggested development solutions sympathetic with the historical fabric, and brought divergent factions together. The studio combined classroom education with local community outreach and provided design assistance to local stakeholder groups, including the city of Greenville, Friends of Springwood Cemetery (a white cemetery), and Friends of Richland Cemetery (an African-American cemetery). This essay also focuses on the importance of logistics in successfully undertaking a master plan project of this nature.

Since the late 18th century, when Johann Heinrich Pestlozzi, the renowned Swiss educational theorist, asserted that intellectual understanding should emerge from a balance of head, hands, and heart, educators have understood the importance of direct observation and real-world experience. By the 1930s, John Dewey's theories helped establish the value of community-based projects as a means of providing grounded learning but also as a method of combining education with an imperative for social action. American universities in the 1960s began a fuller development of service-learning as an effective teaching method capable of benefiting students and communities alike.

Clemson University is South Carolina's land-grant institution and has a heritage of applied research and active involvement with residents; service-learning has long held a central place in the university's mission. The Department of Planning and Landscape Architecture has undertaken numerous service-learning projects of various types and scales in the United States and abroad. Unlike the curricula in other disciplines, service-learning in the department has been directly aligned with the core studio courses. In those projects faculty have had their share of successes and failures. Because service-learning projects carry high expectations from students, teachers, and community participants, far too often one or more groups leave the process disappointed. For example, a focus on educational objectives can sometimes pull the energy of the class far away from the general expectations of the community. By the same token a heavy emphasis on providing a product for a community can easily shortchange the student experience. In the span of a single semester the Greenville project was successful in meeting the expectations of all parties as a consequence of close attention to logistics. A plan for the semester was carefully laid out ahead of time, and early in the semester students were informed about the complexity of the project and the importance of staying on task.

The master plan project — which included the preservation of the cemeteries as valued public places, had a clear goal of community participation and design for student education, and dealt with a complex political environment — required an interactive and participatory approach. In response to growing concerns among the individuals, the community, and the local government, the third-year landscape architecture studio employed a complex design process. Throughout the project, students were able to communicate directly with the stakeholders through extensive interviews. Those interactions enabled them to develop the project program and identify design objectives, while interpreting and resolving conflicting views. The master plan solution offered by students and faculty suggested thoughtful development at the edge of the cemeteries and site preservation to ensure continuous care into the future.

In the following sections, we establish the context for the project with a short examination of community and site history as well as contemporary factors that led to the initiation of the project. We follow with an exploration of project planning and the various components of the project itself and conclude with a discussion of outcomes. We also offer a perspective on how attention to logistics can dramatically increase the likelihood of success.

Community and Site History

The community originally platted as the village of Pleasantburg in the late 18th century soon was officially renamed Greenville (Ebaugh 1966). Greenville experienced steady growth throughout the first half of the 19th century, increasing to a total population of 21,892 (14,631 white, 212 free African American, 7,049 African-American slaves) just prior to the Civil War (Richardson 1980). Much of the economy was built on agriculture and a substantial milling industry dependent upon the waterpower of the Reedy River. Like most Southern towns, the pattern of dwelling and development in Greenville reflected the segregated nature of society. At the heart of the pattern were race separation and the construction of two of nearly everything. That pattern, as a clear reflection of the "Jim Crow" policies of the age, is still legible in the landscape of Greenville.[1] Duplication and separation were also carried through in places of interment, which explains why the Springwood and Richland cemeteries were developed only several hundred yards apart.

Springwood Cemetery was originally laid out as a burial ground in 1829 and numerous additional parcels were added over the years. In 1876, architect Godfrey Norman developed a design for the cemetery, which became the place of burial for the rich and famous of Greenville for many years thereafter (Ward 2003). A few African Americans were buried in a commingled unmarked arrangement on a far corner of the site. Richland Cemetery, named for Richland Creek, a Reedy River tributary, also dates to the mid-19th century but was then part of Springwood. It was officially dedicated as an independent African-American cemetery in the early 20th century, again in keeping with the segregationist policies of the age.

In recent years both cemeteries have become neglected if not forgotten landscapes, in part because burials today occur on the edges of the community in well-manicured lawn cemeteries. Both Richland and Springwood cemeteries have also been poorly maintained over the last several years. In the case of Springwood, major road construction has essentially divided the cemetery from the surrounding urban context. The problem is even more pronounced at Richland because the entire area has been treated as a utility and storage zone — piles of gravel, rusted vehicles, and other unsightly objects fill the spaces around the cemetery where members of the African-American community once lived and worked. The lack of attention to the edge condition of the site has exacerbated the damage and vandalism because people who care about the site do not live in close proximity.

The idea for engaging Clemson in the project was originally developed over a year earlier, when faculty joined Friends of Springwood Cemetery on a trip to Mount Auburn Cemetery in Cambridge, Massachusetts. Afterwards a few prominent white residents approached the Department of Planning and Landscape Architecture at Clemson for assistance in preserving the site and envisioning a better future for the cemetery. In recent years, the Friends of Springwood Cemetery have generated community interest and developed a following. The department, in collaboration with the city of Greenville, established criteria for involvement in the project. For example, it was determined that Springwood Cemetery had to be explored within a larger physical and social context. From a physical perspective its potential linkage to other public open spaces seemed important. More important was the city's determination that Springwood should only be studied and improved if Richland Cemetery were also included as a part of the project. That decision is important in reflecting the current political situation in Greenville, but is also related to the city's reconsideration of the linking of all of its open spaces including parks, river edges, and cemeteries.[2]

Another nonprofit organization, the Friends of Richland Cemetery, was organized more recently than the Friends of Springwood. While the Friends of Richland have garnered some political support, they have had difficulty in raising public awareness and money. Their strongest advocate has been Councilwoman Chandra Dillard, who has argued persistently for the need to develop a plan for both cemeteries that would fit into the larger context of the community.

Course Planning and Project Development

While the Greenville stakeholders had clear objectives, the Department of Planning and Landscape Architecture, intent on making sure that students also gained from the experience, carefully planned the sequence of the semester. The Alliance for Service-Learning in Education Reform (ASLER) has defined service learning as

> a method by which young people learn and develop through active participation in thoughtfully organized experiences: that actually meet community needs, that are coordinated in collaboration with school and community, that are integrated into each young person's curriculum, that provide structured time for young people to think, talk, and write about what they did and said during the service project, that provide young people with opportunities to use newly acquired academic skills and knowledge of real life situations in their communities, that enhance what is taught in school by extending student learning beyond the classroom, and that help to foster the development of a sense of caring for others. (ASLER 1994)

The components of that definition served as guidelines for the student experience in the Greenville project. Ultimately the task was to work in a systematic way for the benefit of all parties — Clemson students, city of Greenville, residents of Greenville, Friends of Richland, and Friends of Springwood.

With that general direction in place, 14 students from the department set out to provide a master plan for the cemeteries and surrounding urban fabric. While the department has a long history of service-learning projects including international projects,[3] the stakes were very high in this case because the city desired workable guidelines and a clear direction by the end of the semester (Yilmaz 2003). For that to happen, two groups who had heretofore had nothing to do with each other had to be brought together. Students also had to engage in a multifaceted approach including research, interviews, design, and presentation. The participatory nature of the project assured that students would need to leave egos aside and gain a realistic perspective on the appropriateness of various approaches.

As a critical aspect of quality service-learning programs, the faculty placed great emphasis on the preparation phase. Since the contract and budget with the local government were finalized before classes started, faculty were able to plan in great detail the tasks based on the client's expectations, the timelines associated with completion of tasks, the responsibilities for everyone involved, and the outcomes of the project. From the students' perspective, equity (equality in the way tasks were assigned) was another important aspect of preparation because the students worked in groups as well as individually during different phases of the project. A list of key persons in the community identified by faculty later became the pool for interviewees during the oral history documentation.

The course syllabus acted as the "class contract" with the students and identified clear goals for everyone involved. After the students were familiarized with the syllabus, the faculty provided an orientation session on expectations, deadlines, and final products. Students were randomly assigned to the tasks identified by faculty, first in groups and then individually.

Other activities during the preparation phase included securing an exclusive classroom space for the service-learning project. Students had their own individual study areas throughout the semester, which helped them use studio time effectively. Dedicated space for the project also facilitated community involvement during all phases of design. Community members and local officials were able to participate on several occasions while the students continued to work in the studio.

Faculty aimed at having the city accept a master plan and guidelines as the end goal. They laid out a set of tasks that included site reconnaissance, site analysis (determination of opportunities and constraints), literature review (archival research), interviews, public meetings, development of the master plan and guidelines, and dissemination (Yilmaz 2003). Interviews were conducted individually and in small groups. In some of the interviews and group meetings, students sought opportunities to bring people together for the purpose of building a common base of support. Many of the interviews revealed a perspective on loss, grieving, memory, and heritage shared by all residents, black or white (Yilmaz 2003).

Planning and design issues, goals, and objectives were identified and the project program was developed in light of the interviews with community members, city officials, and students' own research and analyses. Based upon the program, 14 planning areas were defined in a design charrette and one student was assigned to work on each zone. All 14 students worked in the studio collaboratively in order to make the planning areas consistent and complementary prior to assembling their individual designs into a composite master plan. The danger in having students work individually on small portions of the site was that the plan might easily become fragmented. That possibility was countered in the overall delivery of the course: as a consequence of interviews, planned meetings, lectures, and research, all of the students clearly understood the big picture. Larger issues were also reinforced frequently during the numerous pinups and reviews held during the semester. Periodic review meetings during the planning and design process brought community groups and city officials together and provided opportunities for the exchange of ideas, as well as social interaction between the members of two groups and others in the larger community.

**Figure 1. Student Venessa Ciaccio
interviewing Rev. J.W. Henderson**

Master Plan and Guidelines

The final plan used a comprehensive approach to master planning and direct community participation to suggest preservation of the existing cemetery layouts and solutions for future needs identified by the community. The plan responded to such planning issues as pedestrian and vehicular circulation, access, safety, aesthetics, land uses and development phasing, historic preservation, and maintenance. The two cemeteries, consolidated into a contiguous space and integrated with parks and public places, were surrounded with proposed land uses that introduced compatible functions at the edges to facilitate historic preservation. The proposal minimized the potential threats posed by incompatible uses to the cemeteries, while creating smooth transition areas from the cemeteries to the outlying intense land uses.

In Richland Cemetery, the design proposal suggested the development of a funeral parlor, a small-scale single-family residential neighborhood, and a community garden along the western cemetery boundary, where currently a vacant building and an auto body shop exist. The houses with their porches and front yards were designed to create a watchful eye on the cemetery across the proposed community green space, while maintaining a buffer between the cemetery edge and a busy road. Along the southern edge of the cemetery, the design proposal focused on new land uses that would contribute to improvements for the cemetery and creation of new public spaces and gateways into the cemetery. Attractive sidewalks surrounded a proposed mixed-use building with retail at ground level, offices on the first floor, and residences on the upper floors. And a stepped pedestrian promenade with plazas and outdoor sitting places connected the sidewalks on both sides of the building.

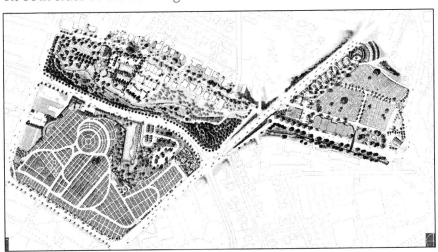

Figure 2. Illustrative master plan

Design proposals for Springwood Cemetery included development of two mausoleums that responded to the expansion needs, site improvements that respected and enhanced the characteristics of the cemetery, and a small chapel that was identified as a need by the Friends of the Cemetery. The students also proposed edge amenities, such as improvements for traffic circulation and effective boundaries between the cemetery and the surrounding uses. A critical aspect of the master plan, establishing the connection between Springwood and Richland cemeteries, was accomplished by creating a safe and attractive pedestrian underpass through the park between the two cemeteries. In all design proposals, the needs of the friends of the cemeteries and the historical and natural features of the individual design areas dictated the design concepts.

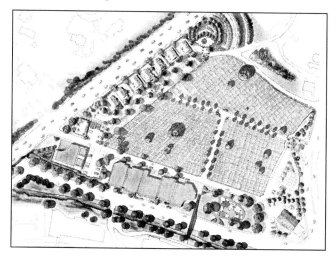

Figure 3. Proposed land uses at the perimeters of Richland Cemetery

Student concepts for the cemeteries were well received for two reasons: (1) they placed the cemeteries in a larger spatial context, linking them together within a system of open space, and (2) the design was built on the economic realities of place in the suggestion that for preservation to happen development near the sites was necessary.

The Outcomes

With direct participation of the community, local government, and students, this project was completed and approved within 16 weeks. The method used and the plan and guidelines it produced provided different factions in the community with a common vision toward the same goal. In bringing divergent groups as well as local officials and university representatives together, the project created a sense of group ownership of the ideas developed in the design process. On May 13, 2003, the Greenville City Council unanimously adopted the

Springwood and Richland Cemeteries Master Plan and Guidelines. The council also allocated additional funding to publish the results of the service-learning project. Outcomes of the project include the preservation of the cemeteries and bringing populations together as well as benefits to students and service learning lessons.

Historic preservation sometimes emphasizes the bygone at the expense of the present. Heritage accepts the past as a part of the present; the past provides a means of establishing identity and a method of bringing people together (Lowenthal 1996). The perspective on history developed in this project moved beyond a focus on objects and prior eras to an understanding of how a living history might be incorporated into the fabric of community, thereby assuring a higher level of maintenance, if not perpetual care. Oral histories developed by the students clearly revealed the power that the places held in the minds and hearts of advocates for both of the cemeteries. In the following quotation, Anna C. Smith spoke to student David Cosstlett about her connections to Richland Cemetery:

> OK, this is my daddy's twin sister. I don't know how they have her name wrong. He was Albert, and she was Alberta. And this is my uncle; he died before I was born. This is my grandmother and grandfather, and my great aunt. And I believe my great grandmother is buried here somewhere, because they lived close. And this is my uncle, T. Arthur, and this is reserved for my aunt who lives in Philadelphia. I believe there is one vacant, and I do not know, it will probably be reserved for my son if he is not married by then and [does not] have anybody of his own.

Similar information was gathered from people concerned with Springwood Cemetery. The realization that everyone shared those emotional bonds made it possible to think about the preservation of both sites together.

At the final student presentation, when John M. Dillard, treasurer of the white Friends of Springwood Cemetery, and African-American councilwoman Chandra Dillard met and discovered they had the same last name, Ms. Dillard, to everyone's delight, exclaimed, "Maybe we are related." That encounter is symbolic of the overall effect of the process. Because the groups had a common cause they were pulled together as never before. At all of the meetings, members from each cemetery group were found sitting next to one another. That interaction led to dialogue and a groundswell of support that resulted in enough political clout to win council approval for the plan. During the process, student involvement was given public attention and the coverage in the press had significant impact, which may have influenced the positive vote by the council.

The students benefited from the service-learning experience, which added to their knowledge of the course content. They were not only exposed to complex planning, design, and historic preservation issues throughout this real-world project, but they also actively participated in the process. They learned the role of community participation in consensus building and responsive design, gained skills in project coordination, and grasped the importance of teamwork. Class discussions moved beyond design to the integral aspects of citizen participation and service-learning as a concept. Course logistics were also openly discussed and students participated in the numerous subtle shifts that inevitably occur during a semester. They clearly learned the benefit of staying focused as a consequence of close involvement in a transparent process.

This third-year design studio is one of the required core courses in a five-year professional landscape architecture program. The studio is heuristic in nature and designed to explore, discover, evaluate, interpret, and communicate the design process; help students develop a vocabulary useful in the further study or professional practice of landscape architecture; and strengthen students' skills and confidence at working individually and in team or group settings. The students develop their own personal design process under the guidance of the course instructor. While the focus is on design and its application to complex landscape and environmental issues, faculty add the important layer of community interaction and participatory design.

During the course-planning phase of a service-learning studio project, special attention is given to structuring the design phases and a first delineation of study sub-areas, so that all students participate equally in the service-learning process. This extra attention to the logistics eliminates the piecemeal approach to problem solving, which often produces individual designs that do not create a harmonious whole. As one student participant in the cemeteries project remarked, "I have never worked on a project of this scale, nor have I delved as deeply into each and every step of a design. I think the constant focus on the site throughout the semester did lead to a better design in the long run. I also had help from all of the students, especially those I shared borders with, and the professor himself was no stranger to the work, contributing freely and making himself available. I hope my project lived up to the city's expectations, as well as my studio's. I know our work lived up to, and shattered my expectations. If our work is ever put to use in the area, I will be thrilled." An organized debriefing produced numerous similar comments from students as a part of the planned reflection process.

Students often feel frustrated when their service experience fails to connect the educational experience to any tangible real-world results (Wade 2000). The Greenville cemeteries project revealed that it is possible for students to learn a great deal consistent with the pedagogical goals, while advancing the development of their skills as aspiring design professionals and also providing useful ideas to the community. The key is thinking through all aspects of the service-learning project ahead of time and laying the groundwork, then keeping the lines of communication with the community and the students wide open throughout the semester. Beyond that, the success of this project depended on the interest of community stakeholders. In the case of both the Friends of Richland Cemetery and the Friends of Springwood Cemetery, strong advocates were unwilling to let a good opportunity pass them by.

Notes

1. The Department of Planning and Landscape Architecture and the Center for Community Growth and Change at Clemson, for example, recently completed a large Reedy River project that considered community linkages and recreational amenities provided by the riverine environment.

2. The landscapes and architecture of segregation have recently become the subject of scholarship. Robert Weyeneth, a noted University of South Carolina public historian, is writing a book on the subject.

3. An international service-learning project led by Yilmaz in Santiago Texacuangos, El Salvador, in fall 2001, was a collaborative effort between Clemson University's Department of Planning and Landscape Architecture, the Asociacion Maria Madre de los Jovenes, the mayor and council of Texacuangos Santiago, and the Stone Institute (the sponsor) in Greenville, South Carolina. The project involved a comprehensive town master plan and site plans designed by the students in the landscape architecture program and won two national student awards.

References

Alliance for Service-Learning in Education Reform (ASLER). (1994). *Standards of Quality for School-Based and Community-Based Service-Learning.* Alexandria, VA: The Close Up Foundation.

Ebaugh, L.S. (1966). *Bridging the Gap: A Guide to Early Greenville, South Carolina.* Greenville, SC: Greater Greenville Chamber of Commerce.

Glassburg, D. (2001). *Sense of History: The Place of Past in American Life.* Amherst, MA: University of Massachusetts Press.

Lowenthal, D. (1996). *Possessed by the Past: The Heritage Crusade and the Spoils of History.* New York: Free Press.

Richardson, J.M. (1980). *History of Greenville County, South Carolina.* Greenville, SC: Reprint Company Publishers.

Wade, R.C, ed. (2000). *Building Bridges: Service-Learning in Social Studies.* Washington, DC: National Council for Social Studies.

Ward, L.P. (2003). *God's Little Acre on Main Street: Springwood Cemetery.* Greenville, SC: A Press.

Yilmaz, U. (2003). "Springwood and Richland Cemeteries Master Plan." www.greater-greenville.com/neighborhoods/master_plan.asp.

Contributors

James J. Abernethy
Professor
College of Architecture and Design
Lawrence Technological University
21000 West Ten Mile Road
Southfield, MI 48075-1058
abernethy@ltu.edu

Anne Beamish
Assistant Professor
Community and Regional Planning Program
School of Architecture
University of Texas at Austin
1 University Station B7500
Austin TX 78712
abeamish@mail.utexas.edu

Daniel Bennett
Dean
College of Architecture, Design & Construction
Auburn University
202 Dudley Commons
Auburn, AL 36849-5313
bennedd@auburn.edu

Julie A. Dercle
Assistant Professor
Department of Urban Studies and Planning
California State University, Northridge
18111 Nordhoff Street
Northridge, CA 91330-8259
julie.dercle@csun.

Keith Diaz Moore
Assistant Professor
Architecture & Landscape Architecture
Interdisciplinary Design Institute
Washington State University Spokane
PO Box 1495
Spokane, WA 99210-1495
keithdm@wsu.edu

Sharon L. Gaber
Associate Dean
College of Architecture, Design & Construction
Auburn University
202 Dudley Commons
Auburn, AL 36849-5313
gabersl@auburn.edu

Mary C. Hardin
Professor
College of Architecture and Landscape Architecture
University of Arizona
Tucson, AZ 85704
mchardin@u.arizona.edu

Kara Heffernan
Project Manager
Center for Neighborhood Technology
2125 West North Avenue, Chicago, IL 60647
kara@cnt.org

Paula Horrigan
Associate Professor
Department of Landscape Architecture
Cornell University
440 Kennedy Hall
Ithaca, NY 14853
phh3@cornell.edu

Lorlene Hoyt
Assistant Professor
Department of Urban Studies
Massachusetts Institute of Technology
77 Massachusetts Avenue, Room 9-528
Cambridge, MA 02139
lorlene@mit.edu

Joongsub Kim
Assistant Professor
College of Architecture and Design
Lawrence Technological University
21000 West Ten Mile Road
Southfield, MI 48075-1058
j_kim@ltu.edu

Jacqueline Leavitt
Director
Community Scholars Program
Department of Urban Planning
UCLA School of Public Affairs
3250 Public Policy Building
Box 951656
Los Angeles, CA 90095-1656
jleavitt@ucla.edu

Hollie Lund
Assistant Professor
Urban and Regional Planning
California State Polytechnic University, Pomona
3801 West Temple Avenue
Pomona, CA 91768
hlund@csupomona.edu

Daniel J. Nadenicek
Professor and Chair
Department of Planning and Landscape Architecture
Clemson University
121 Lee Hall
Clemson, SC 29634-0511
dnadeni@clemson.edu

David R. Riley
Associate Professor
Department of Architectural Engineering
Pennsylvania State University
104 Engineering Unit A
University Park, PA 16802
DRiley@engr.psu.edu

Michael Rios
Assistant Professor
School of Architecture and Landscape Architecture
Pennsylvania State University
University Park, PA 16802
mxr43@psu.edu

Anthony Schuman
Associate Professor
School of Architecture
New Jersey Institute of Technology
Newark, NJ 07102-1982
Schuman@adm.njit.edu

Darius Sollohub
Associate Director
Infrastructure Planning
School of Architecture
New Jersey Institute of Technology
Newark, NJ 07102
sollohub@njit.edu

Gwen Urey
Professor of Urban and Regional Planning
California State Polytechnic University, Pomona
3801 West Temple Avenue
Pomona, CA 91768
gurey@csupomona.edu

David Wang
Associate Professor and Graduate Coordinator of Architecture
Interdisciplinary Design Institute
Washington State University Spokane
PO Box 1495
Spokane, WA 99210-1495
davewang@wsu.edu

Scott Wing
Associate Professor
Department of Architecture
Pennsylvania State University
302 Engineering Unit C
University Park, PA 16802
sww10@psu.edu

Umit Yilmaz
Associate Professor and Director of Landscape Architecture
Department of Planning and Landscape Architecture
163 Lee Hall
Clemson University
Clemson, SC 29634-0511
uyilmaz@clemson.edu